DEMEI

Living in ᵤₕₑ
Memories of God

John Swinton

scm press

This book is dedicated to my friend Peter Barclay.
Peter, you may, for now, live in the land of forgetfulness,
but you are not forgotten.

© John Swinton 2012

First published in the USA in 2012 by Wm. B. Eerdmans Publishing Co.

This Edition published in 2012 by SCM Press
Editorial office
Invicta House, 108–114 Golden Lane, London, EC1Y OTG

SCM Press is an imprint of Hymns Ancient and Modern Ltd (a registered charity)
13a Hellesdon Park Road, Norwich, Norfolk, NR6 5DR

www.scmpress.co.uk

British Library Cataloguing in Publication data

A catalogue record for this book is available
from the British Library

978-0-334-04672-1
Kindle edition 978-0-334-04673-8

Printed and bound by
CPI Group (UK) Ltd, Reading

Contents

Acknowledgments

A s with all things, this book was a collaborative effort. There are many people who deserve thanks for their advice and their contribution to the process of writing this book. It is not possible to mention all of them here. However, there are some for whom extra thanks is due. I owe much of what is written in this book to my experiences with many people with dementia that I have ministered with over the years in my capacity as a psychiatric nurse and later as a mental health chaplain. Looking back, in many ways I wonder how useful my ministry was to them at the time. If I knew then what I know now, things might have been different. But I hope that it was useful. My memories of them and the experiences that we had together have been central to what I have tried to capture in this book. Most of these people will have passed on by now, but I hope that as they live out their new lives in God's memory that they will forgive me for my mistakes and that this book will go some way to compensating for them. I would like to acknowledge with special thanks my friend and colleague Brian Brock for his continuing encouragement, sharp comments, and wonderful theological mind. Thanks also to Eric Stoddart, Aileen Barclay, Donald Meston, and Trevor Adams for taking the time to read through and comment on earlier drafts of this book and to offer me invaluable guidance, comment, and critique. I value your thoughts and your friendship. I am grateful to my friend and colleague Stanley Hauerwas for discussing some of the underlying issues that permeate this book during what was a fascinating time together with Jean Vanier at his home at L'Arche in Trosly, France. I am also grateful to Jean Vanier for the conversations that we have had about the lives of people with severe intellectual disabilities.

The stories of such people are not the same as those stories that are lived out by people with dementia, but the resonance is clearly there. The question "What does it mean to know God when you don't have the intellectual capacity to understand who God is?" is not a million miles away from the question "What does it mean to know God when you have forgotten who God is?" Jean's kindness, deep experience, and beautiful insights have helped me at various levels as I have wrestled with the complicated issues that emerge when we try to reflect theologically on the experience of dementia. I am also grateful to Professor Elizabeth MacKinlay at the Centre for Ageing and Pastoral Studies in Canberra, Australia, for giving me some important opportunities to share some of this material at various conferences and workshops in Australia. These experiences were invaluable in terms of shaping and forming this book over time. As always, I am eternally grateful to my family — to my wife, Alison, whose love is my life, and to my children, Paul, Ryan, Kerri, Micha, and Naomi. You guys are my inspiration and a constant source of confidence within a life that is often filled with self-doubt. Thank you. More than anything else I am thankful to Jesus for being patient with me and for remembering me when I have forgotten whose I am.

A Note on Inclusive Language

Throughout this book I have tried to use gender-inclusive language as much as possible. However, in some cases, for the sake of retaining the integrity of certain texts, I have left some quotations in their original gender-specific form. Gendering God is an aspect of the construction of our image of God which is clearly open to abuse and misrepresentation. I hope that the reader will not be distracted by the approach of those theologians and philosophers quoted in this book for whom the gendered nature of language had not yet become an issue. I want to acknowledge the inherent problems with non-inclusive language. This is particularly so with regard to people with dementia, who, as we will see, constantly have false identities implicitly and explicitly forced upon them.

Introduction: Being Loved for Who I Am

Neither height nor depth, nor anything else in all creation, will be able to separate us from the love of God that is in Christ Jesus our Lord.

ROMANS 8:39

The bottom line is — I'm in God's hands . . . and the medical community's. And hopefully they're in God's hands.

BUTCH NOOAN, A PERSON WITH DEMENTIA[1]

In 2009 I was asked to take part in a program on BBC Radio 4 called *Beyond Belief*. The topic of the program was the theological issues surrounding dementia. The program was a three-way conversation between me (in the studio in Aberdeen, Scotland) and two psychiatrists, one a Muslim and the other a Hindu. Before the interview began, the host of the show, Ernie Rea, told the three of us that we would be asked one final question at the end of the interview and that it might be useful to begin to think about it before the interview started. The question was this: "If you ended up having dementia, how would you like to be treated?" Great question! But most distracting when you're supposed to be participating in a

---

1. Quoted from Elisabeth Peterson, *Voices of Alzheimer's: Courage, Humor, Hope, and Love in the Face of Dementia* (Cambridge: Da Capo Press, 2004), p. 57.

complicated and sometimes difficult discussion about the theological dynamics of the human experience of dementia. The interview went quite well, and toward the end of it the host asked the question. I still wasn't sure what to say. Then, from nowhere, I found myself saying something like this: "If I do get dementia, I hope that I will be loved and cared for just for who I am, even if who I am is difficult for me and for others." The interview ended, and we all went home.

Who Am I?

As I was driving home, I began to think back on what we had been talking about. My words returned to me, and they troubled me. "Loved and cared for just for who I am . . ." The words were simple, but their practical meaning was profoundly complicated. My mind was drawn to one of Dietrich Bonhoeffer's prison poems titled "Who Am I?":

> Who am I? This or the other?
> Am I one person today and tomorrow another?
> Am I both at once? A hypocrite before others,
> And before myself a contemptibly woebegone weakling? . . .
> Who am I? They mock me, these lonely questions of mine.
> Whoever I am, Thou knowest, O God, I am Thine![2]

Bonhoeffer's question "Who am I?" rings strangely true for many modern people. In an age where people constantly try (and fail) to discover who they are and constantly strive to re-invent themselves (because they assume that autonomous self-construction is a real possibility), this question carries the weight of much cultural desire. However, the apparent simplicity of the question is deceiving. Am I the same person I was twenty, thirty, forty years ago? How can I be the same person when almost all of the cells in my body have been replaced? I bear some resemblance to my "previous self," but I don't look the same. I certainly don't think in the same ways that I did when I was thirteen, and I don't have the same priorities, values, desires, or physical capacities. Psychologically, I really don't see

---

2. From Dietrich Bonhoeffer, *Who Am I?: Poetic Insights on Personal Identity* (Minneapolis: Augsburg Books, 2005), pp. 8-9.

the world in the same way that I did when I was a child. And yet, despite the fact that there is little physical or psychological continuity between the "then me" and the "now me," *that* which was *was "me!"* "I" *was* thirteen, and "I" am no longer that age. "I" remain "me" in spite of all of the changes. And yet, when I lay my life out in such ways, I'm still not completely sure who "I" really am.

The question of who I am is complicated at the best of times. It would become even more complicated if I was to develop dementia. Who will I be when I have forgotten who I think I am? Who will I become when that last tentative connection between who I thought I was then and who I think I am now has been severed? The more I thought about my statement on the radio, the less clear I became about exactly what I was asking people to do when I asked that they love and care for me just for who I am. To ask people to continue to love me "even if who I am is difficult for me and for others" is a pretty big request. What would that look like? If dementia leads me to become a radically new "me," how could I expect people to love this stranger? Why would they? How could they? Who would they be loving? Who will "me" be? Yet, I want them to keep on loving me. I don't want to be forgotten or abandoned. I'm just not sure what it would look like to remember me when I have forgotten who I am and who they are, and . . . who my God is. The psalmist puts it this way: "Can the darkness speak of your wonderful deeds? Can anyone in the land of forgetfulness talk about your righteousness?" (Ps. 88:12, NLT).

The Complexities of Love

Of course, remaining loved is not always a safe place to be. Some might seek to love the "me-with-dementia" by offering comfort, solace, and friendship in my times of struggle. But others might see my dementia as a fate worse than death, and assume that death would be a blessed release for me.[3] In the name of love and compassion, dementia might *seem* to be a good reason for justifying euthanasia.[4] My loved ones might abandon me

---

3. For example, recent developments in Holland indicate that enabling people with dementia to end their lives may be becoming an accepted practice. See Tony Sheldon, "Euthanasia Endorsed in Dutch Patient with Dementia," *British Medical Journal* 10, no. 319 (July 1999): 75.

4. Stanley Hauerwas has noted the way in which compassion has become dangerous for

because they think that I am no longer there, that I'm already dead. My silent pleas that "It's still ME, Lord . . ."[5] may fall on deaf ears. I could find myself standing in the shoes of the psalmist when he cries out, "My loved ones and friends stay away, fearing my disease. Even my own family stands at a distance" (Ps. 38:11, NLT). Perhaps, even if I can no longer speak the words, I will agree with the psalmist's fateful resignation: "You have taken away my companions and loved ones. Darkness is my closest friend" (Ps. 8:18, NLT). When those days come, who will be my voice? Who will be my protector? Who will be my God?

So, I might want to be careful about precisely what I mean when I say that I would like to be loved for who I am! But is it actually fair to ask anyone to love me even when the "me" that they used to love seems distant and perhaps even absent? If our life together now is really not what they signed up for, how could I expect them to love me and remain faithful to me in the midst of my plight? It might be understandable and appropriate for me to ask those who have loved me in the past to continue to love me. But what about those strangers who will seek to care for me when my family can't? I may end my days in the company of strangers; caregivers who have never known me apart from what they see me as now: a "victim of dementia." What does it mean for them to love me and for me to ask for their love? What kind of love could such strangers give to me . . . and I to them?

Loved by God

Bonhoeffer's answer to the question "Who am I?" is to find peace and rest in the assurance that, despite his own confusion, his identity, who he truly

---

vulnerable people in modernity. In his essay "Killing Compassion," he notes that compassion has become a cardinal virtue. At heart, compassion is perceived as a way of ridding the world of unnecessary suffering. However, without the presence of Christian virtue, particularly the virtue of patience, it can quickly evolve into a dangerous and destructive practice. In the name of compassion we might feel quite comfortable aborting babies and ending the lives of people with dementia. See Stanley Hauerwas, "Killing Compassion," in Stanley Hauerwas, *Dispatches from the Front: Theological Engagements with the Secular* (Durham, N.C.: Duke University Press, 1994).

5. "It's still ME, Lord . . ." is the title of a DVD that focuses on spirituality and dementia produced by the CARITAS, an aspect of the Roman Catholic Church in England; the DVD focuses on issues of social justice. Access the DVD at http://www.caritas-socialaction.org.uk/pages/dvd_.html.

is, is known and held only by God. Here he resonates with the prophet Jeremiah's affirmation that human identity is divinely shaped and held:

> "But blessed are those who trust in the Lord
> and have made the Lord their hope and confidence.
> They are like trees planted along a riverbank,
> with roots that reach deep into the water.
> Such trees are not bothered by the heat
> or worried by long months of drought.
> Their leaves stay green,
> and they never stop producing fruit.
> The human heart is the most deceitful of all things,
> and desperately wicked.
> Who really knows how bad it is?
> But I, the Lord, search all hearts
> and examine secret motives.
> I give all people their due rewards,
> according to what their actions deserve." (Jer. 17:7-10)

In the end only God knows who we are; only God can search our hearts and recognize who we really are. God creates us, sustains us, and knows us. Bonhoeffer may well be correct: "Whoever I am, Thou knowest, God, I am Thine!" Nothing can destroy such divine recognition (Rom. 3:39). Here Bonhoeffer finds peace. Perhaps here also those suffering with dementia and those who accompany them on their journeys can also find peace. But what would such peace look like? What does it mean to be known, loved, and held by God when you have forgotten who God is and you can no longer recognize yourself or those whom you once loved?

I was still turning these questions over in my mind when I turned into the driveway of my home. It was then that I realized I had to write this book.

Dementia: A Theological Condition?

It is important to be clear from the outset that this is a self-consciously theological book. It is written for Christians and is firmly located within that faith. It is true that throughout it engages with a wide range of disciplines, primarily within the fields of philosophy, psychiatry, neurology, and psychology. However, the core of the Christian argument and the heart of the book relate to developing a specifically theological perspective on dementia. Such a perspective takes seriously established knowledge, but seeks to enable the discovery of options, possibilities, and perspectives which are not available from other sources of knowledge but which are crucial for a truly Christian understanding of dementia and the development of authentically Christian modes of dementia care. The book is not therefore interested in broad forms of "spirituality" which claim to be generic and neutral.[6] Such approaches to spirituality may well have their place within the overall arena of how human beings care for those whose lives are marked by dementia; these approaches make people aware of hidden dimensions of the experience of dementia and open up important spiritual spaces within health and social care services, which have a tendency toward the secular and the mundane.[7] But the focus here will be on quite specific forms of spirituality and theological understanding of the world that emerge from a perspective which is deeply informed by, although not uncritical of, the Christian tradition; a perspective that presumes that the world is created by God, broken by sin, and in the process of being redeemed through the saving works of Jesus.

This basic premise provides the book with a particular orientation and dynamic and presents the relationship between theology and the other disciplines involved in the diagnosis and care of dementia in a particular way. The book does *not* focus on how medicine can use theology to bring benefits to patients with dementia. That dynamic is quite different — and wrong-headed. For example, many of the participants of the growing religion-and-health conversation in the United States and Europe make a fundamental mistake in seeming to assume that the goals of religion should echo and contribute to the goals of medicine and cul-

6. For a useful review of some of the literature that takes this approach, see L. Beuscher and C. Beck, "A Literature Review of Spirituality in Coping with Early-Stage Alzheimer's Disease," *Journal of Clinical Nursing* 17 (2008): 88-97. See also John Swinton, *Spirituality and Mental Health Care: Rediscovering a Forgotten Dimension* (London: Jessica Kingsley Publishers, 2001), pp. 165ff.

7. For a critique of generic approaches to spirituality as they relate to health care, see John Swinton and Stephen Pattison, "Moving Beyond Clarity: Towards a Thin, Vague, and Useful Understanding of Spirituality in Nursing Care," *Nursing Philosophy* 11, no. 4 (2010): 226-37.

ture.[8] If religion eases depression and anxiety, then it should be grafted in as a resource for modern medical approaches to care and intervention.[9] If it helps people cope better with suffering, then we should seek to develop interventions that enable effective coping.[10] If forgiveness is good for our mental health, then it should be incorporated into therapy.[11] From this perspective, it might seem natural to assume that if theology can help enhance the well-being of people with dementia, we should use it as an aspect of our current medical understanding and practice. However, what is rarely considered is the fact that the goals of medicine and theology and their respective definitions of health and well-being may be significantly different. Grafting theology into the goals of medicine simply on the grounds of potential therapeutic benefit will inevitably lead to confusion, dissonance, distortion, and contradiction.

At a very basic level, well-being within Christianity is not gauged by the presence or absence of illness or distress. Religious beliefs and practices may well have therapeutic benefits, but that is not their primary function or intention. Nor is the efficacy of a "spiritual intervention" theologically determined according to criteria such as reduced anxiety, better coping, or a reduction in depression, important as these things may be at a certain level. Theologically speaking, well-being has nothing to do with the *absence* or reduction of anything. It has to do with the *presence* of something: *the presence of God-in-relationship.* Well-being, peace, health — what Scripture describes as *shalom* — has to do with the presence of a specific God in particular places who engages in personal relationships with unique individuals for formative purposes.[12] Rather than alleviating anxiety and fear, the presence of such a God often brings on dissonance and

8. For a deeper critique of this movement, see Joel James Shuman and Keith Meador, *Heal Thyself: Spirituality, Medicine, and the Distortion of Christianity* (New York: Oxford University Press, 2003).

9. H. G. Koenig, D. B. Larson, and M. E. McCullough, *Handbook of Religion and Health* (New York: Oxford University Press, 2001).

10. K. I. Pargament, "The Bitter and the Sweet: An Evaluation of the Costs and Benefits of Religiousness," *Psychological Inquiry* 13 (2002): 168-81.

11. G. Bono and M. E. McCullough, "Positive Responses to Benefit and Harm: Bringing Forgiveness and Gratitude into Cognitive Psychotherapy," *Journal of Cognitive Psychotherapy* 20 (2006): 147-58. For a powerful theological critique of this approach, see L. Gregory Jones, *Embodying Forgiveness: A Theological Analysis* (Grand Rapids: Wm. B. Eerdmans, 1995).

12. John Swinton, *From Bedlam to Shalom: Towards a Practical Theology of Human Nature, Interpersonal Relationships, and Mental Health Care* (New York: Peter Lang, 2000).

psychological disequilibrium, but always for the purpose of the person's greater well-being understood in redemptive and relational terms.[13]

This is not to suggest that there cannot and should not be a creative and healing conversation between medicine and theology. There is much that these two disciplines can learn from each other. It is the grounds upon which such a conversation should be built that are crucial. *We do not do theological reflection on dementia within a medical, psychological, or neurobiological context.* In other words, these disciplines do not set the context into which theology speaks. Rather, theology provides an understanding of the basic context into which the medical sciences speak. *These disciplines are practiced within the context of creation and under the providential sovereignty of God.* This is so even if that theological context is not formally acknowledged.[14] If we truly are relational, dependent creatures, created by a God who remains steadfastly at the helm of creation, moving it toward its final destiny, then a person's neurobiological state is not a-theological, and scientific explorations of that neurobiology are not pre-theological. In a real sense, *neurology is theology.*[15] It is in this sense that the book assumes that dementia is a thoroughly theological condition. It makes a world of difference to suggest that dementia happens to people who are loved by God, who are made in God's image, and who reside within creation. The task of theology is to remind people of that distinction and to push our perceptions of dementia beyond what is expected, toward the surprising and the unexpected.

13. Job 28:28: "And this is what he says to all humanity: 'The fear of the Lord is true wisdom; to forsake evil is real understanding.'"

14. John Howard Yoder states, "The distinction between church and the world is not a distinction between nature and grace. It is, instead, a distinction that denotes the basic personal postures of men, some of whom confess and others of whom do not confess that Jesus Christ is Lord. The distinction between church and the world is not something that God has imposed upon the world by prior metaphysical definition, nor is it only something which timid or pharisaical Christians have built up around themselves. It is all of that in creation that has taken the freedom not yet to believe" (John Howard Yoder, *The Original Revolution* [Scottdale, Pa.: Herald Press, 1971], p. 116). If this is the case, then practitioners may exert their freedom not to believe, but that does not alter the fact that they continue to practice within creation.

15. I am not referring to the popular movement of neurotheology. (See, for example, Andrew B. Newberg, *The Mystical Mind: Probing the Biology of Religious Experience* [Minneapolis: Fortress Press, 1999].) My point is that we are embodied creatures, and that what occurs within our bodies inevitably has theological significance.

The Challenge to Theology

A basic premise of this book is that standard neurobiological explanations of dementia are deeply inadequate for a full understanding of the nature and the experience of dementia. What is required is a different approach that not only includes the biological, psychological, and social dimensions of dementia, but also understands and recognizes the critical theological aspects. It is only as we develop this "whole sight" that we can really understand what it means to be a person with dementia living in God's creation. However, this book is more than a challenge to medicine and medical approaches to dementia; it is also a challenge to theology. In his book *Forgetting Whose We Are: Alzheimer's Disease and the Love of God*, David Keck describes Alzheimer's disease as the "theological disease."[16] He perceives dementia as differing from many other forms of disease insofar as, in his opinion, it erodes the very essence of the self and raises profound existential questions about personhood, love, sin, and salvation:

> This disease does differ from other examples of disease, anguish, and death. The unusual situation of a prolonged mental deterioration and the need for sustained caregiving over many years means that we can no longer presume the existence of the cognitive subject when we are thinking theologically.[17]

Keck's point is an interesting one. He asserts that the subjective, cognitively aware "I," which is the central focus of much contemporary and historical theology, is not available or at least is radically revised within the lives of people in the advanced stages of dementia. When we put aside for now whether or not Keck is correct, his observation is worth unpacking. A good deal of theology (and, indeed, much of our worship activity[18]) hinges on

16. David Keck, *Forgetting Whose We Are: Alzheimer's Disease and the Love of God* (Nashville: Abingdon Press, 1996), p. 15. Keck's book focuses specifically on Alzheimer's disease, and it is important to note that Alzheimer's is just one form of dementia. The fact that it has, in the eyes of many, come to name all forms of dementia is an interesting phenomenon that will be discussed more fully as the book moves on.

17. Keck, *Forgetting Whose We Are*, p. 15.

18. For example, a song such as Darlene Zschech's "Shout to the Lord" assumes a self-aware, cognizing self. A line such as "My Jesus, my savior," makes sense only if one has the cognitive capacity to recognize and conceptualize the "me" who is praising, and who Jesus

the assumption that the theologian is addressing an individuated, experiencing, cognitively able self, perceived as a reasoning, thinking, independent, decision-making entity. This cognitively able self is assumed to have the potential to know and understand certain things about God, a God who is available at an intellectual level through such things as revelation, prayer, observation, and other forms of self-conscious spiritual experience. Knowledge of God, sin, salvation, discipleship, sanctification, and justification, are all assumed to relate to a fully cognizant being who can understand certain things, who can avoid or engage in certain ways of thinking and acting, and who is able to make particular choices which have positive and negative implications and consequences for now and into eternity. Even at a basic level, the assertion "If you confess with your mouth, 'Jesus is Lord,' and believe in your heart that God raised him from the dead, you will be saved" (Rom. 10:10) requires a certain level of subjectivity, awareness, and cognitive competence. If the criterion for salvation is what we read in Romans 10:13 — "Everyone who calls on the name of the Lord will be saved" — then those whose intellect, cognition, and memory have been devastated by dementia have a serious problem. How can they claim to love God when they have forgotten who God is?

Subjectivity and Self

Such a focus on subjectivity and the emphasis on the cognitive self are common themes within theology. For example, at the outset of his *Institutes of the Christian Religion,* John Calvin states,

> Nearly all the wisdom which we possess, that is to say, true and sound wisdom, consists of two parts: the knowledge of God and of ourselves. But, while joined by many bonds, which one precedes and brings forth the other is not easy to discern.[19]

---

is. It has spiritual power only if one can remember what such knowledge might mean for one's salvation. (See "Shout to the Lord," words and music by Darlene Zschech, 1993.) Such a way of framing Christian worship is indicative of the kind of theological dynamic that we are exploring here.

19. John Calvin, *Institutes of the Christian Religion* (Philadelphia: Westminster Press, 1960), p. 35.

For Calvin, knowledge of God and knowledge of ourselves (self-knowledge) are wholly intertwined: we can know who we are and why we have what we do only if we look at ourselves in the light of God:

> . . . no one can look upon himself without immediately turning his thoughts to the contemplation of God, in whom he "lives and moves" (Acts 17:28). For, quite clearly, the mighty gifts with which we are endowed are hardly from ourselves; indeed, our very being is nothing but subsistence in the one God. Then, by these benefits shed like dew from heaven upon us, we are led as by rivulets to the spring itself.[20]

As we recognize our dependency, our contingency, and our location within God, so we are freed to see our true state. As we come to know God, we discover who we are. The more we know of God, the more we realize the depth of our own depravity; the more we recognize the depths of our depravity, the more we are drawn toward the wonder of God's grace and sanctifying love. Knowledge of God leads to worship and an awareness of who we are before God. I have no difficulties with Calvin's suggestion regarding the contingent nature of human beings, a suggestion that is key for the argument of this book. Likewise, I recognize that knowing God leads to worship. But it is easy to see problems when we apply Calvin's ideas about knowledge of God to the lives of people with dementia. If knowledge of God is necessary for knowledge of self, and if the only way to access who we are is through active contemplation of who God is, then we have a problem. What happens when one can no longer remember either self or God? How can I know God if I can no longer contemplate God? Can I no longer know God?

A similar emphasis on the knowing self is found in this oft-quoted observation from Augustine:

> Great are you, O Lord, and exceedingly worthy of praise; your power is immense, and your wisdom beyond reckoning. And so we men, who are a due part of your creation, long to praise you — we also carry our mortality about with us, carry the evidence of our sin and with it the proof that you thwart the proud. You arouse us so that praising you may bring us joy, because *you have made us and drawn us to yourself, and our heart is*

20. Calvin, *Institutes of the Christian Religion*, p. 35.

unquiet until it rests in you. Grant me to know and understand, Lord, which comes first. To call upon you or to praise you? To know you or to call upon you? Must we know you before we can call upon you? Anyone who invokes what is still unknown may be making a mistake. Or should you be invoked first, so that we may then come to know you? But how can people call upon someone in whom they do not yet believe? And how can they believe without a preacher? But scripture tells us that those who seek the Lord will praise him, for as they seek they find him, and on finding him they will praise him. Let me seek you then, Lord, even while I am calling upon you, and call upon you even as I believe in you; for to us you have indeed been preached. My faith calls upon you, Lord, this faith which is your gift to me, which you have breathed into me through the humanity of your Son and the ministry of your preacher.[21]

If our hearts are restless until they discover God, and if the human vocation is to know and to worship nothing but God,[22] then at best, people with advanced dementia are destined to be eternally restless, and at worst, they are never going to find or rediscover the place of heart-to-heart peace within the heart of God. If finding God requires that we actively seek after God, then those who can no longer remember what it might mean to do so find themselves trapped in a place of eternal lostness and hopelessness. If we cannot seek the Lord, how can we praise God? If we cannot know and praise God, then how can our hearts be anything other than restless?

If then, as Anselm[23] in like vein suggests, faith has to do with seeking understanding — that is, "an active love of God seeking a deeper knowledge of God" — then it is clear that people with advanced dementia have no real way of finding God. The experience of seeking understanding is precisely what is being lost as one encounters the latter stages of the process of dementia. It would appear that people who are losing their sense of self (at least that sense of self which is addressed in a good deal of theol-

21. St. Augustine, *Confessions,* in *The Works of Saint Augustine: A Translation for the 21st Century,* 2nd ed. (New York: New City Press, 2001); italics added.

22. *Westminister Shorter Catechism:* "Q. 1. What is the chief end of man? A. Man's chief end is to glorify God, and to enjoy him forever." Access at http://www.reformed.org/documents/index.html?mainframe=http://www.reformed.org/documents/WSC_frames .html.

23. Anselm of Canterbury, *Proslogion,* trans. M. J. Charlesworth, in *The Major Works,* ed. Brian Davies and G. R. Evans (New York: Oxford University Press, 1998).

ogy) will struggle to access God, who, it appears, directly addresses only the cognitively able, and who offers no real way to access people for whom selfhood might have a radically different meaning.

Problems arise even in theological ideas that at first might seem to lend themselves positively to the losses that accompany dementia. For example, Friedrich Schleiermacher argues that God is given and present in and with the feeling of "absolute dependence." As an existential experience that resonates in interesting ways with the experience of advanced dementia, discovering God in absolute dependence has the potential to be helpful. Indeed, it is precisely an outworking of this suggestion that underpins much of what is to come in this book. Absolute dependence is the true state of all human beings, and that radical dependency has important implications for how we frame dementia. The problem is that, for Schleiermacher, the awareness of God is the *feeling* of absolute dependence:

> The feeling of absolute dependence, accordingly, is not to be explained as an awareness of the world's existence, but only as an awareness of the existence of God, as the absolute undivided unity.[24]

Such a feeling requires an awareness of the nature of God, and such awareness requires a person to have the cognitive capacity to develop the conceptual language necessary to be aware and to feel dependent on God. How does one know God when one cannot understand or conceptualize the meaning of absolute dependence or interpret and make sense of such a feeling? Despite the fact that the lives of people with advanced dementia are profoundly marked by the experience of "absolute dependence," it is not the absolute dependence that Schleiermacher speaks of.

Toward a Practical Theology of Dementia

These theological problems are not simply dissociated "academic" arguments. They are in fact deeply practical in consequence and orientation. David Keck notes,

---

24. Friedrich Daniel Ernst Schleiermacher, *The Christian Faith* (London: T&T Clark, 1928), p. 132.

> The loss of memory [in dementia] entails a loss of self, and we can no longer be secure in our notions of "self-fulfillment." Indeed, our entire sense of personhood and human purpose is challenged. Because we are dealing with the apparent disintegration of a human being — indeed, the apparent dissolution of many human beings — a thorough reconsideration of many fundamental theological questions is not entirely out of order.[25]

If the primary focus of theology is on the cognitively aware subjective self, and if that very self is perceived to be dissolving as the process of dementia works itself out, then the forgetfulness that marks dementia will inevitably be mirrored by the ways in which theology forgets the experiences of people with dementia. This dual forgetfulness — one the product of neurology, the other the outcome of hyper-cognitive theological assumptions — will inevitably lead to practices which are ill-informed, theologically naïve, and potentially destructive. Keck is correct in suggesting that what is required is a thorough reconsideration of some fundamental theological questions. The intention of this book is to explore what that might look like.

However, while Keck is right on this point, it is not at all clear that Keck's statement that the self is dissolved in the context of advancing dementia is in fact true. If we are our memories, if our sense of who and what we are in the world is determined by what we can remember about ourselves and the world around us, then Keck is correct: losing our memory will inevitably mean losing our selves. If "our selves" are perceived as isolated islands of memories, then we will inevitably disappear when these memories abandon us. In this sense dementia does indeed seem to dissolve our selves, challenge our cultural assumptions of what it means to be human, and force us to question the meaning of a life well-lived. However, as will become clear, human beings are much more than bundles of memories. The key in Keck's statement lies in the word *apparent*. There is a world of difference between an *apparent* dissolution of a human being and the *actual* dissolution of that person. As this book will show, while many things might seem "apparent" when we encounter people with dementia, if we go deeper, if we listen to people and are prepared to give them the benefit of the doubt, that which at first seems "apparent" is quickly re-

25. Keck, *Forgetting Whose We Are*, p. 15.

vealed to be much more complex, opaque, and surprising. It is true that when we encounter people with dementia, we can no longer be secure in our notions of self and self-fulfillment, but that is at least partly because such notions may be false perceptions based on false premises. It will be one of the tasks of this book to show that, devastating as dementia undoubtedly is, the human beings experiencing it do not dissolve. They are certainly changed, and there is much suffering and cause for lament. *But these people remain tightly held within the memories of God.* It is our ideas about what humanness, the nature of the self, and self-fulfillment mean that will have to be dissolved and re-created.

In giving voice to certain key questions that arise in the context of the experience of dementia, particularly advanced dementia, the intention of this book is to provide a practical and theological re-orientation that moves beyond current tendencies to perceive the subjective, self-aware, cognitive self as the necessary qualification for humanness and theological construction, and to open up the possibility that knowing *about* God may not be as important as *knowing God,* and that knowing God involves much more than memory, intellect, and cognition.

1. A Practical Theology of Dementia

Do not conform any longer to the pattern of this world, but be transformed by the renewing of your mind. Then you will be able to test and approve what God's will is — his good, pleasing, and perfect will.

ROMANS 12:2

We are to attempt an answer to the questions, "What is there within the Bible? What sort of house is it to which the Bible is the door? What sort of country is spread before our eyes when we throw the Bible open?"

KARL BARTH

In essence this book develops what one might describe as a practical theology of dementia. As a theological discipline, practical theology seeks to explore the interface between the practices of the church and the practices of the world with a view to enabling faithful participation in God's redemptive practices in, to, and for the world.[1] Practical theology is that as-

---

1. John Swinton and Harriet Mowat, *Practical Theology and Qualitative Research Method* (London: SCM Press, 2006), p. 6. Here the term "practices" relates to forms of divinely inspired human action (individual and communal) which are rooted in Christian beliefs about the world and the way that God and human beings perceive and act within the world. Such an understanding of practices assumes that all forms of human action, includ-

pect of theology which seeks to bring together theology and practice in an attempt to describe and redescribe the world in order that the practices of Christians can remain true to the practices of God in, to, and for the world. Theology has to do with knowledge of God. However, such knowledge is not simply intellectual. Knowledge *about* God should lead to and indeed requires knowledge *of* God, and knowledge *of* God is necessarily experiential, practical, and transformative.[2] Theology provides us with a lens through which we can look at the world. It offers us a perspective on the way things are which scripts and guides Christian thinking, perception, and living. The object of this book is to use this lens to develop a theological redescription of dementia which is shaped by a different script. Such a description acknowledges the pain and suffering that this condition brings to those with dementia and their families, but offers an alternative theological reading of the condition within which hope and new possibilities — in the present and for the future — remain even in the midst of deep forgetfulness. This different view of dementia will enable us to respond to it differently.

Redescription as a Mode of Practical Theology

A central aspect of the approach of this book is what I will describe as "theological redescription." In his book *Redescribing Reality: What We Do When We Read the Bible*, Walter Brueggemann proposes that the task of Scripture is not simply to offer moral guidance and tell us things about God, although it certainly does these things. In addition, Scripture's task is to *redescribe the world*. The Christian's task is to enter into the strange world of the Bible and to allow that world to redescribe reality. It is as we learn to

---

ing the actions of Christians, are value-laden. Christian practices emerge from a variety of traditions and perspectives, all of which serve to shape and form the ways in which we see the world and the forms of action that we may or may not deem appropriate for our encounters with the world. We practice what we believe in quite literal ways. In this sense, Christian practices are embodied theology which can be read, interpreted, and understood in a way similar to the way in which we read and interpret texts.

2. The apostle James observes that anybody can know things *about* God: "You say you have faith, for you believe that there is one God. Good for you! Even the demons believe this, and they tremble in terror" (James 2:19). Knowledge *about* God is useless without knowledge *of* God. To *know* God is something quite different from knowing *about* God.

live in this redescribed world that we encounter God and one another in fresh and challenging ways and find the resources for faithful discipleship.[3]

Brueggemann argues that we make sense of the world by utilizing a variety of implicit and explicit scripts (stories that form our worldview). These scripts help us to define, negotiate, act on, and make sense of the world. So, for example, nationalism, religion, capitalism, psychology, and biomedicine would be five primary scripts that form the epistemological context of Western liberal cultures. Such scripts are so powerful and so deeply ingrained in our thinking that we often don't recognize the impact that they have on the ways in which we see and understand the world, including the ways in which we see and understand Scripture. Many of us no longer recognize that these scripts have been taught to us by people and systems that have quite particular goals, intentions, and worldviews.

However powerful and apparently decisive these defining scripts may seem to be, their claims are always open to counterclaims which may challenge or even overpower their definitions of the way the world is. The Christian narrative is one such counterclaim. Scripture calls the church to live by a different script, which emerges from within "the strange new world within the Bible."[4] This script offers a radical redescription of the world, turning it from a place of individualism and competitiveness, a place where autonomy, freedom, and choice reign supreme, into a place where we discover the sovereignty and majesty of God, who has created all things. In this new space of creation, we discover that salvation comes through brokenness,[5] strength comes through weakness,[6] and gentleness is revealed as an ontological aspect of the Messiah-who-is-God.[7] It is impor-

---

3. Walter Brueggemann, *Redescribing Reality: What We Do When We Read the Bible* (London: SCM Press, 2009).

4. Neil MacDonald, *Karl Barth and the Strange New World within the Bible: Barth, Wittgenstein, and the Metadilemmas of the Enlightenment* (Cumbria: Paternoster Press, 2006).

5. John 12:24: "I tell you the truth, unless a kernel of wheat is planted in the soil and dies, it remains alone. But its death will produce many new kernels — a plentiful harvest of new lives" (NLT).

6. 2 Corinthians 12:9: "But he said to me, 'My grace is sufficient for you, for my power is made perfect in weakness.' Therefore I will boast all the more gladly about my weaknesses, so that Christ's power may rest on me" (NIV).

7. Matthew 11:29: "Take my yoke upon you. Let me teach you, because I am humble and gentle at heart, and you will find rest for your souls" (NIV). The statement "I am humble and gentle at heart" is profound. Jesus who *is* God claims that in his very essence he is hum-

tant for our current purposes to note that this strange world is a place where intellect and human wisdom are perceived as barriers rather than as aids to faithfulness.[8] Dementia will inevitably look different within such a strange new world. That being so, the practical theological task will be one of offering critical redescriptions of the world in the light of the new script of the gospel. The task is to *redescribe the world* in the light of Scripture and tradition and to look carefully at what dementia *really* looks like within this strange new world.

Challenging the World

Brueggemann's point is similar to the point made in the previous chapter regarding the relationship between theology and medicine. The Christian task is not to try to make the Bible relevant to society — quite the opposite. Christians are called to help society to recognize that it actually already lives within the strange world that is described in the Bible. It has just forgotten this primal fact. The Bible is not just inspirational and hopeful; it is revelatory and transformative. Put in terms of the intentions of this book, our task is not simply to see how the Christian story can contribute to our current understandings of dementia, although this is certainly important. But the deeper task is to see what our current understandings of dementia and the practices that emerge from them look like when they are viewed and redescribed from the perspective of the strange biblical world.

Brueggemann suggests that " . . every time the church takes up Scripture, it undertakes a serious challenge to dominant characterizations of our social world. It dares to propose an alternative reading of the world, an alternative version that is in fact a sub-version that rests beneath the dominant version in a less aggressive form."[9] So, for example, he points to the words of Psalm 119:105: "Your word is a lamp to my feet and a light to my path." This text powerfully asserts that the Torah, the most important Jew-

---

ble and gentle. Somewhere within the heart of God, humility and gentleness reign. To be humble and gentle is to be like God.

8. 1 Corinthians 3:19: "For the wisdom of this world is foolishness to God. As the Scriptures say, 'He traps the wise in the snare of their own cleverness'" (NLT).

9. Walter Brueggemann, *Redescribing Reality*.

ish teaching tradition, is the *lamp* and the *light* that guides people in the world. It redescribes the basis of power and the nature of the world. In the midst of the many competing claims about what the world is and how humans should function within it, the Torah (and in similar fashion, the gospel) reveals in fresh and radical ways the meaning of living well in sickness and in health.

In seeking to redescribe dementia using Scripture, theology, and tradition, this book will aim to protest against negative and misleading descriptions, insisting that "the initial presentation of reality is not an adequate or trustworthy account."[10] If the cultural narrative that underpins our perceptions of dementia is that dependence is something to be feared, and that autonomy and freedom are things to be desired, the basic assertion that we live in *creation* offers a radical redescription. Autonomy and freedom are meaningful only as they relate to the contingency of human beings before God. If God is the Creator, and if we live in a creation which God says is good,[11] then at the very least we know that we are created out of love and loved beyond all measure.[12] If God knew us when we were still in the womb (Ps. 139), and if God does have plans for us to prosper,[13] then neurological decline cannot separate us from the love of God and our ongoing vocation as human beings. Lives that are touched by profound forms of dementia have meaning and continuing purpose.

The redescriptions of dementia that will be offered in the following chapters will not, of course, be wholly independent of the old descriptions. The old descriptions may turn out to be necessary, but they are insufficient. Like the resurrection body (1 Cor. 15), the art of theological redescription recognizes that the redescribed world will have continuity and discontinuity with what has gone before. The old descriptions retain some degree of utility and value but are transformed in important ways. The new description, as Brueggemann explains, "employs in fresh ways speech that is already known and trusted. In order to serve as 'redescription,' however, the

10. Walter Brueggemann, *The Word that Redescribes the World: The Bible and Discipleship* (Minneapolis: Augsburg Fortress Press, 2006).

11. Genesis 1:31: "God saw all that he had made, and it was very good. And there was evening, and there was morning — the sixth day" (NLT).

12. John 3:16: "For God so loved the world that he gave his one and only Son, that whoever believes in him shall not perish but have eternal life" (NIV).

13. Jeremiah 29:11: "'For I know the plans I have for you,' declares the Lord, 'plans to prosper you and not to harm you, plans to give you hope and a future'" (NIV).

already trusted speech must be uttered in daring, venturesome ways that intensify, subvert, and amaze."[14]

Whether the thoughts presented in this book serve to intensify, subvert, and amaze is for the reader to decide! In this book I will listen carefully and critically to the known and trusted scripts that have been constructed around the nature of the experience of dementia. However, rather than simply uncritically reiterating the standard accounts of dementia, I will redescribe the condition in ways that are recognizable but have become intense, subversive, and, perhaps, amazing as they encounter the radical script of Scripture, theology, and tradition. Such redescription will enable dementia to look and indeed to *be* something quite different from the culturally constructed norms of it. This, I hope, will lead to responses which are caring, compassionate, and, above all else, faithful.

To summarize, I'll provide the definition of redescription as a practical theological method:

> Redescription is an interdisciplinary approach to practical theology that seeks, in the light of Scripture and Christian tradition, to redescribe objects, actions, situations, and contexts in ways that reveal hidden meanings, modes of oppression and misrepresentation, with a view to offering a fuller and more accurate description that highlights alternative understandings and previously inconceivable options for theory and action.

The Stories That We Tell

Central to the approach of redescription as it will be worked out here is the significance of stories. In developing this point, it will be helpful to return to the question that opened this book: Who am I? One way of answering that question is that we are the stories that we tell about ourselves and that are told about us. Human beings are natural storytellers. We live in a world that is profoundly shaped and formed by the stories we tell about ourselves and one another. We tell stories to identify ourselves — stories about our past, stories about our hoped-for futures, stories about what is happening

---

14. Walter Brueggemann, "Cadences Which Redescribe: Speech among Exiles," *Journal for Preachers* 27, no. 3 (Easter 1994): 10-17.

in the here and now. We continually move backward and forward in time as we use our stories to describe who we were, who we are, and what we hope we will become. Storytelling reveals the inherent timelessness of human existence. With just a few words we can traverse years, racing backward toward our memories or shifting forward toward infinite possible futures. We perceive ourselves as existing in the present, but at any given time a story can take us backward or forward in time, revealing old or new experiences, opening us to future worlds that contain possibilities we hadn't even considered before. Some of the stories we tell and that are told about us are true, some of them are imaginative, and others are just plain false. Nonetheless, all of them come together to give us a sense of who we are and where we are located within the ongoing stories of our lives.

The Power of Counter-Stories

While our identity, in a sense, may change over time (I say "in a sense" because the question of identity over time will become significant and much less obvious as the book moves on), we normally remain aware that certain stories, whether they be about ourselves, others, or the world around us, are true and others are not. We can be mistaken or deceived, but we still continue to believe or disbelieve them. Even illusory stories, if we believe them, are true in their consequences. Under normal circumstances, most people are able to effectively negotiate their narrative worlds and gain and retain a more or less realistic sense of who they are. In whatever flawed way, they can articulate this sense of self-in-the-world in ways that present and maintain their identity within the public and the personal realms. This in turn protects them from the imposition of false identities that may be inaccurate or dangerous. Not all stories are true. Some stories need to be countered. The key to holding onto one's identity, even if one is not entirely sure of who one is, lies in the art of being able to effectively tell counter-stories that correct the picture.[15]

However, there are circumstances within one's life where one — literally or by default — loses the ability to tell one's own story. Dementia is

---

15. I am indebted to Hilde Lindemann for this idea of counter-stories that serve to heal broken narratives. See Hilde Lindemann Nelson, *Damaged Identities, Narrative Repair* (New York: Cornell University Press, 2001), especially chapters 3 and 5.

one of these circumstances. If one has been diagnosed with dementia, the availability of plausible, positive counter-stories is not always apparent. One of the problems for people with dementia is that they gradually begin to lose the ability to tell their own stories. Over time it is the stories of others that shape their experiences and place the parameters on their identity, personhood, and experiences. Particularly those people with advanced dementia simply do not have the ability to articulate counter-stories in ways that provide them with enough social power to sustain their identities as valuable and capable human beings.[16] The various stories told by the powerful others that surround them — doctors, neurologists, nurses, society, media, family, friends — eventually overwhelm their own stories, leaving them echoing author Christine Boden's words — "Who will I be when I die?"[17] — and resonating in a strange way with Jesus' question to his disciples: "Who do you say I am?"[18] Even if people with dementia have important stories to tell about themselves and others, who will listen? Gradually the question changes from that which is asked by all people — "How can I tell my story well?" — to a new and more complex question: "*Who* will tell my story well?" Having to ask the latter question puts one in a position of tremendous vulnerability. In a culture which prizes memory, intellect, freedom, reason, and autonomy, what kinds of stories will be told about those who seem to be losing these things? Their question is haunting: *Who will tell our stories well when we have forgotten who we are?*

16. If the reader finds himself or herself pulled up by the suggestion that people with dementia are not "capable human beings," this essentially makes the point. Precisely what is it that makes them incapable? Is the term "incapable" an all-inclusive adjective, or does it refer only to certain faculties that we perceive have been lost? Which story drives our perception of capability?

17. Christine Boden, *Who Will I Be When I Die?* (Melbourne: HarperCollins, 1998). Boden was diagnosed with dementia when she was only forty-six; in this book she details the beginning of her illness.

18. Matthew 16:13-16: "When Jesus came to the region of Caesarea Philippi, he asked his disciples, 'Who do people say the Son of Man is?' They replied, 'Some say John the Baptist; others say Elijah; and still others, Jeremiah or one of the prophets.' 'But what about you?' he asked. 'Who do you say I am?' Simon Peter answered, 'You are the Messiah, the Son of the living God'" (NIV). The key thing for Jesus here was that in the midst of confusing narratives and possible identities, Peter alone noticed who Jesus *really* was and bore witness to that fact. There is a powerful principle here for dementia care.

Story, Counter-Story, Revelation

This book will suggest that some of the central stories we have been accustomed to using to explain the phenomenon of dementia are at best inadequate and at worst deeply flawed. They require counter-stories that will correct, enhance, and transform them. In a real sense we need to re-narrate dementia in the light of the coming kingdom of God. For the reasons highlighted thus far, I will argue that it is the Christian story which offers real possibilities in terms of the development of transformative counter-stories. When spoken into the experience of dementia, the Christian story has the potential to reveal and reframe dementia in vital ways. Such a counter-story offers a radical redescription of the world and of dementia. It challenges accepted stories of biomedical determinism, inevitable neurological decline, the nature of suffering, the prioritization of the intellect, the role of memory, the potency of individualism, competitiveness, and autonomy, and the value of freedom. The counter-story of God does the work of repairing broken or misleading narratives and as such will become a place of rupture, resistance, and change. This new counter-story will not be read and understood apart from the old narratives. Neurology, psychology, biomedicine, and psychiatry all remain important aspects of dementia care, but they will be seen in a different light. Instead of providing a script that shapes and determines our understanding of dementia, they themselves will be called to learn a new script.

In a sense, this book will engage in a process that Gilles Deleuze and Félix Guattari have described as *deterritorialization*, a process "whereby certain framings of ideas, people, ways of being (and so on) are undermined by reconfigurations of those elements that frame them in those particular ways."[19] This will mean that dementia remains within the general frame of neurological disorder marked by decline, loss of cognitive faculties, suffering, disease, and so forth. Aspects of this large standard story of dementia remain significant, although always open to challenge and counter. However, it will be assumed throughout this book that "there is . . . nothing given about any configuration and thus it is possible to reconfigure the framing of dementia using different elements."[20] This means that we can take elements of

19. Quoted in Clive Baldwin and Andrea Capstick, *Tom Kitwood on Dementia: A Reader and Critical Commentary* (Maidenhead: Open University Press, 2007), p. 17. The idea is developed in detail in Gilles Deleuze and Félix Guattari, *A Thousand Plateaus: Capitalism and Schizophrenia* (London: Continuum, 2004).

20. Baldwin and Capstick, *Tom Kitwood on Dementia,* p. 17.

knowledge from standard stories and use them in the service of God to create a different story which redescribes dementia in new, challenging, and more faithful ways. The point of this book is not necessarily to take territory away from established understandings, but to retake territory that rightly belongs to the story of God and the practices of the church.

Listening to Stories

One final observation is important to bear in mind. While the primary counter-story is the story of the gospel, throughout this book I will be using smaller, personal stories which also function as powerful counter-stories to some of the more oppressive stories that surround dementia. It would be a mistake to read these stories as simply illustrating the points that are being made, or as neutral foci for theological reflection. These stories are themselves strong counter-stories that will help to redescribe dementia in important ways and will enable readers to see the practical relevance of the broader and wider counter-story of God's actions in the world. As we engage with these stories, it will be helpful if readers bear in mind that each story contains and reveals deep insights into the nature and character of God and human beings, and the nature and character of God's practices in, to, and for the world. Karl Barth observes that we cannot know God apart from that which God chooses to reveal:

> God is known only by God. We do not know Him, then, in virtue of the views and concepts with which in faith we attempt to respond to His revelation. But we also do not know Him without making use of His permission and obeying His command to undertake this attempt. The success of this undertaking, and therefore the veracity of our human knowledge of God, consists in the fact that our viewing and conceiving [are] adopted and determined to participate in the truth of God by God Himself in grace.[21]

God is known only according to what God chooses to reveal. God is known as God acts. One way to frame the various stories presented in this

---

21. Karl Barth, *Church Dogmatics*, 4 vols., ed. Thomas F. Torrance, trans. Geoffrey W. Bromiley (London and New York: T&T Clark, 2009), II/II.1, p. 179.

book is to say that they are places of revelation, places where God in some sense is acting and revealing. God acts in the big stories in history — in those of the Exodus, the Cross, and redemption. But God also acts in and through the smaller stories of human life. If we take time to listen and to reflect, we can discover God's practices of revealing and acting in the strangest of places.

2. Redescribing Dementia: Starting from the Right Place

The process of scientific discovery is, in effect, a continual flight from wonder.

ALBERT EINSTEIN

I am gentle.

JESUS OF NAZARETH, MATTHEW 11:29

L ike any journey, traveling toward an understanding of dementia requires that we start at the right place, follow the most appropriate
routes, and read the correct maps. If I'm flying to Boston, I need to be in
the right airport and make sure I get on the right plane. If I get on the
wrong plane, I'm not going to reach my destination. I may well end up in
interesting places, and indeed I might even convince myself that these interesting places are actually parts of Boston, even though those who actually live in Boston know very well that they are not. But in the end, I'll still
be in Pittsburgh! (I hasten to add that there's nothing wrong with arriving
in Pittsburgh as long as that's your destination.) Understanding dementia
is a bit like that. If we get on the wrong track or follow the wrong road
map, we'll end up in the wrong place. We'll see some interesting things
along the way, but in the end we won't know what dementia is because we
won't really have visited it. In this chapter I will present a revised map of
the territory of dementia. This map will take full consideration of the

other maps and perspectives that surround our understandings of dementia. However, it will present the beginning of a fresh route, which suggests that theologians and pastoral carers might be wise to start their journey in a different place from where they might "naturally" assume they should begin. This place might seem a little strange and unnatural, but if we go there, we'll find that our journey into dementia will reveal important new territories which will bring fresh understanding and, perhaps, revelation.

It is important to be clear about the intention of this chapter. Although I will be offering some challenges to established models of dementia and standard ways of understanding it, I do not intend my tone to be polemical toward medicine, psychiatry, neurobiology, psychology, or any of the other established disciplines that are focused on helping us understand the nature of dementia. But I will be suggesting that these disciplines are not necessarily the best place for theologians and pastoral carers to begin their journey into dementia, and that there is a need, at times, for challenge and critique. I am not, however, suggesting that they are unimportant aspect of the process of mapping and understanding dementia. This chapter is written *for* theologians and pastoral carers and not *against* any other perspectives. Dementia is a multifaceted condition. Problems arise when a single facet is prioritized (culturally or medically) and assumed to be definitive of the whole explanation. My suggestion is that this easily happens with dementia and that there are good reasons why this is an unwise theological and pastoral move. In beginning to tease this out, we must start with a story: a *counter-story*.

Two Ways of Looking

Michael Ignatieff's book *Scar Tissue* is a powerful and moving semi-autobiographical account of a son's experience of his mother's development of Alzheimer's disease and her eventual untimely death. It tracks the complex emotions that families go through as they wrestle with the difficult issues that emerge from watching and being with someone who is forgetting all that once made her the person they remembered and loved. It is a beautiful and somewhat disturbing reflection on the nature of the self and the processes that serve to "self" and "un-self" people experiencing advanced dementia. At the heart of the story are two sons and two quite different relationships. The story pivots around the sons' shared experience of their mother's dementia and the very different ways in which they deal with it. One son (the narrator of the story) is a philosopher; his brother is a medical doctor and a hard-nosed scientist. The book offers two ways of looking at dementia that result in two quite different stories that can be told about it. The philosopher son narrates the world in terms of ideas, emotions, and alternative possibilities using sources of knowledge that are not determined by the boundaries of scientific method, knowledge, and inquiry. For him it is the experience of dementia — both his experience and his mother's experience — that is of paramount importance. The scientist son inhabits a story that perceives the world primarily in objective and empirical terms. There is no mystery or wonder in this story — just hard, cold facts. What is true about dementia is that which is empirically provable and evidentially the case. This brother resides in a world where the scientific method and the technology that emerges from it reign supreme. It is perhaps not inconsequential that while he desires to know a great deal about the etiology and prognosis of his mother's illness, he rarely visits her.

Both brothers share the same mother, but in her now primary role as a person with dementia, they see her very differently. The doctor sees dementia as a medical entity that requires the marshaling of all the technical resources available in order to do battle with the condition that is destroying his mother. Though he rarely visits her, he nonetheless constantly pushes for increased medical contact and clinical intervention. The philosopher experiences his mother's dementia quite differently. For him, dementia is deeply personal, wrapped up in his day-to-day life with his mother, whom he refuses to abandon to negative external assessments of the disease. He knows that what dementia is cannot be separated from who his mother is and is becoming, and he sees dementia as personal and relational. He visits his mother every day — in fact, his insistent desire to visit his mother strains his marriage to the breaking point. He visits her so often that, eventually, the reader begins to realize that he is in fact visiting his own future. In the last few pages of the book, he talks about the scar tissue within his own brain; dementia has not yet emerged, but it is on its way.

Giving the Benefit of the Doubt

Unlike his medical brother, the philosopher chooses not to accept uncritically the stories he is told about his mother by the professionals he encounters. His mother's true self has *not* gone; the mother he once knew and loved is *not* gradually disappearing. She is *not* losing her self. It may appear that way to some, but he knows something different because he knows her. He knows what happens and what he sees when he comes close. *He wants to give her the benefit of the doubt.* However, suggesting that she should be given the benefit of the doubt is a hard story to sustain in the face of powerful stories that have already decided what she will inevitably become. Ignatieff narrates a powerful and revealing encounter between the philosopher son and one of his mother's doctors:

> I want to say that my mother's true self remains intact, there at the surface of her being, like a feather resting on the surface tension of a glass of water, in the way she listens, nods, rests her hand on her cheek, when we are together. But I stumble along and just stop.
>
> The doctor tries to help me out. "This seems to matter to you." "Because," I say, "a lot depends on whether people like you treat her as a human being or not."
>
> She is too clever to rise to this. She deals with beleaguered and hostile relatives all the time. "This is difficult for you. I know that. My job is to give you the facts."
>
> "She needs respect," I say, unsure why I am saying it.
>
> "Of course." And then she says, reflectively, "Though who knows what 'respect' means."
>
> "Just giving her the benefit of the doubt. Just assuming there might be some method in her madness."
>
> The doctor smiles. "So act 'as if' she is rational. Behave 'as if' she knows what she is saying."
>
> "Exactly."
>
> I tell her how mother goes in and out of the bathroom five times an hour because she does not want to wet herself but can't tell when she last went to the bathroom. So her strategy is to behave "as if" she needs to go to the bathroom, whenever the thought occurs to her. There is a method here. This is not random, panic-stricken behavior. Self-respect is in play here. This is how she manages to avoid making a mess of herself. My voice rises at this point, and both of us go silent.
>
> "From a clinical point of view," she says, taking up the thread, "disinhibition begins with disintegration in the frontal lobes. Your mother's frontal lobes are not yet affected," the neurologist goes on, "which would help to explain why she is continent and why she is gentle."

"She is gentle," I say, "because that's the kind of person that she is."

"I know how you must feel."

"Besides," I say, "disinhibition is such an ugly word. . . . Disinhibition suggests that everything is beyond her. Actually she is struggling."

It is pointless to go on, and we both know it. The doctor looks at Mother's PET scan and sees a disease of memory function, with a stable name and a clear prognosis. I see an illness of selfhood without a name or even a clear cause.[1]

Both the son and the doctor are looking at the same person, but both see radically different things. I use the term "radical" in its basic form as relating to the very root of a thing. At root, they are looking at the same person and seeing things totally differently. One sees disease and disintegration and names it with technical terms; the other sees his mother, with all that such recognition implies.

The son's task of positively recognizing and remembering his mother is a difficult one. The apparent "obviousness" of the cause of her dementia and the "clear" meaning of her neurological decline do not lend themselves easily to a different interpretation of her experiences, particularly when the naming power within the conversation is clearly to the advantage of the specialist:

"Take the business about her language," I say. "She can't maintain a conversation, but the way she listens, and laughs when you say something that amuses her, nods to let you know she's following what you say."

The doctor seems interested. "Her semantic and syntactic memory functions have collapsed, but prosodic variation is still intact."

"Prosodic variation?"

She means tone of voice, facial expression, gestures. Some patients begin to drawl or stutter in a voice that they have never used before. "They hear themselves speak," she says, "and they think, 'Who is this?'"

"That's not my mother. She still knows who she is. She may not talk correctly, but she's still able to take part in a conversation. She still has her social skills."

The doctor is good-naturedly persistent. "Her prosodic variation is still intact."

1. Michael Ignatieff, *Scar Tissue* (London: Penguin Books, 1993), pp. 58-60.

It is the word "still" that bothers me. *"You keep telling me what has been lost, and I keep telling you something remains."*[2]

Digitizing Mother

At one point, the brother who is a doctor insists that their mother has a series of neurological tests to see what's going on within her "failing brain." He recognizes there is no cure, but seems driven to look and see what's going on. His philosopher brother has no desire for such tests but goes along with them in spite of himself:

> . . . neurological investigations are humiliating. "Urine samples, blood samples, X-rays, CAT scans, PET scans. Christ, what do we need this for?" . . . And so it proved. Mother was led, naked and uncomprehending, into a tiled room and sealed inside a machine that resembled one of those iron lungs in a B-movie. I stood in the control room, on the other side of the glass, watching her terrified glances as her head was placed inside an instrument to measure cerebral activity. Like a fool, I began to wave, though she couldn't see me. Her legs made small struggling gestures of fear, and a technician flicked on the intercom and told her not to. I stood there, beyond the glass, wanting to kill my brother for putting her through this. Then the sedation took hold, and she lay awake but motionless, while a stream of images of the neurochemical activity within her brain flowed across the monitors in the control room. The technicians were talkative. They told me what to look for: bright blue for the skull casing, red for the cerebral lobes, purple for the tracer. I stood there watching brightly colored neural images of Mother's fear and dread.[3]

The medical procedure presumed to show that dementia was best understood in terms of damaged neurons. The tests, machines, and chemicals drew a beautiful picture of the neurological architecture of a failing brain. The technology noted and tracked the neurochemical activity and neatly recorded the structures of the mother's brain so that her defects could be

---

2. Ignatieff, *Scar Tissue*, p. 58; italics added.
3. Ignatieff, *Scar Tissue*, p. 55.

named accurately. The technician saw neurological defect and decline and named it dementia. The son saw his mother, someone whom he loved who was experiencing fear and dread. The technology did not tell him anything about her that he didn't already know, other than that her fear and dread could now be seen and measured. But could it be understood?

Ignatieff's narrative of the two brothers' experience of their mother's dementia illustrates well the difficult tension between the standard story of dementia, with its focus on the specifics of neurological decline and technological intervention, and the "hidden" story that trundles along beside, through, and underneath it. The hidden story sometimes sounds quite ridiculous. It is easily silenced by the skillful use of technical language. And yet, the experience of the philosopher son tells us some deep things about the nature of dementia even if his language and experience do not correlate well with the medical account. In order to understand why there is often such a disjunction and a tension between medical accounts of dementia and the lived experiences of dementia, we need to spend some time reflecting on how the concept of dementia comes into existence in the first place and why the process of naming particular human experiences like dementia might be more complicated and deceptive than it first appears.

Naming Dementia: The Question of Definition

Let us begin with the question of exactly what dementia is. The criteria used by health care professionals to define dementia have been collated, assimilated, and laid out in quite specific ways. Richard Cheston and Michael Bender note the following:

> At present two important systems of classifying psychiatric illnesses exist. The World Health Organization sponsored the development, in 1948, of the International Classification of Diseases (ICD);[4] in the U.S. a

4. *The ICD-10 Classification of Mental and Behavioral Disorders: Clinical Descriptions and Diagnostic Guidelines* (Geneva: World Health Organization, 1992). According to the World Health Organization, "The ICD is the international standard diagnostic classification for all general epidemiological, many health management purposes and clinical use. These include the analysis of the general health situation of population groups and monitoring of the incidence and prevalence of diseases and other health problems in relation to other variables such as the characteristics and circumstances of the individuals affected, reimburse-

slightly different system emerged known as the American Psychiatric
Association Diagnostic and Statistical Manual (DSM).[5] Both of these
systems have gone through many variations, with some illnesses being
abandoned, others brought into being, and most altered, some radically.
The latest versions are ICD-10 and DSM-IV.[6]

These diagnostic criteria represent formal attempts to try to bring together
and make sense of a variety of different human experiences (memory loss,
disorientation, social and relational difficulties, and so forth) — experiences that have been perceived as problematic by the people who have
them, as well as their families and society. The specific collation and
grouping of these experiences form the diagnostic criteria which a consensus of professionals has agreed to use. Although based on scientific research and observation, the process of defining and naming what are and
what are not the constituent parts of dementia is not an objective process.
The difficult history of the development of such criteria indicates that
there is often little consensus among doctors concerning what should or
should not be included within any given form of categorization. In other
words, definitions always emerge from a context of contention and sometimes widely differing opinions. This is not to suggest that the general approach is not scientific. It is, however, to point out that the politics that
surrounds the ways in which scientific data is worked with in this context
is not objective or value-free. Warren Kinghorn puts this point well in his
reflections on the origins and purpose of the DSM criteria:

> The truth is that the *DSM*, like any psychiatric diagnostic classification,
> has never been an "objective" document in this sense. It has always been
> a pragmatic tool of a particular clinical community — starting with
> American psychiatry and extending, in recent years, to global psychia-
> try, to the nonpsychiatric mental health professions, and to medicine as
> a whole — useful for fostering interclinician communication, for pro-

ment, resource allocation, quality, and guidelines." See http://www.who.int/classifications/
icd/en/.

5. DSM-IV is the main diagnostic manual used by psychiatrists to make diagnoses. It is
produced by the American Psychiatric Association and covers all categories of mental health
disorders for both adults and children.

6. Richard Cheston and Michael Bender, *Understanding Dementia: The Man with the
Worried Eyes* (London: Jessica Kingsley Publishers, 1999), p. 51.

viding an operational base for the organization of research, for self-regulating and disciplining diagnostic practices, and for proposing to the public that particular states of affairs are best interpreted within the language-game of psychiatry.[7]

Kinghorn highlights the important point that classificatory systems such as the DSM or the ICD are intended as *practical tools for mental health-care professionals,* beginning with psychiatrists and moving outward from there into the perceptions of wider society. They are not intended as neutral descriptions that can be used as explanatory frameworks for all people in all contexts at all times, although in practice that is often how they are perceived.[8] They are constructed *specifically* as pragmatic responses to particular needs that have been recognized and named in specific ways by particular professional disciplines.

This observation has two consequences. First, it should make those who do not belong to this particular community of reference wary of sim-

7. Warren Kinghorn, "Ordering 'Mental Disorder': Theology and the Disputed Boundaries of Psychiatric Diagnosis." Unpublished paper presented at the Society for Spirituality, Theology, and Health, 3rd Annual Meeting, Durham, North Carolina, 17 June 2010. Kinghorn also astutely observes, "[That] the *DSM* categories have so deeply pervaded public discourse about human suffering as to affect the way that questions are framed, so that the *DSM* is conveniently able to provide the answers to what turn out to be its own questions, only adds to its power." For a further elaboration of this point and a deepening of the overall argument within a broader mental health context, see Warren Kinghorn, "Whose Disorder?: A Constructive MacIntyrean Critique of Psychiatric Nosology," *Journal of Medicine and Philosophy Advance,* February 28, 2011, pp. 1-19.

8. Ethan Watters makes this point very well in his book *Crazy Like Us: The Globalization of the American Psyche* (New York: Free Press, 2010). Watters lays out a convincing argument to suggest that America in particular is exporting its own understandings of what constitutes mental suffering. DSM categories are worked out within a Western, primarily American context and then exported to other cultures. The power of such diagnostic enterprises is such that local understandings and definitions of mental distress are overpowered and subsumed by the powerful Western models. Consequently, he argues, there is an ongoing process of homogenization of the mind whereby one particular set of understandings about the workings of the mind is coming to have universal significance and acceptance, despite the fact that it is just that: one particular understanding of mental health and mental health problems. Waters sees this colonialization of the mind as dangerous, not least because, as we have seen, such diagnostic categories are inevitably deeply culturally bound. The homogenization of mental illness brings with it a homogenization of culture which is deeply problematic.

ply taking up such definitions and applying them as if they were intended as universal explanatory frameworks. Second, the ongoing controversies regarding the construction of these definitions and the ways in which diagnoses and categories shift and change over time should alert us to the subjective and fallible nature of such ways of defining dementia. Cheston and Bender correctly make this point:

> No matter what criteria are developed, the process whereby a diagnosis is reached is inevitably a subjective one carried out by fallible human beings. Moreover, it is these fallible human beings who have to decide what is and is not an illness. Over time these decisions about illness and symptoms have changed, so that we now recognize sets of behaviors that even 20 years ago would have been disregarded or seen as evidence of moral weakness.[9]

Cheston and Bender highlight the case of the ongoing creation of Alzheimer's as indicative of the fallible and political nature of the construction of dementia. For many contemporary people, the term "Alzheimer's disease" has become, at least linguistically, synonymous with dementia. However, the complex history of the development of the category of Alzheimer's disease reveals a less-than-straightforward story. Cheston and Bender observe,

> In the 1970s, before the third edition of the DSM, Alzheimer's disease was defined as a pre-senile dementia: an illness which only affected younger people. Later editions of the DSM have defined Alzheimer's disease in a much broader and therefore more inclusive way. . . . The reasons for this shift are complicated but have much to do with the need to define dementia in a way that will be attractive to potential sources of research money. After all, you can claim to be able to find the cure for a disease in a way that you cannot for old age or senility.[10]

9. Cheston and Bender, *Understanding Dementia*, pp. 50-51.
10. Cheston and Bender, *Understanding Dementia*, p. 51. One of the most interesting and compelling critiques of the construction of Alzheimer's is offered by Daniel George in his book *The Myth of Alzheimer's: What You Aren't Being Told about Today's Most Dreaded Diagnosis* (New York: St. Martin's Press, 2008). Readers interested in this line of thinking will also find helpful a book by Nancy Harding and Colin Palfrey: *The Social Construction of Dementia: Confused Professionals?* (London: Jessica Kingsley Publishers, 1997). In particular, their reflection on Patrick Fox's critique of the construction of Alzheimer's disease opens up

The point is that naming dementia as a specific disease makes it more attractive for potential funders. If it is a disease, there might be the possibility of a cure. In a socio-cultural milieu that tends to fear aging, this can easily be heard and processed in terms of a cure for old age.[11]

This is not to suggest that there is no such thing as Alzheimer's disease, or to in any way downplay it as a very real condition. The point here is to question the social power of this particular name for dementia. Why is it that one rarely if ever finds a high-profile campaign that seeks to highlight Lewy bodies, Korsakoff's syndrome, Binswanger's disease, or vascular dementias? Is it coincidental that the *disease* of Alzheimer's often ends up linguistically representing forms of dementia that are not caused by the specific identifiable disease processes that underpin the diagnosis of Alzheimer's? It may simply be a matter of numbers: more people seem to have Alzheimer's than other forms of dementia, although we can't be completely sure even about this, because the only way that one can test for Alzheimer's is either postmortem or via medical technology that most people don't have access to. Or/and it's possible that the more overtly political dimension that Cheston and Bender have noticed is implicitly present within lay and professional discourse.[12] The point is that diagnostic categories are a locus for a complex process of negotiation and a struggle for power and authority which is deeply influenced by such things as cultural expectations, research agendas, and resource allocation. They are considerably less objective and much more flexible than we might at first assume.

---

the issues neatly (pp. 79-82). (See Patrick Fox, "From Senility to Alzheimer's Disease: The Rise of the Alzheimer's Disease Movement," *Milbank Quarterly* 67, no. 1 [1989]: 58-102.)

11. Martin Albert and Bracha Mildworf reflect on the ways in which the etiology of dementia has changed over time (from sin, to moral deficit, to psychological problem, to neurological problem): "One possible interpretation of these historical trends in the definition of dementia is that we are becoming more accurate in our understanding of the problem, i.e., that we are moving closer to the true definition of dementia. Another possible interpretation, however, is that society has simply shifted its historical perspective on the question of who should be considered its authority in matters of mental health, from priests to psychiatrists to neurologists. If the second interpretation is correct, then the definition of dementia is, at least in part, being culturally constructed." See Martin L. Albert and Bracha Mildworf, "The Concept of Dementia," *Journal of Neurolinguistics* 4, no. 3/4 (1989): 301-8. Clearly, making decisions about the nature of mental health problems is a complicated and deeply culturally influenced endeavor.

12. This is one reason why I have chosen to focus on the wider term "dementia" throughout this book.

The category of "dementia" is negotiated into existence and sustained by a common agreement and a shared adherence to specific ways of grouping particular forms of human experience. The shape of dementia is inevitably flexible and permeable, always open to redescription.

Defining Dementia

If we are to begin the process of redescribing dementia, we must first reflect more deeply and critically on the process through which it is currently described and defined. The World Health Organization's International Classification of Diseases (ICD-10) defines dementia in this way:

> [Dementia is] a syndrome due to disease of the brain, usually of a chronic or progressive nature, in which there is disturbance of multiple higher cortical functions, including memory, thinking, orientation, comprehension, calculation, learning capability, language, and judgment. Consciousness is not impaired. Impairments of cognitive function are commonly accompanied, occasionally preceded, by deterioration in emotional control, social behavior, or motivation. The syndrome occurs in Alzheimer's disease, in cerebrovascular disease, and in other conditions primarily or secondarily affecting the brain.[13]

DSM-IV offers a slightly different definition within which chronicity or progression is not required:

A. Impairment in short- and long-term memory.
B. At least one of these:
  1. impairment in abstract thinking
  2. impaired judgment
  3. other disturbances of higher cortical functioning
  4. personality change
C. That the deficit in A and B significantly interferes with work or social activities.

---

13. *The ICD-10 Classification of Mental and Behavioral Disorders: Clinical Descriptions and Diagnostic Guidelines* (Geneva: World Health Organization, 1992). See http://www.who .int/classifications/icd/en/.

D. That these deficits should not be caused by delirium.

E. Either there is evidence for the person's history or a physical examination to show that the deficits are produced by a dementia or these problems cannot be accounted for by any other condition.[14]

The story that underpins these definitions appears quite comprehensive, obvious, and clear. Dementia is a brain disease, the product of brain damage brought on by a variety of different causes. This brain damage leads to serious impairment, particularly of the higher cortical functions of the brain. This in turn results in cognitive impairment that either causes or is preceded by emotional, behavioral, and motivational problems. Within this narrative of loss and inevitable neural destruction, the person will lose control of their emotions and their social skills, and their ability to interact appropriately will begin to decline, as will their motivation for the tasks of living. The definition doesn't mention that dementia is a terminal condition and that the person will eventually lose consciousness and die, but the end of the story is clearly not a happy one, even without drawing the terminal nature of dementia to the reader's attention.

From this core definition, a series of subcategories of dementia are worked out based on various causal factors. Table 1 on page 40 outlines some of the main subcategories.[15] The story that underlies these definitions is precisely the kind of story that guided the doctor in Ignatieff's tale as she tried to describe and explain to the philosopher son the "true" nature of his mother's condition. This is not surprising, given the doctor belongs to the group of professionals for whom such definitions are constructed in the first place. Cheston and Bender suggest that such descriptions reflect what Tom Kitwood has described as the "standard paradigm" of dementia:[16]

The "thing" that is lost in dementia is defined in terms of the person's intellectual, linguistic, and cognitive functioning. These losses are said to arise directly from neurological impairment, the origins of which are beginning to be identified as having genetic, molecular, and cellular in-

14. Cheston and Bender, *Understanding Dementia*, p. 53.

15. The list is produced by the Alzheimer's Society. See http://alzheimers.org.uk/site/scripts/documents.php?categoryID=200362.

16. Tom Kitwood, "The Dialectics of Dementia: With Particular Reference to Alzheimer's Disease," *Ageing and Society* 10 (1990): 177-96.

Table 1: Types of Dementia

Alzheimer's disease This is the most common cause of dementia. During the course of the disease, the chemistry and structure of the brain changes, leading to the death of brain cells.

Vascular dementia If the oxygen supply to the brain fails, brain cells may die. The symptoms of vascular dementia can occur either suddenly, following a stroke, or over time, through a series of small strokes.

Dementia with Lewy bodies This form of dementia gets its name from tiny spherical structures that develop inside nerve cells. Their presence in the brain leads to the degeneration of brain tissue.

Fronto-temporal dementia In fronto-temporal dementia, damage is usually focused in the front part of the brain. Personality and behavior are initially more affected than memory.

Korsakoff's syndrome Korsakoff's syndrome is a brain disorder that is usually associated with heavy drinking over a long period. Although it is not, strictly speaking, a dementia, people with the condition experience loss of short-term memory.

Creutzfeldt-Jakob disease Prions are infectious agents that attack the central nervous system and then invade the brain, causing dementia. The best-known prion disease is Creutzfeldt-Jakob disease, or CJD.

HIV-related cognitive impairment People with HIV and AIDS sometimes develop cognitive impairment, particularly in the later stages of their illness.

Mild cognitive impairment Mild cognitive impairment (MCI) is a relatively recent term used to describe people who have some problems with their memory but do not actually have dementia.

Rarer causes of dementia There are many other rarer causes of dementia, including progressive supranuclear palsy and Binswanger's disease. People with multiple sclerosis, motor neuron disease, Parkinson's disease, or Huntington's disease can also be at an increased risk of developing dementia.

fluences. This is, essentially, the representation of dementia in terms of a disease of the brain.[17]

Few would argue that dementia is related to neurological damage. Nevertheless, as will become clear, the power of this story is greater than its general accuracy.

The Problem of Defectology

The problem with definitions such as these is that they tend to highlight only pathology. They are not designed to enable the reader/user to see those who experience this pathology as unique people with feelings, hopes, loves, and joys. They are designed to facilitate the recognition and effective naming of typical forms of pathology within "typical people." They do not and indeed cannot see "the person" in terms other than his/her deficits because, as pragmatic tools for mental health professionals, that is what such definitions are designed to highlight. This is not necessarily a criticism, but it is a significant fact. Oliver Sacks notes,

> Neurology's favorite word is "deficit," denoting an impairment or incapacity of neurological function: *loss* of speech, *loss* of language, *loss* of memory, *loss* of vision, *loss* of dexterity, *loss* of identity and myriad other lacks and losses of specific functions (or faculties). For all of these dysfunctions (another favorite term), we [neurologists] have privative words of every sort — Aphonia, Aphemia, Aphasia, Alexia, Apraxia, Agnosia, Amnesia, Ataxia — a word for every specific neural or mental function of which patients, through disease, or injury, or failure to develop, may find themselves partly or wholly deprived.[18]

Both the DSM-IV definition and the ICD-10 definition sit comfortably within Sacks's description of such negativizing tendencies (as do the brief descriptions of the types of dementia outlined in Table 1). Dementia is conceived and conceptualized as a series of deficits, malfunctions, and

17. Cheston and Bender, *Understanding Dementia*, p. 67.
18. Oliver Sacks, *The Man Who Mistook His Wife for a Hat and Other Clinical Tales* (London: Picador, 1985), p. 3; italics added to quotation.

losses. Steven Sabat refers to this as *the defectological approach,* wherein "the afflicted person is defined principally in terms of his or her catalogued dysfunctions."[19]

As mentioned, definitions such as ICD-10 and DSM-IV are intended to highlight that which is broken, because they are intended to be helpful to a group of professions for whom pathology and broken neurology are of particularly practical significance. Roy Porter has argued persuasively that psychiatry came into existence as a distinct branch of medicine within nineteenth-century Europe and North America with the primary purpose of meeting the practical needs of the nineteenth-century asylum.[20] Neurology, psychiatry, curative medicine, and psychology, particularly as they occur within mental health care contexts, are specifically focused on identifying and dealing with pathology and disease. That is why these disciplines exist. There would be no need for psychiatry if there were no mental health problems. That is why these disciplines create, require, and are comfortable with definitions that highlight defects over more positive aspects of people.

My point is not that this in itself is necessarily problematic. Nor is my point that mental health professionals don't care about people. In the proper context, this way of describing dementia can be appropriate and helpful. Definitions that highlight and seek to provide explanations for unusual behaviors, forgetfulness, and changes in emotional and intellectual abilities may be helpful for people, particularly in the earlier phases of dementia, and can provide explanations that are helpful for both people going through the experience and those seeking to offer care and support. If one knows the reasons for unusual behavior, it is often easier to cope with it and to make allowances for it. Sally is not just being awkward, clumsy, or deliberately forgetful — she has something significantly wrong with her brain. This may not be the most hopeful explanation, but it is nonetheless a way of helping people to understand mysterious changes in others in ways that make sense according to the medical story in which most of us place our trust. So there may well be some benefit in defining dementia in terms of neurological deficit. Having said that, I am not con-

---

19. Steven R. Sabat, *The Experience of Alzheimer's Disease: Life through a Tangled Veil* (Oxford: Blackwell, 2001), p. 10.

20. Roy Porter, *Madness: A Brief History* (New York: Oxford University Press, 2002), p. 100. My thanks to Warren Kinghorn for highlighting this point for me.

vinced that if I had dementia I would like to see my future mapped out by a definition such as that offered by ICD-10! This is not a flippant point, particularly when, as we will see, there is a tendency for theologians and pastoral carers to begin their explorations of dementia with an uncritical acceptance of standard definitions and descriptions of dementia.

Why Theologians Should Be Wary of Definitions

Given the particular community from which such definitions emerge and the practical ways in which they are intended to feed back into these communities, the tendency toward defectology should not be surprising. What *is* surprising are those times when theologians and pastoral carers assume that an uncritical acceptance of such descriptions (and their implications) is an appropriate starting point for the development of a specifically Christian theological understanding of dementia. So, for example, in Malcolm Jeeves' book *From Cells to Souls — and Beyond: Changing Portraits of Human Nature,* Glen Weaver, a theologian at Calvin College, spends seventeen of the twenty-four pages of his chapter on embodied spirituality in dementia explaining the neurobiology of dementia, complete with charts and photographs of brain scans.[21] Presumably he feels that basic knowledge of the condition is necessary for good care and effective theological reflection. But why would he assume that basic knowledge from the psychiatric community — knowledge which is designed specifically to help that particular community to function according to its internal criteria and goals — is necessarily the best place to begin to reflect theologically on dementia? It's not that such knowledge is necessarily unhelpful; it just might not be the best place for theologians and pastoral carers to begin the journey. Beginning with the basic knowledge given to us from the mental health professions may well feel "natural" and appropriate. It is almost impossible for Western people to think about illness and disease without first thinking about medicine, despite the fact that most healing goes on within the non-professional sectors of the commu-

21. Glen Weaver, "Embodied Spirituality: Experiences of Identity and Spiritual Suffering among Persons with Alzheimer's Dementia," in *From Cells to Souls — and Beyond: Changing Portraits of Human Nature,* ed. Malcolm Jeeves (Grand Rapids: Wm. B. Eerdmans, 2004), pp. 77-101.

nity rather than within professional medicine.[22] Likewise, neurological descriptions of dementia that focus on pathological neurology are turned to first, even though most of the experience of dementia and all of the symptoms of this condition occur in contexts that emerge and are interpreted and lived out quite apart from professional definitions of broken brains. That being so, the desire to begin a theological examination of dementia with an in-depth reflection on the medical story is in some ways understandable.

Nevertheless, one has to ask why a *theologian* would feel the need to spend quite so much time laying out a defectological description of dementia in a non-medical textbook. This seems to me to be a very good example of starting in the wrong place. What is an appropriate place for the beginning of psychiatry's journey into dementia is not necessarily an appropriate place for theology's journey. As one reads Weaver's article, it is interesting to notice that there are no pictures of people with dementia (i.e., the real people behind the brain scans), and no words are recorded from people experiencing dementia. It is stated quite clearly that communication of this sort is not possible for people with advanced dementia. There is no discussion of potentially central theological contributions to understanding dementia such as grace, dependency, contingency, love, and relationship — aspects that are fundamental to the experience of dementia and fundamental to our understanding of Christian theology. In other words, Weaver assumes throughout his article that theology can't tell us much about what dementia actually is. That story has already been fully narrated and fixed within the standard medical account. The words of neurologists are presented as defining the nature of dementia. Carers are given a place to speak on behalf of their loved ones who have dementia; persons with dementia remain silent. Theology is brought in to reflect on a context that has already been defined by powerful defectological stories which presume they can know what dementia is without knowing persons with dementia.

One can see the tendency to begin with dementia as a medical problem in a good deal of the pastoral literature. In her excellent book on caring for the spiritual needs of people with dementia, Eileen Shamy begins

---

22. Arthur Kleinman, *Patients and Healers in the Context of Culture: An Exploration of the Borderland between Anthropology, Medicine, and Psychiatry* (Berkeley and Los Angeles: University of California Press, 1980).

by pointing out that medicine is not her area of expertise. She suggests that she is "not qualified" to provide a detailed study of the various conditions that come under the banner of "dementia." Nonetheless, she begins the book with what she describes as "key information" about what dementia is. She points out,

> Contrary to general belief, dementia is not the name of any disease. Rather, it is a name given to a set of symptoms indicating a need for investigation by a competent doctor trained in this field of medicine.[23]

In this understanding, dementia is a name given to a set of human experiences (symptoms) by doctors who are specifically trained in "this field of medicine," the field presumably being some aspect of neurology or psychiatry. It is true that this is an aspect of dementia, but why are the negative aspects of dementia considered to be *key* aspects, and why, bearing in mind the complex cultural and political contexts that underlie the process of definition, would theologians and pastoral carers simply uncritically accept this description as a given?

We find this medical/defectological dynamic in what is otherwise an excellent book of essays on dementia edited by Donald McKim: *God Never Forgets: Faith, Hope, and Alzheimer's Disease.*[24] This book is a serious attempt to reflect theologically on dementia and to offer fresh Christian perspectives on this form of human experience. But why does it open with a chapter that focuses on the medical aspects of dementia? One could of course argue that this is necessary in order for people to understand what the condition is and then to respond appropriately. However, such a response would make my point. It is of course helpful to have the medical perspective. But why put it in Chapter 1 and not Chapter 6? It *feels* appropriate to begin with a defectological account, but the question is this: *Is that the primary story that should be told first about dementia?*

---

23. Eileen Shamy, *A Guide to the Spiritual Dimension of People with Alzheimer's Disease and Related Dementias: More than Body, Brain, and Breath* (London: Jessica Kingsley Publishers, 2003), p. 45.

24. Donald McKim, ed., *God Never Forgets: Faith, Hope, and Alzheimer's Disease* (Louisville: Westminster John Knox Press, 1998).

Patients or Persons?

One more example will help to make my point. David Keck in his otherwise very helpful and deeply theological book on Alzheimer's disease refers throughout the book to people with dementia as "patients."[25] To name someone as a patient is to position them in a particular way. Positively, the term "patient" can relate to the ability to bear suffering. It could certainly be argued that this description fits the experience of many people with dementia, particularly in the earlier stages, when the burden of the condition is becoming clear. But for the most part, the term "patient," at least in common parlance, relates to someone who requires medical care. Why would a *theologian* desire to identify someone with dementia according to their need for *medical* care? Most people with dementia are not cared for within health care establishments beyond diagnosis (there is actually not very much that medicine can currently do for people with dementia), so this seems a rather odd choice of language. The fact that many of us have become attuned to associating health and illness with professional medicine is interesting. The fact that people quite often unthinkingly encapsulate such assumptions in the language we use is worrisome. As will become clear, the words we use and the concepts we assume to guide our interpretation of the world and our perceptions of dementia have an impact not just on what we see and don't see, but also on what is actually there. The full impact of this point will become clear in Chapter Four. Here the thing to keep in mind is that *our words shape our worlds*. Words matter. The language we choose to describe dementia matters.

Where Should Theology's Journey into Dementia Begin?

At this point it will be helpful to summarize what has been said. Medicine — in the case of dementia, psychiatric medicine — is a recognized tradition or set of traditions that produces its own forms of accepted knowledge and worldviews, which in turn leads to particular ways of looking at human beings and human experience. A defectological perspective on dementia is a natural outcome of the form that psychiatric medicine has

25. David Keck, *Forgetting Whose We Are: Alzheimer's Disease and the Love of God* (Nashville: Abingdon Press, 1996).

come to adopt over time. There is nothing inherently wrong with this, and I would stress once again that my point is not in any sense intended to be perceived as anti-psychiatry. Such medical knowledge is important as a contribution to human well-being, and knowledge of the neurobiology of dementia is an important dimension of understanding dementia. That aspect of the territory — to use the metaphor of Gilles Deleuze and Félix Guattari discussed in the previous chapter — remains in place, although, as we will see in the following chapter, it requires significant modification. The emphasis on defectology does, however, require a degree of deterritorialization. The nature of medical knowledge and medical training means that those working within the field of mental health are often schooled to see some things and, by implication, not others. They are called to make sense of a cluster of human experiences according to the particular theoretical framework(s) that they have been trained to use to see and describe the features of illness. When I say that people are trained not to see certain other things, I mean simply that the specific focus of the professional gaze will by definition exclude certain things which may be vitally important. It is unlikely, for example, that such things as God, faithfulness, discipleship, sin, and love (central theological concepts) will emerge as part of a medical definition of any form of illness. Unhappiness and relational disconnection might, but sin and love? Such things are not being looked for, so they are not perceived as significant within that context. The fact that it might seem strange and counterintuitive to the reader to suggest that something like sin, love, or the presence or absence of God might be a central part of a medical definition of dementia makes the point, and indicates the boundaries of medical diagnosis and the limited intentions that such a process has. Such an observation should alert us to be more than a little suspicious about why we (the "we" here being theologians and pastoral carers) might uncritically accept a medical definition of dementia as an appropriate starting point for a theological understanding of dementia. Medical definitions are helpful for medical purposes, but they may be considerably less helpful for working through the contribution of theology and pastoral care to the process of defining and responding to dementia.

Let me be clear: I am not arguing that psychiatric medicine and theology cannot cooperate or communicate around issues pertaining to dementia. There's plenty of room for creative and critical discussion between the two, but only if both are clear as to what it is that they are looking at.

Also, both must realize that, as with the philosopher son and the doctor, two descriptions of the same thing may be both radically divergent and therapeutically similar. In order for this to happen, we need a bigger story of dementia.

3. The Fragmentation of Persons and the Creation of "Typical" People

So out of the ground the LORD God formed every animal of the field and every bird of the air, and brought them to the man to see what he would call them; and whatever the man called every living creature, that was its name.

GENESIS 2:19 (NRSV)

"But what about you?" [Jesus] asked. "Who do you say I am?"

MARK 8:29

Perhaps the main problem for theology (and probably also for medicine) is the way in which our attempts to describe and categorize dementia tend to result in a deep fragmentation and reduction of human persons. We are used to having our experience of physical and psychological malfunction defined by others according to criteria that are general rather than specific to our situations. Rarely do we step back and wonder what it actually means to create and apply a generic term such as "dementia" to an unusual and deeply personal set of human experiences. Categorization is deeply interested in that which is general and universalizable. Theology and pastoral care are deeply interested in that which is particular and unique. The two positions are not necessarily exclusive of each other, but it is difficult for them to negotiate meaningfully with each other. The purpose of any process of categorization is to allow us to take elements such as ideas, objects, and experiences, to observe their similarities and differences and, then to place them within particular schema, the boundaries of which are marked out according to perceived correspondences of kinds. The category of "dementia" thus indicates a particular form or configuration of relationships between personal experiences that are recognized and formalized in ways which allow for similarities to be noted, general explanations to be applied, and responsibility for care and intervention to be allocated.

A central aspect of the process of diagnosis and categorization is the breaking down of the human person into his/her constituent parts. Steven Sabat, a psychologist who specializes in issues of the nature of the self within dementia, suggests that in the assessment and diagnosing of dementia, personal psychological life is made generic and broken down into certain components, such as the cognitive component, the intellectual component, the emotional component, and so on. These components, Sabat explains, are then broken down further into "elements such as memory, language functions, calculation, attention, general intelligence, the organization of movement, orientation to time and place, and the like. . . . Each of these elements is examined separately through the use of standardized tests in a setting such as a hospital clinic."[1] A good example of this is found in the DSM-IV criteria for the diagnosis of dementia of the Alzheimer's type. Here this subcategory of dementia is described as follows:

A. The development of multiple cognitive deficits manifested by both:
 1. Memory impairment (impaired ability to learn new information or to recall previously learned information)
 2. One or more of the following cognitive disturbances:
   (a) aphasia (language disturbance)
   (b) apraxia (impaired ability to carry out motor activities despite intact motor function)
   (c) agnosia (failure to recognize or identify objects despite intact sensory function)
   (d) disturbance in executive functioning (i.e., planning, organizing, sequencing, abstracting)

1. Steven R. Sabat, *The Experience of Alzheimer's Disease: Life Through a Tangled Veil* (Oxford: Blackwell, 2001), p. 4.

B. The cognitive deficits in criteria A1 and A2 each cause significant impairment in social or occupational functioning and represent a significant decline from a previous level of functioning.

C. The course is characterized by gradual onset and continuing cognitive decline.

D. The cognitive deficits in Criteria A1 and A2 are not due to any of the following:

    1. other central nervous system conditions that cause progressive deficits in memory and cognition (e.g., cerebrovascular disease, Parkinson's disease, Huntington's disease, subdural hematoma, normal-pressure hydrocephalus, brain tumor)

    2. systemic conditions that are known to cause dementia (e.g., hypothyroidism, vitamin B or folic acid deficiency, niacin deficiency, hypercalcemia, neurosyphilis, HIV infection)

    3. substance-induced conditions

E. The deficits do not occur exclusively during the course of a delirium.[2]

The emphasis on defects in this definition is obvious, as is the compartmentalization of the different components of "typical patients." Sabat says that these components are measured according to the results of various psychological and neurological tests. Scores are then aggregated, and an overall picture of the person is constructed in comparison to a "typical dementia patient." The assumption is that dementia has a natural history which can be identified, tracked, and predicted, and which applies to all individuals who experience similar types of brain damage. The various tests that lead up to the diagnosis of dementia are designed to compare the experiences and capabilities of the individual to an average norm, and assess and record the individual's current state on the basis of that norm. Once certain divergences from the norm have been identified, the task is then to establish the specific etiology of the condition — that is, to track a line of causality leading from the observation of particular experiences, which are indicative of some form of brain damage, to the identification of the condition's formal cause. This in turn leads to some form of prediction about the future for all people with this condition, based on previous ex-

2. *Diagnostic and Statistical Manual of Mental Disorders,* 4th ed. (Washington, D.C.: American Psychiatric Association, 2000).

perience of "typical" patients. This explanatory framework enables the doctor to understand the causes that lie behind an individual's manifest difficulties irrespective of the particularities of his/her circumstances and to look into and articulate the presumed nature of the person's future.

This process of etiological determination, diagnosis, and prognosis is intended to capture and communicate the essence of the phenomenon of dementia. It is an epistemological and hermeneutical process intended to bring about clear understanding and accurate diagnosis leading to effective categorization and appropriate treatment. It is epistemological in that by configuring and naming a cluster of phenomena or experiences, it creates a new entity which in turn provides new knowledge. It is hermeneutical in that the new entity becomes the primary interpretative principle that is used for interpreting the emerging situation and the continuing experiences of the person. In this sense this process shapes a worldview. Breaking down the person into his/her various components, renaming his/her experiences, and laying out the formal configuration of dementia in this way brings dementia into existence — medically and culturally — in a quite precise form. It is perceived to be a medical condition with distinct and universal features that are located specifically or at least primarily within the human brain.

It is interesting to notice at this point that dementia is a diagnosis by exclusion:

> It is what you have left when you have excluded all other sources of confused behavior. This is an important point. . . . Essentially it means that a diagnosis of dementia is often reached when the person doing the diagnosis cannot find any other explanation for the problems the person is experiencing.[3]

Most people with dementia don't go through the types of testing that the mother in Ignatieff's story was subjected to. Dementia is inferred when other possibilities are ruled out. Through this process of exclusion it is then presumed that we know what dementia is and what it is not. It is *not* temporary amnesia or delirium; it is *not* schizophrenia or bipolar disorder; by omission, it is *not* a social or spiritual disease. The one assumed cer-

---

3. Richard Cheston and Michael Bender, *Understanding Dementia: The Man with the Worried Eyes* (London: Jessica Kingsley Publishers, 1999), p. 53.

tainty is that it is neurological through and through. Any emotional, spiritual, or social aspects are presumed to be epiphenomenal to the central neurological root. If such things are noticed or taken seriously, they must be read through the lens of the neurological definition, which perceives them primarily as the products of failing neurology rather than as causal or explanatory aspects of the condition. This is what I mean when I suggest that the process of naming and categorization shapes a worldview. By reducing the core meaning of dementia to the universal and the biological, other potential core meanings and possibly vital dimensions of the syndrome of dementia are excluded or at best downgraded. Thus, in the story that opened the previous chapter, the mother's gentleness — gentleness being a trait that Jesus ascribes directly to the nature of God[4] — becomes a matter of her not yet having experienced frontal lobe dysfunction. Forgetfulness — a profound experience of existential challenge and personal anxiety — becomes the product of a malfunctioning hypothalamus. Agitation is translated into a problem manifesting an underlying neurological pathology rather than a normal response to a frightening experience, or even an understandable response to the ways in which people have begun to treat the person since they "discovered" that she has dementia. The person is assumed to have "deterioration in emotional control, social behavior, or motivation." The fact that such experiences might well be reasonable responses to a frightening life experience — a profound loss of memory — is lost in translation.

We have already seen that worldviews are things that we look through rather than look at. The subtle work carried out by definitions and diagnoses in creating worldviews often has latent malignant functions that are easily hidden beneath apparent manifest beneficence. Definitions and categorizations are designed to provide us with maps that help us to make sense of certain experiences and objects in the world and to respond in effective ways to what we see. We very easily mistake these maps for the terrain itself. The danger is that in concentrating so hard on the maps, we fail to recognize that aspects of the terrain don't quite match up. My point is not that definitions and categorizations are in and of themselves unnecessary or dangerous. I have already indicated why I think they may well be necessary, particularly for psychiatrists, if less so for theologians. Richard Cheston and Michael Bender are correct when they note,

4. Matthew 11:29.

There are good, practical reasons for taking this classificatory approach. If every person is thought of as unique — if there is no way of classifying people at all — then no case law could be built up. In effect, we would be unable to see the wood for the trees. It is only by classifying into categories, then classifying further into subtypes and then investigating each subtype that medical knowledge has been able to progress systematically to a point at which many illnesses can be cured. Essentially, a diagnosis identifies an individual as a member of a specific group of patients.[5]

I don't disagree with this. My point is that definitions and other ways of naming dementia are powerful storytellers that need to be recognized as such and challenged at the points where the story they seek to tell becomes misleading or just plain wrong.

Opening up the Territory: Rethinking "the Obvious"

If the individual person has a tendency to get lost within standard descriptions of dementia used by mental health care professionals, the individual can also find himself/herself lost in a different way within more popular and implicit lay forms of naming. Here the process of losing the person to the name takes on subtle but powerful forms. Take the core meaning of the name "dementia." The literal meaning of the term "dementia" is "deprived of mind."[6] With this understanding, to have dementia is in some sense to lose one's mind. We don't have to look far before we come across this particular way of naming and describing dementia in lay and professional language. The title of Lawrence Broxmeyer's paper on Creutzfeldt-Jakob's syndrome makes this point quite nicely: "Thinking the Unthinkable: Alzheimer's, Creutzfeldt-Jakob, and Mad Cow Disease: The Age-related Re-emergence of Virulent, Foodborne, Bovine Tuberculosis, or Losing Your Mind for the Sake of a Shake or Burger."[7] Not the snappiest of titles! But the tag line at the end draws attention to the issue at hand: *to have dementia is to lose one's mind.*

---

5. Cheston and Bender, *Understanding Dementia,* p. 50.

6. Gloria J. Sterin, "Essay on a Word: A Lived Experience of Alzheimer's Disease," *Dementia* (February 2002): 1.

7. Broxmeyer's paper can be found in *Medical Hypotheses* 64, no. 4 (2005): 699-705.

Even within popular Christian literature that genuinely seeks to advocate for people with dementia, the language of loss of mind can appear with benign intent but more malignant consequences. For example, a book about what it means for Christians to have dementia, written by Louise Morse and Roger Hitchings, is titled *Could It Be Dementia?: Losing Your Mind Doesn't Mean Losing Your Soul.* This is a comforting title in one sense — until one reflects on the underlying assumptions that dementia means losing one's mind, and that the soul is something apart from the mind (and, by implication, the body, the place where the mind is generated and located) and is the particular locus of God's salvific activities. Both of these suggestions, as will become clear as the argument of this book unfolds, are at least open to question, if they are not in fact profoundly mistaken.

Impaired Thinking?

This sense or impression that loss of mind is a central feature of dementia is not confined to lay descriptions. As we have seen, the definitions of dementia by both the DSM-IV and the World Health Organization play into this way of thinking. Both in different ways claim that the syndrome we have named dementia includes impairments in *thinking* and *comprehension*. This assumption is presumably based on the types of tests that Sabat highlighted earlier, designed to assess a person's cognition and comprehension. If the person scores in particular ways on the particular test, he/she is assumed to have an impairment in thinking and comprehension. This appears to make sense. People with dementia clearly do get confused, and certain cognitive tasks become difficult if not impossible. However, there is a significant problem with the global and unreflective ascription of "impaired thinking." How do we actually know that a person's *thinking* is impaired? We can presume that thinking is impaired based on what we see (behavior), what the person says (speech), or how the person responds to certain questions (comprehension), but the former two things are *behaviors,* and the latter can fluctuate based on such things as mood, general interest, or the appropriateness of the subject matter of particular questions to the biography and personality of the individual. None of these things are necessarily good gauges of what a person is actually *thinking.* How do we know that either behavior or linguistic response truly reflects what a person is thinking? We can certainly say that a person has impaired or changed behavior or that the words he/she uses seem not to make sense, or that he/she scores badly on particular tests, but isn't it much more questionable and presumptuous to suggest that we know what they're thinking? Thought processes are an aspect of the mind; they are not visible. They can only be presumed and inferred based on whatever criteria the observer chooses to use to interpret the person's behavior in any given situation.

It could of course be objected at this point that we actually do know more or less what others are thinking from what we see in their behavior. Gestalt psychologist Wolfgang Köhler argues in this way, observing that "not only the so-called expressive movements but also the practical behavior of human beings is a good picture of their inner life, in many cases."[8] Köhler notes that the process of understanding what's going on within the mind of another has less to do with mind-reading and inferring meaning from actions, and more to do with observing behavior without inference. If a friend is startled by a loud noise, we don't infer the emotion of fear — we see it. If someone is in pain, we don't infer the feeling of pain — we see it. If someone is upset because we ask them to do something, we see it rather than infer it from their actions.[9] You don't have to be a mind reader to understand a wide range of human experiences and emotions. That being said, it could be argued that it's quite legitimate to read thinking and distortions of thinking and comprehension into the behaviors of people with advanced dementia. However, there is a crucial hermeneutical problem that needs to be considered. Our reading of behavior is never done in a vacuum. We inevitably approach our subject with particular theories and assumptions in mind. In the case of dementia, most of these tend to be negative.

The Social Construction of Thinking and Humanness

In a fascinating paper titled "Relationships with Severely Disabled People: The Social Construction of Humanness,"[10] social psychologists Robert

8. Wolfgang Köhler, *Gestalt Psychology* (New York: Horace Liveright, 1929), p. 250. In this he anticipates Wittgenstein's later aphorism: "The human body is the best picture of the human soul." See Ludwig Wittgenstein, *Philosophical Investigations*, trans. G. E. M. Anscombe (New York, 1953), p. 178.

9. Ian Hacking, *Autistic Autobiography* (Phil. Trans. R. Soc. B 364, 2009), 1467-1473.

10. Robert Bogdan and Steven J. Taylor, "Relationships with Severely Disabled People: The Social Construction of Humanness," *Social Problems* 36, no. 2 (April 1989): 135-48.

Bogdan and Steven Taylor describe a piece of research they carried out which tried to understand the perspectives of non-disabled people who don't stigmatize, stereotype, and reject those with obvious disabilities. Based on their working alongside families with members who have profound intellectual disabilities, Bogdan and Taylor offer some challenging reflections on the ways in which thinking is attributed to family members with disabilities. They begin by noting that "many [people with profound intellectual disabilities] give few or no obvious signs of experiencing the stimuli presented to them. Most people would say that they lack the ability to think."[11] However, the non-disabled people in their study *believed* and in fact cited evidence that their disabled partners could and did think. Indeed, some stated quite emphatically that they knew exactly what the disabled person was thinking. Others were less certain but were willing, like the philosopher son in Ignatieff's story, to give the disabled person the benefit of the doubt. Bogdan and Taylor note that "what a person thinks is always subjective and never totally accessible to others."[12] That is the case for all of us. We know what other people think or experience by observing the symbols of speech, writing, gestures, or body language that are meaningful to us. The severely disabled people in Bogdan and Taylor's study were "extremely limited in their abilities to move or make sounds and, hence, to produce symbols. Yet this inability did not prevent their nondisabled partners from attributing thinking to them."[13] According to Bogdan and Taylor, the nondisabled people believed that "thinking is different from communicating thought":

> From their perspective, a person can have full thinking capacity, be "intelligent" and reflective, but be locked in a body that is incapable of or severely limited in its capacity for communication. They hold the view that their severely disabled partners are more intelligent than they appear and that their physiology keeps them from revealing their intelligence more fully. . . . Attributing thinking to a person with or without severe disabilities is a matter of reading meaning into the gestures or movements the person makes. That people with severe disabilities may have a limited repertoire of gestures or movements does not prevent the

---

11. Bogdan and Taylor, "Relationships with Severely Disabled People," p. 139.
12. Bogdan and Taylor, "Relationships with Severely Disabled People," p. 139.
13. Bogdan and Taylor, "Relationships with Severely Disabled People," p. 139.

nondisabled people described in this study from recognizing meaning in the gestures and movements they make.[14]

In other words, as insiders who came close to the person on a regular basis, they were noticing things that were invisible to outsiders who popped into the lives of disabled people on a much less intimate level. The tension between the perspectives of the philosopher son and the doctor(s) highlighted in Ignatieff's story shows this dynamic at work. The distance one has from the person provides the particular hermeneutical framework which one uses to interpret behavior and responses. What one thinks and expects to see is probably what one will end up seeing. Coming close or standing back makes a difference.

Ultimately, what one assumes a person is thinking (or not, as the case may be) will be determined by what one *believes* is going on within their actions and behaviors, and what one believes about that will be determined by how one has been taught to understand dementia. In the end, it really all has to do with which story one chooses to put one's faith in. The global and rather vague ascription of "impaired thinking" provides a negative hermeneutic that will inevitably prime a person to see some things and to omit others. Bearing in mind that, at least within the West, thinking has come to be conceived of as a central dimension of the structure and function of the mind — and, indeed, of what is essential to our humanness ("I think; therefore I am") — ascribing impaired thinking to a person with dementia has quite particular connotations: dementia = deprived of mind = deprived of humanness. The suggestion that a person has impaired thinking might be helpful for a psychologist, but it is much less helpful for a theologian with a critical eye on the implications of uncritically accepting such an apparently obvious statement.

Confused Language?

Beyond the issue of the hermeneutics of distance, the fragility of the statement that dementia has to do with impaired thinking is brought into sharp focus in a slightly different way in the work of Steven Sabat. Sabat has shown quite clearly that linguistic confusion is not necessarily indica-

14. Bogdan and Taylor, "Relationships with Severely Disabled People," p. 139.

tive of impaired thinking.[15] A person may struggle for words or even use completely wrong words, but still be clear in what he/she is trying to say. The person needs to be heard on his/her own terms rather than according to standard, preconceived normative assumptions.

Sabat highlights the fact that we should be careful with regard to the ways in which "impaired thinking" is tested. A person might be very unclear in a test situation which focuses on what the researcher/tester considers to be significant, but very clear in other aspects of his/her life which researchers and those who construct tests aren't interested in or don't see as significant. What people like this need is someone to take the time to listen carefully to them and to learn how best to interpret their "linguistic confusion" and "impaired thinking." They need someone who has a map that's open to the type of terrain that they *actually* inhabit rather than a map that points out where they *should* be; they need someone to point out that they may actually be somewhere else and that the map might be flawed or not detailed enough. If theologians and pastoral carers begin their approaches to dementia by simply and uncritically buying into the assumption that they can somehow actually know that the person before them has "impaired thinking," the chances are that that is exactly what they will see. If, on the other hand, they are constantly prepared to give people the benefit of the doubt and to leave open the possibility that what seems to be impaired thinking might in fact be communicating real meaning, surprising things might happen.

Is Anyone There?

Perhaps the most poignant criticism of the suggestion that a person with dementia has lost or is losing his/her mind is the simple observation that none of us really know whether or not anyone has a mind in the first place! It's not at all clear that we know what's going on in anyone's mind other than (perhaps?) our own. This isn't an obscure philosophical point; it is a deeply practical observation. In his study of the social construction of the mind in people with Alzheimer's disease, Jaber Gubrium presents a short

---

15. Steven R. Sabat and Rom Harré, "The Alzheimer's Disease Sufferer as a Semiotic Subject," *Philosophy, Psychiatry, Psychology* 1 (1994): 145-60. For an extended empirical development of this point, see Sabat, *The Experience of Alzheimer's Disease.*

but poignant abstract from an interview with a woman whose husband had Alzheimer's disease. In discussing the complexities involved in understanding her husband, the woman asks,

> How do you really know [his mind has gone]? You don't *really* know for sure, do you? You don't really know if those little plaques and tangles are in there, do you? . . . How do I know that the poor man isn't hidden somewhere, behind all that confusion, trying to reach out and say, "I love you, Sara?" [weeps].[16]

This woman is faced with a very difficult dilemma. Which map will she follow as she tries to negotiate the tragic journey into Alzheimer's disease? She is well aware of the standard story of her husband's situation. She knows all about plaques and tangles and the medical narrative that speaks of her husband's gradual decline and descent into self-less-ness and apparent mindless-ness. But like the philosopher son in Ignatieff's story, she doesn't feel she has to allow that story to be her only interpreter and guide on her journey. She chooses to take a different route and follow a different story.

How are we to understand this woman's statement? Either she is in denial and needs to be informed of the "reality" of her husband's situation, or she needs to be supported in her experience and affirmed that she may in fact be seeing different things than other people are seeing and that what she is seeing may in fact be the case. Denial is always a possibility, but, as Bogdan and Taylor's study has indicated, so also is hidden insight.[17] In the end, like the philosopher son, this woman chooses to give her husband the benefit of the doubt. She doesn't abandon the medical story, but she also doesn't allow it to make her abandon her husband.

The Mysterious Process of Mind Reading!

That's all very well, some might say. Such an interpretation of the state of the thinking of people with dementia is nice and encouraging, but is there any real basis for believing it? Isn't it really just blind faith, denial, or even

---

16. Jaber F. Gubrium, "The Social Preservation of Mind: The Alzheimer's Disease Experience," *Symbolic Interaction* 9, no. 1 (Spring 1986): 37-51.

17. This point gains further poignancy in the light of the previous discussion of the social construction of thinking (see Chapter 2, note 25).

fantasy? One might wish to respond to that question with another question: Why would we assume that the person's mind has gone (or that his thinking is irreparably impaired) when we are in fact deeply unclear about what *anyone's* mind is and the state of *anyone's* thinking? The difference may be that most of us don't get tested. Think of it this way. Human experience and social interaction involve a constant process of mind reading.[18] As we meet one another, we make decisions about what the other is thinking based on how we perceive the situation and what we expect from the encounter, combined with interpretations of behavior, body language, and so forth. Through this complex process of behavioral observation and interpretation, we figure out what's going on within the other person: "He likes me"; "She isn't going to attack me"; "I think that he'd like to be somewhere else"; "She thinks I'm handsome!" Of course, we don't really have any idea what's going on inside another person's head. We're constantly guessing and second-guessing based on the presumption that we have a mind and that those whom we seek to understand also have minds which are similar to ours and which we can in some sense read accurately. Mind reading, like reading behavior, is a complex hermeneutical practice.

Such guessing and second-guessing isn't done in a vacuum. Our guesses are informed by tradition — that is, they're informed and shaped by what Julian Hughes et al. (after Charles Taylor[19]) describe as our "webs of interlocution."[20] Webs of interlocution are the stories, assumptions, concepts, values, and understandings that emerge from the particular

18. Readers might recognize here resonances of the ideas of the Theory of Mind (ToM). ToM argues that in order to communicate effectively, human beings need to be able to read the body language, intonation, and intentions of the other and from this infer particular insights into the mind of the other. In this way we develop a theory of the mind of the other — that is, a theory which assumes that other people have minds more or less similar to our own. In order for us to effectively communicate and interact, it is necessary to read the mind of the other and to anticipate and infer what they are thinking, what their behavior means, and the nature of their intentions. In other words, we work with a theory which assumes that other people have minds that are similar to our own and that we can read them as we endeavor to communicate. See *Understanding Other Minds: Perspectives from Developmental Cognitive Neuroscience,* 2nd ed., ed. S. Baron-Cohen, H. Tager-Flusberg, and D. J. Cohen (Oxford: Oxford University Press, 2002).

19. Charles Taylor, *Sources of the Self: The Making of Modern Identity* (Cambridge: Cambridge University Press, 1989).

20. Julian C. Hughes, Stephen J. Louw, and Steven R. Sabat, *Dementia: Mind, Meaning, and the Person* (London: Oxford University Press, 2006), p. 70.

epistemological communities that orient us toward what we come to perceive is and is not the case about the world. Put slightly differently, we make assumptions about the nature, function, and presence of other minds according to the particular narratives that shape and form our ways of seeing and being in the world. Ideas about what does and doesn't go on in our minds and the minds of others are therefore constantly being constructed according to perception and expectation rather than what may actually be going on. Our creative mind-reading skills are firmly rooted in the stories that we use to make sense of the world. The stories we believe about others will determine how we read their minds. Because of this, whatever mind-reading skills we have are inevitably flawed, fallible, and open to misrepresentation and manipulation. To suggest that a person with dementia has "lost his mind" may actually relate to the inadequacies of the particular stories that we're using to make sense of our encounters with those who bear the name "dementia."

Giving Our Minds Away

An interesting way of drawing this point out is to think about what we do when we visit a counselor or a psychotherapist. We tell the therapist our stories — in other words, we give them the content of our "minds." They filter this content through whatever theoretical framework they have been trained to see the world through and then give us back our minds in a revised form. If we don't agree, we are told we are in denial! Now of course that is a rather crass caricature, but it contains truth and helps to make the point. The mind is both an individual and a social/communal entity. If it actually exists, then it certainly could be argued that it is the product of an individual's neurology. But this isn't the only place where the mind exists. Minds also have an existence outside of our individual bodies within the perceptions and presuppositions of our culture and those who surround us as they read our minds into our actions and behaviors. Indeed, strange as it may initially seem, culture comes before mind. As Wittgenstein has ably shown, we experience first and then later we develop minds which reflect on that experience.[21] The content of our minds emerges from the lan-

21. Ludwig Wittgenstein, *Philosophical Investigations,* 4th ed., trans. G. E. M. Anscombe, P. M. S. Hacker, and Joachim Schulte (Oxford: Wiley-Blackwell, 2009).

guage we use and the cultures within which we exist rather than the other way around. As we learn language, we also learn that we have minds; as we engage with culture, the contents of our minds are shaped and formed.[22] Development of the mind is a second-order activity that emerges from community learning and living. In this sense there is no such thing as an "individual." We are all deeply interconnected even in those apparently private inner places we ascribe to our minds.

That being so, in order to make a statement such as "She has lost her mind" or even "His thinking is impaired," we make three key assumptions. First, we assume that we are competent to make such a judgment — and my point is that we are not. Second, we assume that the mind resides only within the boundaries of the individual's head. Again, it would appear that this is not in fact the case. Third, we have a cultural tendency to assume that the mind is the essence of the person and that losing the ability to think clearly and intellectualize effectively is particularly important for who the person is and how his/her quality of life can be judged. As the book moves on, it will become clear that this also is not the case. On all three points we would do better to give the person the benefit of the doubt and see where that takes us. My overall point is that the suggestion that people with dementia lose their minds is highly questionable. Even if that were the case, it is debatable whether it would actually be possible for anyone to make that judgment. The very name "dementia" — "deprived of mind" — is a misnomer.

Higher Cortical Functions?

Before we move on to explore how we might go about redescribing dementia in ways that help to overcome some of the difficulties highlighted thus far, there is one further observation that will be helpful. The ICD-10 definition of dementia is "a syndrome due to disease of the brain, usually of a chronic or progressive nature, in which there is disturbance of multiple higher cortical functions, including memory, thinking, orientation, comprehension, calculation, learning capability, language, and judgment." We have already looked at why one aspect of this definition — impaired

---

22. David G. Stern, *Wittgenstein on Mind and Language* (London: Oxford University Press, 1985).

thinking — is open to challenge and reinterpretation. There is, however, another aspect that is highly problematic and deeply pertinent for people experiencing dementia within Western cultures in particular. This aspect relates to how this kind of definition emphasizes the significance of the "higher cortical functions." This emphasis is also apparent in the DSM-IV's highlighting of disturbance of higher cortical functions as significant for defining the parameters of dementia. Why is it that, when the definition is clearly intended to suggest objectivity, scientific rigor, and technical accuracy, the authors use the spatial metaphor of "*higher* cortical functions"? Higher than what? The lower ones, presumably, but why are these particular capacities considered higher? This point is more than mere semantics. Stanley Jacobson and Elliot Marcus describe higher cortical functions this way:

> What is a higher cortical function? As one examines the abilities of a human, one is struck by our ability to use tools and create wonderful buildings or works of art. However, our ability to communicate by speaking and writing and reading, we believe, is the best example of a higher cortical function.[23]

The expression "we believe" in this statement is worthy of note. Higher cortical functions seem to be higher because they allow humans to do things that other animals cannot do — in particular, to speak, write, and read. The authors of the ICD-10 definition consider "higher" functions to be "memory, thinking, orientation, comprehension, calculation, learning capability, language, and judgment." But why? What makes such capacities *higher* than the capacities to love, relate, touch, and feel — all aspects of experience that people with dementia hold onto throughout their journey? Why are capacities like orientation and comprehension higher than the capacity to weep and feel distress for the loss of those things that remain valuable but seem distant in the midst of profound memory loss?

The use of the term "higher cortical functions" implies that this aspect of the brain, the cerebral cortex, came into existence late in the evolutionary process and that its functions are advanced in comparison to other aspects of the brain, which have not developed as fully or as comp-

---

23. Stanley Jacobson and Elliot M. Marcus, "Higher Cortical Functions," *Neuroanatomy for the Neuroscientist*, January 2008, pp. 375-95.

lexly as this part. We will return to the cultural power of the cerebral cortex later in the book. Here the question to focus on is this: *Why call this aspect of the brain's development "higher"?* Surely the essence of the theory of evolution, at least in its secular form, is that there is no such thing as progress in the sense that we are consciously or intentionally advancing from a state of primitiveness toward a state of higher consciousness, awareness, or capability. What there is, it is argued, is a process of random mutation and genetic change which occurs over huge periods of time in response to the environment; this process leads to the development of genetic formations, traits, and configurations that enhance functional effectiveness and enable adaptation and survival. In this sense our brains are no higher or lower than they were at the beginning of the evolutionary process; there is nothing to progress toward or away from. We can't move upward or downward; we just move on! The spatial language of "higher cortical functioning" must at best be metaphorical. If it is metaphorical, then those who use it are clearly trying to make a point — but what is it? Is it coincidental that the capacities that are highlighted as emerging from the area of the brain that produces the "higher cortical functions" are precisely the capacities that are highly valued by contemporary Western societies? More precisely, capacities such as memory, thinking, orientation, comprehension, calculation, learning capability, language, and judgment are the aspects of human beings that are deeply prized by intellectuals, academics, and academic researchers — the very people who construct such definitions. In other words, this aspect of the definition is clearly culturally bound and value-laden. This observation about the emphasis on the cerebral cortex will become important later, when we discuss issues of personhood. Here we must note that to indicate that acquiring dementia includes losing one's higher cortical functions is a much deeper and altogether more alarming statement than it might at first appear to be. Hidden in the midst of this apparently objective and scientific statement is the subliminal suggestion that people with dementia are losing those aspects of being human which are perceived as more important than the other capacities humans might have. They are losing that which society prizes. Receiving such a diagnosis puts people in a tricky position which has both neurological *and* social implications. Definitions are not value-neutral. Often they are value-forming.

Moving beyond the Standard Story

This chapter and the previous one have tried to show how important it is for theologians and pastoral carers to start their journey into dementia from the right place. They have shown some of the problems that are tied up with the process of naming and defining dementia and have offered critical perspectives on commonly held assumptions about dementia that make all the difference in terms of getting to the correct destination. The point is not that theology cannot or should not converse creatively with the other disciplines involved in naming and caring for people with dementia. It is clear that such disciplines as psychology, neurology, and psychiatry contain much that is important and valuable to all parties concerned. However, the grounds on which to build that conversation need to be established carefully and critically, and the territory inhabited by each discipline needs to be clearly delineated and thought through. We have yet to develop the precise form of the contribution that theology makes to the process of naming and redescribing dementia. Suffice it to say for now that theology is not medicine, and the territory inhabited by medicine, while important for theology, is not definitive of either its starting point or its goal. From the perspective of theology, beginning the journey into dementia using the standard story as the primary map and guide will not take us to the right destination. Cheston and Bender's table (see Table 2 on page 67), which helpfully lays out the standard paradigm of dementia care, makes that clear.

Categorizing and focusing on neurobiology are to an extent helpful for the mental health professions as they focus on pathology and treatment. But even here definitions can be deceiving if their inherent and often hidden moral thrust isn't recognized. The inner world of the person with dementia and its deep and intimate connections with the world outside are not inconsequential to what dementia is and cannot be narrated by neurobiology alone. Neurology may well keep telling us what has been lost, but, as Ignatieff's philosopher son knows, there is a need to keep telling the world that something remains. The story of what remains is a vital constituent of the definition of dementia that needs to be reclaimed. It is to the construction of such a story, or better, such a *counter-story,* that we must now turn.

Table 2: The Standard Paradigm of Dementia Care

	Main Features	*Implications for Care Management*	*Implications for the Internal World of the Sufferer*
Causation	Only neurological changes are of interest. Cell destruction due to plaques, tangles, and vascular destruction. Neurological changes due to biochemical and genetic factors.	The disease is seen as progressive and degenerative, so once established, little can be done to affect prognosis. The aim of care is essentially to make life as tolerable as possible.	The internal world is of no consequence to the disease process, so it is seen as being of little or no relevance to the process of care.
Psychological Features	Brain damage, especially alteration in cognitive functioning, personality, and memory, is equated with destruction of the mind. Dementia is seen as the death of the person.	Emphasis on diagnosis — a need for the assessment of cognitive functioning in order to distinguish between dementias and pseudo-dementias. The individual is seen as unable to make decisions about his/her own care.	The internal world of the person with dementia lacks validity, due to the damage to his/her brain. All necessary decisions should be agreed on between professionals and relatives/carers.
Symptomatology	Many, varied, and usually strongly negative. Includes confusion, wandering, disorientation, and aggression.	Assessment of problematic behaviors. Medication and behavioral management. Advice and support to carers.	Individual has little meaningful (conscious) control over his/her actions. The only valid role is that of "patient." Relationships are invalidated.

Table adapted from Richard Cheston and Michael Bender, *Understanding Dementia: The Man with the Worried Eyes.* London: Jessica Kingsley Publishers, 1999, p. 68.

4. Moving Beyond the Standard Paradigm: From Defectology to Relationships

My charge is not simply to coalesce our societal understanding about dementia around more positive imagery, but rather to endow health professionals, families, and individuals affected by brain ageing with different linguistic choices that can better align our habits of speech with scientific fact and shared humanity. Choosing new language patterns can reshape our thoughts, attitudes, and actions towards our ageing neighbors and our own ageing brains, giving rise to a slightly different and more life-affirming reality that connects us to those who are ageing instead of hastening their social death.

DANIEL R. GEORGE, "OVERCOMING THE SOCIAL
DEATH OF DEMENTIA THROUGH LANGUAGE"

This trail of unraveled brain structure and mounting dysfunction is, in physical terms, only one of inches; yet its silent, implacable wrecking creates entirely new conditions for living life and being with others.

ARTHUR KLEINMAN, "CAREGIVING"

Enlarge the place of your tent, stretch your tent curtains wide, do not hold back; lengthen your cords, strengthen your stakes.

ISAIAH 54:2

I t has become clear that the way in which we define things and the expectation that such defining creates will determine what we see and how we respond. This is so with dementia, but it is probably the case with all things. The importance of this point is illustrated well in Jonathan Franzen's 2001 article in the British newspaper *The Guardian* titled "The Long Slow Slide into the Abyss." For the most part, Franzen offers a positive reflection on his experiences with his father, who had Alzheimer's disease. He makes a series of important and quite positive points about the retention of selfhood, the complexities of memory, and the importance of recognizing what remains available when people go through dementia. However, toward the end of the article, as he starts to reflect differently on his father's experience, his tone begins to change. He had developed his more positive perspective on dementia when he was younger. Now that he is a little older and wiser, things look different:

> From my current vantage, where I spend a few minutes every month fretting about what a self-righteous 30-year-old I was, I can see my reluctance to apply the term Alzheimer's to my father as a way of protecting the specificity of Earl Franzen from the generality of a nameable condition. Conditions have symptoms; symptoms point to the organic basis of everything we are. They point to the brain as meat. And, when I ought to recognize that, yes, the brain is meat, I seem instead to maintain a blind spot across which I interpolate stories that emphasize the more soul-like aspects of the self. Seeing my afflicted father as a set of organic symptoms would invite me to understand the healthy Earl Franzen (and the healthy me) in symptomatic terms as well — to reduce our beloved personalities to finite sets of neurochemical coordinates. Who wants a story of life like that?[1]

Who indeed? The young Franzen was reluctant to take the suggestion that the organic basis of all human existence determines what human beings are. He recognized that ascribing the label "Alzheimer's" to his father's behavior would diminish his specificity and draw all that he was into the totalizing power of the diagnosis. Instead, he focused on those aspects of

---

1. Jonathan Franzen, "The Long Slow Slide into the Abyss," *The Guardian,* 15 December 2001; access at http://www.thelancet.com/journals/lancet/article/PIIS0140-6736(10)61286-X/fulltext.

his father's experience which he considered to be "soul-like," by which he presumably meant, among other things, not wholly explicable by or reducible to neurological changes. However, with the passage of time he has learned to see things differently:

> Even now, I feel uneasy when I gather facts about Alzheimer's. Reading, for example, David Shenk's excellent new book, *The Forgetting: Alzheimer's: Portrait of an Epidemic,* I'm reminded that when my father got lost in his own neighborhood, or forgot to flush the toilet, he was exhibiting symptoms identical to those of millions of other afflicted people. There can be comfort in having company like this, but I'm sorry to see the personal significance drained from certain mistakes of my father's, like his confusion of my mother with her mother, which struck me at the time as singular and orphic, and from which I gleaned all manner of important new insights into my parents' marriage. My sense of private selfhood turns out to have been illusory.[2]

Now, finally persuaded by the explanatory lure of the medical story, Franzen sees things differently. As a consequence, his perceptions of the thoughts and actions of his father have shifted. Gone are the apparently idealistic hopes that his father's actions might be meaningful and undetermined by failing neurology. Now he has come to realize that his father's behavior is nothing more than the symptoms that are experienced by countless other people with Alzheimer's disease. His father's private actions have become public "symptoms" of a most feared disease. The story of his experiences with his father has shifted in quite profound ways.[3]

Franzen's experience is no different from the experience of many people. He changed his mind because he was persuaded by a story that was more powerful than his initial story of hope and "soulishness." But there is good reason for him to change his mind back again. This chapter will argue that, if his father's condition is described and understood properly, there is reason for hope. It will show that Franzen's reflections on his father's experience are both correct and incorrect. Dementia is *not* not neurological; dementia is not only or, perhaps, not even primarily neurological. Such paradoxical statements seem somewhat counter-intuitive. How can Franzen be

2. Franzen, "The Long Slow Slide into the Abyss."
3. Franzen, "The Long Slow Slide into the Abyss."

right and not right? How can dementia be neurological and not essentially neurological at the same time? In this chapter we will explore and develop an interesting and important perspective that takes seriously the neurological dimensions of dementia but offers a significant reframing of them in terms of causality, experience, and response. Dementia is neurological, but it is much more than that. There are similarities among the experiences of people with dementia, but there are no "typical dementia patients." Even those similarities that do exist may not always relate to similar changes within individual brains. Something else is going on. To draw on Isaiah 54:2, the tent curtains of dementia need to be stretched and its cords lengthened. Our definition of dementia needs to be expanded. *We need a counter-story.*

Redescribing Dementia

Two voices in particular have been deeply influential in providing the basis for such a counter-story: those of Tom Kitwood and Steven Sabat. Both are psychologists, one from the U.K. (Kitwood) and the other from the U.S. (Sabat). Both in different but deeply connected ways have challenged the standard story of dementia and offered important alternative ways of looking at, describing, and defining dementia. For both Kitwood and Sabat, dementia is as much *relational* and *social* as it is neurological. The two dimensions are inseparable for a proper understanding of dementia. Both thinkers argue that in order to understand dementia, one needs to look beyond neurology toward the complex network of relationships that surround the person who is the recipient of the diagnosis. It is there, and not simply within the brains of individuals, that we discover the true meaning of dementia. A key point to bear in mind as we proceed through this chapter is that relationships may not be important simply because it is not good that people with dementia should be alone (although, as we shall see, it is not). Rather, the assertion is that relationships may be both *causative* and *formative* within the development of the syndrome of experiences and neurological damage that forms dementia. In other words, relationships are part of what dementia *actually is,* not just an aspect of how we should offer care to people once the nature of the condition has been defined. Both Kitwood and Sabat want to expand the definition of what dementia is to include the significance of such things as love, relationships, and care. This, I will argue, is a much stronger and more appropriate place for theology and pastoral care to begin the journey into dementia. Let us begin by thinking through the implications of Kitwood's suggestion that dementia has to do with relational disorder and his attempts to develop what he describes as a "neurology of personhood,"[4] that is, a model of what he describes as personhood, which recognizes and seeks to brings to the fore the intimate connection between neurology and social experience.

Tom Kitwood on Dementia

Challenging the Standard Paradigm

At the heart of Kitwood's project is his desire to persuade health and social care services to recognize the personhood of people with dementia and to provide a firm practical and theoretical foundation which will open up the possibility of carers engaging in forms of personal relationships that are not unnecessarily influenced by the tendency toward defectology that was noted in previous chapters. Kitwood describes the established medical approach to dementia as "the standard paradigm."[5] This approach, he suggests, has emerged from classical science. It proposes that there is a straightforward, linear connection between brain pathology and the behaviors and experiences that we choose to name as dementia. The pattern moves from causal phenomena to neuropathic change to dementia.[6] The progression is linear, moving from brain pathology (neurological damage, malfunction, or deficit, disease, genetics, and so forth) directly to the manifestations of the symptoms of dementia. All of this remains internal to the individual's brain. Dementia is thus located firmly within individual selves. Standard procedures designed to describe, identify, and treat the condition of dementia are then applied on the understanding that we're dealing with a specifically neurological condition which has some form of identifiable biological basis and which is in principle open to neurological, pharmacological, or genetic intervention. Kitwood notes,

4. Tom Kitwood, *Dementia Reconsidered: The Person Comes First* (Buckingham: Open University Press, 1997), p. 19.
5. Tom Kitwood, "The Dialectics of Dementia: With Particular Reference to Alzheimer's Disease," *Ageing and Society* 10 (1990): 177-96.
6. Clive Baldwin and Andrea Capstick, *Tom Kitwood on Dementia* (Maidenhead: Open University Press, 2007), p. 74.

The paradigm of course allows many variants, and there is controversy among investigators about the details of the process they postulate. In pure research the aim is to identify X [X = causal factors] as a set of necessary conditions, together with the precise causal mechanism; in drug research the aim is to prevent or retard the efficacy of X, ideally with the causal process sufficiently elucidated; and in genetic research, the ultimate aim is to remove X altogether. In all of this the basic linear sequence remains largely unchallenged.[7]

Within this paradigm, the fact that human beings with dementia live in social contexts rather than as isolated monads is presumed to be unimportant for understanding the key elements of what dementia is and how it should be responded to.

Influential as this paradigm has been, Kitwood notices that it has significant flaws. He highlights three problematic areas in particular that have relevance for the purposes of this chapter:

1. *The lack of continuity between the level of neurological damage and the manifestations of dementia.* There are cases in which people have gone through the manifestations of dementia only for it to be discovered that they have no more neurological damage than a person of similar age without the manifestations of dementia.[8] The usual response to such experiences is to suggest that the initial diagnosis was flawed. In other words, the tendency of those who adhere strictly to the standard paradigm when faced with challenge is not to question the paradigm but to assume that the phenomenon in question was mistakenly included and needs to be placed in a different category. Kitwood argues that there may be a different and more radical explanation. Something else may be at work in bringing about the experience of dementia, something that includes but is not fully explained by models that focus on linear causality.

2. *The issue of rapid decline.* A second concern raised by Kitwood is the well-documented observation that "some people with dementia, under certain conditions, deteriorate in their functioning very much

7. Baldwin and Capstick, *Tom Kitwood on Dementia,* p. 74.
8. Ann C. Homer et al., "Diagnosing Dementia: Do We Get It Right?" *British Medical Journal* 297 (October 1998): 894-96.

faster than can be attributed to the consequence of progressive degeneration of nervous tissue."[9] For example, when a person with dementia loses a loved one or is taken out of the familiarity of his/her home environment and placed in a care facility, it is not uncommon for him/her to move quickly into a more advanced stage of his/her dementia. If dementia has a natural history that is bound by an inflexible theory of inevitable neurological decline which progresses through recognizable stages, why is it that exacerbation and escalation can be brought on quickly by social change and uncertainty?

3. *The phenomenon of stabilization.* This point relates to the virtual arrest of deterioration under certain conditions. Here Kitwood draws on some tantalizing evidence which suggests that given an appropriate social, relational, and spiritual environment, a degree of *rementing* can take place. In particular, he examines the work of Andrew Sixsmith and colleagues, who undertook a study of "homely homes" where the care was of a very high quality. They found "clear examples of 'rementing,' or measurable recovery of powers that had apparently been lost; a degree of cognitive decline often ensued, but it was far slower than that which had been typically expected when people with dementia are in long-term care."[10] This process of rementing is recognized within the literature but remains under-researched.[11] This is not to suggest that dementia can somehow be cured through relationships. It is however to suggest that relationships may have a larger role than is generally recognized in the creation and maintenance of the symptoms of dementia.

Kitwood argues that evidence such as this indicates that the standard paradigm is lacking on both conceptual and empirical grounds. A framework that has greater explanatory power is required; a different story needs to be told.

Kitwood's point is not that dementia has no neurological basis. Indeed, he has been criticized for accepting the medical model of dementia rather than going for a full-blown social constructionist approach.[12] He

9. Baldwin and Capstick, *Tom Kitwood on Dementia*, p. 75.

10. Kitwood, *Dementia Reconsidered*, p. 62.

11. Andrew Sixsmith, John Stilwell, and John Copeland, "'Rementia': Challenging the Limits of Dementia Care," *International Journal of Geriatric Psychiatry* 8, no. 12 (December 1993): 993-1000.

12. Dennis Greenwood, "A Review of 'Dementia Reconsidered: The Person Comes First,'" *European Journal of Psychotherapy and Counseling*, 1988, pp. 154-57.

is, to an extent, comfortable with holding on to the types of understanding we explored in previous chapters that frame dementia as a neurological condition which has multiple causes. It is the singularity and directness of the line of causality that is of particular concern for him. The standard paradigm focuses its gaze on such things as neurological damage caused by strokes, Alzheimer's disease, pathogenic genetic configurations, and so forth. Here, as we have seen, the line of causality is assumed to be quite straightforward: pathology + brain damage = dementia. However, Kitwood argues that such linear configurations of causality fail to take into account the relationship of the brain to the mind and the relationship of the mind and the brain to society. He presents us with an alternative story: The mind (via the receiving and processing of experience it receives from its encounters with society) actually impacts the neurology of the brain. Put differently, the experiences and the relationships we have impact deeply the ways in which our brains come to be structured. That is so for everyone. However, Kitwood proposes that the particular ways in which people with dementia experience their social worlds and in particular the negative ways in which they are framed and treated by others have an impact on the structures of their brains and *cause,* or at least exacerbate, the process of neurological decline, and shape and form the symptoms that emerge within the lives of people with dementia. If this is the case, our understanding of the direction of the progression from neurological damage to dementia might require an added dimension that acknowledges the impact of the mind on the brain and the relationship of the mind to society.

Exploring the Problem of the Mind-Brain Connection

At the heart of Kitwood's understanding is the recognition that there is an implicit dualism at work within biomedical understandings of dementia. In response, his intention is to help move people's thinking about dementia away from a Cartesian separation of the body from the mind and toward a monistic position that assumes the human being is a single complex organism within which there is no ontological or substantial separation between the mind and the body. Mind and body cannot be separated; thus neurology cannot be understood without reference to other dimensions of the human person and his/her experiences. To focus simply on the neurobiology of dementia and ignore the significance of the mind is to misunderstand what dementia is and what its causes might actually be.

Kitwood's starting point is important for his understanding of the relationship between neurology, psychology, and social relationships. Kitwood's basic assumption is that "any psychological event (such as deciding to go for a walk) or state (such as feeling hungry) is also a brain event or state. It is not that the psychological experience . . . is causing the brain activity . . . or vice versa; it is simply that some aspect of the true reality is being described in two different ways."[13] Every psychological experience is at the same time a neurological experience and vice versa; the two simply represent two descriptions of the same event. Psychology and neurology are thus seen to be inseparably interlinked.

What is important to notice is Kitwood's basic assumption that "any mental state is also a brain event or state, instantiated in a brain with such-and-such a structure, which is the consequence of both developmental and pathological factors."[14] There are two things to notice here. First, there is the close tie between the mind and the brain. Our experiences leave a physical mark on our neurology. Second, and connected with this, mental states and brain events take place within a discrete brain which has developed in unique and particular ways according to the types of experience that a person has encountered during his/her life. That being so, some people will be less likely to succumb to the type of brain damage that forms the syndrome of dementia because of the ways in which their brains have been structured through their experience over time.[15] No two brains are

13. Kitwood, *Dementia Reconsidered,* p. 17.

14. Baldwin and Capstick, *Tom Kitwood on Dementia,* p. 77.

15. A good example of this is found in what has come to be known as "The Nun Study." This study, which was carried out initially in the 1990s, involved 678 American nuns in the School of Notre Dame religious congregation. Researchers found that nuns who had a low level of education or who had low linguistic abilities were most likely to experience dementia. The study compared the autobiographies written by nuns in the 1930s with those written by the same nuns in the 1990s. This comparison showed a clear relationship between linguistic ability in early life and the level of cognitive function and dementia in later life. None of the nuns with good linguistic capabilities who died during the research period showed any evidence of dementia when their brains were dissected. The implication is that actively and intentionally using one's brain from an early age protects against dementia. This is particularly convincing because so many other variables in the study were the same for the group: the nuns shared the same environment, food, social climate, and so on. See Kathryn P. Riley

the same, and therefore no two brains respond in the same way to the neu-rological trauma that initiates the process of dementia. Such an observa-tion means that some people will be more vulnerable to the effects of brain damage, and others will be more resilient.[16] Thus there is no such thing as a "typical dementia patient," even if people do at one level share similar forms of brain damage. The behavior of Franzen's father may have shared similarities with that of other Alzheimer's sufferers, but that does not make it the same.

So, while dementia clearly does relate to neurological damage and change, the actual impact of particular damage will be variable and per-sonal. This is why some people can have quite extensive brain damage and not manifest dementia while others with relatively little damage do ex-hibit the features of dementia. Kitwood's perspective is important be-cause it suggests that the causal direction of neurological damage may not be straightforward. It may be that events which are experienced outside of the body can actually impact what's going on inside the brain. In order to understand the importance of such observations, we need to begin by thinking about the way in which the brain comes to develop the structure that it has.

Understanding the Plastic Brain

According to Kitwood, brain events take place within a particular appara-tus — the human brain — which has both structure and architecture:

> The key functioning part is a system of around ten thousand million . . . neurons, with their myriads of branches and connections, or synapses. A synapse is a point at which a "message" moves from one neuron to an-other, thus creating the possibility of very complex "circuits." So far as is known, the basic elements of this system, some general features of its development, and most of the "deeper" forms of circuitry (older in evo-

---

et al., "Early Life Linguistic Ability, Late Life Cognitive Function, and Neuropathology: Findings from the Nun Study," *Neurobiology of Aging* 26, no. 3 (2005): 341-47.

16. For a very useful exploration of the significance of resilience for dementia and de-mentia care, see Murray Lloyd, "Resilience Promotion and Its Relevance to the Personhood Needs of People with Dementia and Other Brain Damage," in Albert Jewell, *Spirituality and Personhood in Dementia* (London: Jessica Kingsley Publishers, 2011), pp. 141-53.

lutionary terms) are genetically "given." On the other hand, the elaboration of the whole structure and particularly the cerebral cortex is unique
to each individual and not pre-given. The elaboration, then, is epi-
genetic, subject to processes of learning that occur after the genes have
had their say. Each human face is unique; so also is each human brain.[17]

Unlike other organs, the brain (like the nervous system) is plastic. By that I
mean that its shape, form, and development are responsive to and formed
by the environment and the physical and psychological experiences that a
person has throughout his/her lifetime. Unlike toenails or hair, which just
grows according to a predetermined genetic pattern, a person's brain from
birth is shaped by his/her experiences. What happens in the world around
us, our experiences, relationships, feelings, and so on are all registered in
and impact the developing neurology of our brains. *We are our experiences*
in a very concrete way.

An example will help to make this point clear. Neurologist Sir John
Eccles offers a particularly illuminating case study:

> A child, Genie, was deprived of all World 3 influences by her psychotic
> father. She was penned in isolation in a small attic of his house in Los
> Angeles, never spoken to, and minimally serviced from the age of 20
> months up to 13 years, 8 months. On release from this terrible depriva-
> tion, she was of course a human being, but not a human person. . . .
> Since then, with dedicated help by Dr. Susan Curtiss, she has been
> slowly climbing up that ladder to personhood. The linguistic depriva-
> tion seriously damaged her left hemisphere, but the right hemisphere
> stands in for a much depleted language performance. Yet, despite this
> terribly delayed immersion in World 3, Genie has become a human per-
> son with self-consciousness, emotions, and excellent performances in
> manual dexterity and visual recognition. We can recognize the necessity
> of World 3 for the development of the human person. The brain is built
> by genetic instructions (that is, by nature), but development of human
> personhood is dependent on World 3 environment (that is, Nurture).[18]

17. Kitwood, *Dementia Reconsidered*, p. 18.
18. John C. Eccles, *Evolution of the Brain: Creation of the Self* (London: Routledge,
1991), pp. 221-22. Eccles here is using Karl Popper's representational model of human neurological evolution. According to this model, the human brain evolves in three stages, or

For reasons that will become clear in the following chapters, I do not agree with Eccles's criteria for personhood. Nevertheless, his key point remains pertinent: emotional and intellectual development and their neural correlates are essentially communal and physical from the earliest stages of infancy. In order to develop the capacity to speak, one needs to be spoken to. In order for one's brain to develop effectively, one needs certain forms of relationship and experience. Relationships have neurological as well as psychological and social significance.

These observations pertaining to the plasticity of the brain are important with regard to dementia for at least two reasons. First, as mentioned, it means that the structures of people's brains will differ quite significantly not only according to their genetic endowment but also according to the levels of learning and the types of experience that they have had. Kitwood puts it this way:

> Neuroscience now suggests that there may be very great differences between human beings in the degree to which nerve architecture has developed as a result of learning and experience. It follows that individuals may vary considerably in the extent to which they are able to withstand processes in the brain that destroy synapses, and hence in their resistance to dementia.[19]

Thus, resilience will differ from person to person.

---

worlds. World 1 is the world of physical objects and states, including human brains. World 2 is the whole world of physical subjective experiences or states of consciousness — i.e., perception, thinking, emotions, memories, imagination, and so on. World 3 is the world of knowledge in the objective sense — i.e., the whole manmade world of culture, including language. According to Eccles and Popper, it is in the interplay between World 2 and World 1 that a person develops a sense of self and a conscious place in the universe. Persons create World 3 experiences by using World 2 experiences. World 3 experiences in turn affect World 2 experiences in a continuing dialectical process which constitutes cultural and *active* human evolution (Eccles, pp. 72-74). A further explanation of human evolution will clarify this point. *Passive* evolution is an opportunistic process whereby organisms seek to adapt to a particular environment in an attempt simply to survive. *Active* evolution demands a higher level of consciousness, and occurs when organisms, primarily human beings, seek out particular ways of living and places to live according to personal, self-conscious values and purposes. Eccles argues that it is primarily in this second sense that human evolution continues in the present.

19. Kitwood, *Dementia Reconsidered*, p. 19.

Second, and consequently, there may be a much closer correlation between the *experience* of dementia and the neurological damage that persons experience. In other words, it may be that one's social experiences in some sense reinforce or perhaps even cause or exacerbate neurological damage and deterioration which originally may have stemmed from different causes.

Exploring the Connection between Dementia and Malignant Social Psychology

Kitwood's point in re-narrating the causal factors that lie behind the development of dementia is twofold. First, he wants to loosen the hold that the standard paradigm has on our understanding of dementia and create a space for a different approach that takes care and relationships as seriously as neurological decline, deficit, and damage. He wants to initiate a new story which will present us with a new worldview. Second (and this is a connected goal), he wants people to realize that they may be implicit in the creation of the symptoms of dementia. No longer can we avoid responsibility for dementia by blaming it all on neurology. If Kitwood is correct, then society may well have a profound responsibility for *causing* the symptoms of dementia rather than simply responding to them. The symptoms of Franzen's father might not only have been more than a particular manifestation of a generalized syndrome; they may also have been the product and a manifestation of the society within which he lived, breathed, and experienced dementia.

In making the claim that relationships are in fact central to what dementia is, Kitwood wishes to make us aware of the ways in which people relate to those who have dementia and the implications that such relating has for the development of the condition physically, psychologically, and socially. In particular, he wants his readers to notice the profoundly negative ways in which relationships with people who have dementia often work themselves out. The term "dementia" does not just describe a set of symptoms. It also describes a quite particular way of being in the world that has cultural significance. To become deeply forgetful and intellectually vulnerable within liberal Western cultures that prioritize intellect and reason over other aspects of being human has quite specific meaning, and that meaning is deeply negative. Stephen Post puts it this way:

We live in a culture that is the child of rationalism and capitalism, so clarity of mind and economic productivity determine the value of human life. The dictum "I think, therefore I am" is not easily replaced with "I will, feel, and relate while disconnected by forgetfulness from my former self, but I am." Neither *cogito* (I think) nor *ergo* (therefore), but *sum* (I am). Human beings are much more than sharp minds, powerful rememberers, and economic successes.[20]

Post identifies the key problem for people with dementia living within such a cultural milieu as the general tendency toward *hypercognition*.[21] The idea of hypercognition relates to the tendency within Western liberal cultures to isolate intellect, reason, and rationality and identify these aspects of human beings as having particular moral and social significance.[22] A life which is truly valuable and worth living is fundamentally defined by the ability to function effectively on the level of intellect and reason. Such hypercognitive cultures will inevitably construct dementia in particularly negative terms. This construction will necessarily impact how people respond to those who receive the name "dementia." Thus there is an explicit and implicit negative cultural bias toward diseases which involve deterioration in intellect, rationality, autonomy, and freedom, those facets of human beings that Western cultures have chosen to value over and above others. It is Kitwood's intention to sensitize us to the clinical and relational implications of such negative psychological and sociological processes.

Kitwood suggests that this cultural bias means that many of us are programmed to think of dementia negatively, which inevitably means that our relationships with people who bear the diagnosis have a tendency toward negativity. Kitwood offers a story that illustrates this point:

A . . . day centre was approached by an agency concerned to promote awareness about Alzheimer's disease and similar conditions. Could the day centre provide some photographs of clients, to be used for publicity purposes? Permission was sought and granted; the photographs were duly taken and sent. The agency, however, rejected them, on the ground

20. Stephen G. Post, *The Moral Challenge of Alzheimer Disease: Ethical Issues from Diagnosis to Dying* (Baltimore, Md.: Johns Hopkins University Press, 1995), p. 3.

21. Post, *The Moral Challenge of Alzheimer Disease*, p. 3.

22. By "liberal cultures" I mean forms of liberal democracy, a system of democracy based on autonomy and individual rights and freedoms.

that the clients did not show the disturbed and agonized characteristics that people with dementia "ought" to show, and which would be expected to arouse public concern. The failure of the photographic exercise, from the standpoint of the agency, was a measure of the success of the day centre from the standpoint of the clients. Here was a place where men and women with dementia were continuing to live in the world of persons, and not being downgraded into the carriers of an organic brain disease. Alzheimer's victims, dements, elderly mentally infirm — these and similar descriptions devalue the person, and make a unique and sensitive human being into an instance of some category devised for convenience or control.[23]

The tension between the hypercognitive cultural story with its expectations and demands for loss and devastation to be the prevailing script and a counter-story of love and possibilities couldn't be starker. Kitwood names such negative relational processes forms of *malignant social psychology*. The term refers to social environments in which the forms of interpersonal interactions and communications that occur diminish the personhood of those people experiencing that environment. Its features include relationships which lead to treachery, disempowerment, infantilization, intimidation, labeling, stigmatization, outpacing, invalidation, banishment, objectification, ignoring, imposition, withholding, accusation, disruption, mockery, and disparagement.[24]

A simple example of malignant social psychology would be not thinking twice about talking *about* a person as if he/she were not there: "He won't remember!"; "She can't understand"; "He's not really the person he used to be, so . . . ?" Of course we don't know the truth of any of these statements; they are simply assumptions we make based on the content and meaning that we have ascribed to the name "dementia" and the presumptions we have about the connection between dementia and "loss of mind and self." Similarly, we might find ourselves making comparisons between the individual with dementia and a child: "She's just like a child. It's like caring for a one-year-old." But of course she's not "just like a child." Even if her behavior does seem analogically childlike, she is an adult with a history and a story that make her who she is. She isn't growing into and learning

23. Kitwood, *Dementia Reconsidered*, p. 7.
24. Kitwood, *Dementia Reconsidered*, p. 47.

about the world as a child does. She's been in the world for a long time. Even if her brain can no longer hold onto memories, her body remains formed and available in a world which has bodily familiarity even if that familiarity can no longer be named. She isn't moving backward toward childhood; she's moving forward toward her new future self. Similarly, we may belittle this person by ignoring her, by not consulting her about things that are important in her life, or by acting treacherously by tricking her into situations "for her own good." "We're just going for a Sunday drive," we might say to her — when in fact we're taking her to a care home where she'll spend the rest of her life with strangers. All of these things are examples of not giving people the benefit of the doubt. And, as will become clear, there is in fact plenty of room for doubt.

Malignant interactions need not be perpetrated out of malice. Often they occur because of thoughtlessness, lack of insight, or lack of awareness about the negative effects of particular attitudes, actions, behaviors, and relationships. Often they're the product of underlying cultural assumptions about worth and value. As we have seen, if we're taught to see people with dementia in particular ways, we'll assume that we should respond to them accordingly. Because we tend to look through rather than look at the things we are taught about dementia, we often have no way of knowing how destructive some of our everyday assumptions and attitudes actually are. All of these things have the cumulative effect of depersonalizing the individual with dementia and placing him/her in situations where relationships subtly and sometimes quite rapidly move from "I-Thou" to "I-It"; from the personal to the objectified impersonal. The implication here is that it is malformed relationships rather than pure neurology that lie behind many of the symptoms and experiences of dementia. If this is so, it may be that a changed relational context might bring about changed behavior and a reduction in symptoms. If this is so, then we should be concentrating as much on care as on neurology. Relationships and care need to become aspects of how we describe, define, and seek to understand dementia.

Kitwood summarizes his overall position and revised definition of dementia in the form of an equation: D = NI + PH + B + MSP. He uses this shorthand: D = Dementia; NI = Neurological Impairment; PH = Physical Health; B = Biography; MSP = Malignant Social Psychology. Dementia (D) relates to neurological impairment (NI). This impairment is impacted by a person's general physical health (PH) combined with his/her previous biography (B), wherein the particular neurological configurations that have occurred function in various ways in developing the brain's structure and architecture, thus accounting for variation in resilience to the process of dementia. In order to understand the experience of dementia, we need first of all to understand the person's story.[25] The experience of dementia is in turn deeply impacted by the person's experience of malignant social psychology (MSP). It is as these various elements interact with one another that the full nature of dementia begins to emerge. Experience and biography matter for the ways in which we conceptualize, understand, and respond to dementia.

Establishing What's Needed

An Expanded Medical Perspective   It is important to notice that the arguments presented thus far do not suggest that medical understandings of dementia should be rejected. Kitwood's position does, however, suggest that they require expansion and modification. For Kitwood this means opening up the possibility that malignant social psychology may in fact impact people with dementia at the level of experience *and* of disease:

> A malignant social psychology may actually be damaging to nerve tissue. Dementia may be induced in part by the stresses of life. Thus anyone who envisages the effects of care as being "purely psychological," independent of what is happening in the nervous system, is perpetuating the error of Descartes in trying to separate mind from body. Maintaining personhood is both a psychological and a neurological task.[26]

Kitwood thus brings together standard accounts of dementia as a neurological condition and adds a new aspect: *dementia as a psycho-neurological condition.* In this way he shifts some of the territory away from neurology and resituates dementia within a psycho-neuro-relational framework that includes but is not defined by neurological decline. Kitwood's point is not that dementia is basically a neurological condition and that it is necessary to take note of the psychological and social consequences of this. His suggestion is much more radical: Malignant social interactions are not epi-

---

25. Kitwood, *Dementia Reconsidered,* p. 51.
26. Kitwood, *Dementia Reconsidered,* p. 19.

phenomenal to or a consequence of the neurological decline that is observed in dementia; they may actually be causally implicated in the neurological damage. Although Kitwood has been criticized for not offering enough empirical evidence to support this claim, there is evidence available.

An Understanding of Dementia and Loneliness   Loneliness is a central experience for many people with dementia. This has partly to do with the way in which one's social network shrinks as one gets older and one's friends die. But it has also to do with the ways in which malignant social psychology drives one's friends away. The suggestion that people with dementia might be lonely and socially isolated is no small point in the light of the arguments that have been presented thus far on the effect of relationships on neurology. A 2007 article in the *Archives of General Psychiatry* focused on the role of loneliness in the development of Alzheimer's.[27] It indicated that people who are lonely are twice as likely to develop Alzheimer's disease. Professor Wilson, professor of neuropsychology at Rush University Medical Center, was asked to comment on the implications of the study:

> "There are two ideas that we should take away. Number one is it suggests that loneliness really is a risk factor, and secondly in trying to understand that association we need to look outside the typical neuro-pathology." He said the results ruled out the possibility that loneliness is a reaction to dementia. It may be that loneliness may affect systems in the brain dealing with cognition and memory, making lonely people more vulnerable to effects of age-related decline in neural pathways, he suggested. "We need to be aware that loneliness doesn't just have an emotional impact but a physical impact," he said.[28]

Rebecca Wood, chief executive of the Alzheimer's Research Trust, also commented on the study, as did Dr. Susan Sorensen:

> "This is an impressive study. It follows a large group of people for a significant period of time and comes up with startling findings that back

27. Robert S. Wilson et al., "Loneliness and Risk of Alzheimer Disease," *Archives of General Psychiatry* 64, no. 2 (2007): 234-40.
28. BBC News, "Loneliness Link with Alzheimer's"; access at http://news.bbc.co.uk/1/hi/6332883.stm.

up earlier studies examining social interaction and Alzheimer's risk. What I find particularly interesting about this study is the fact that it is an individual's perception of being lonely rather than their actual degree of social isolation that seems to correlate most closely with their Alzheimer's risk." Dr. Susan Sorensen, head of research at the Alzheimer's Society, agreed: "The study demonstrates a clear link between less social activity and a higher risk of dementia symptoms. However, it is interesting that the people who died during the study and had demonstrated symptoms of dementia did not have relatively more physical signs of Alzheimer's disease in the brain."[29]

That is indeed interesting. The resonance with Kitwood's propositions is obvious and quite startling. The thing to note here is that although the study didn't claim that loneliness is one of the leading causes of dementia, it is very clear that, as Professor Wilson highlights, the impact of loneliness is not only emotional — it's physical. If this is the case, it would at minimum add some support to the suggestion that there is a two-way process at work in the formation of the biology of dementia. The study also supports the suggestion that human beings are relational beings. Even in the midst of cognitive decline and an apparent "loss of the person," we need others in order to live well. But where are the others in the lives of people who have dementia? On the positive side, this study indicates that Kitwood's hypothesis about the centrality of relationships in neurological development and change may be valid. People do require relationships — healthy relationships — to be who they are and to sustain a sense of well-being. On the negative side, the fact that the research notices the significance of loneliness indicates that many people *are* lonely; many people do not have and perhaps cannot attain the types of relationships that are vital for their well-being. Malignant social psychology provides one reason for this. But there is much more to be said about malignant social interactions.

29. BBC News, "Loneliness Link with Alzheimer's."

Steven Sabat on Dementia

Exploring "Excess Disability" and Malignant Social Positioning

Steven Sabat takes up, develops, and in important ways offers further verification of Kitwood's thinking. Central to Sabat's thinking is the idea of "excess disability":

> . . . there has been considerable reason to have at least some doubt that the myriad symptoms observed in AD sufferers are due to brain pathology alone. More than a quarter of a century ago Brody[30] coined the term excess disability to describe what he called "the discrepancy that exists when a person's functional incapacity is greater than that warranted by the actual impairment." But if there is such excess disability, there would seem to be only one possible realm in which that disability is rooted, and that would be the social world in which the person with AD dwells.[31]

Excess disability relates to manifestations of incapacity that do not relate directly to any physical damage that might have occurred to an individual. So, for example, the social isolation and exclusion that come from being labeled "schizophrenic" emerge not only from the condition itself but from people's reaction to the label.[32] Schizophrenia is certainly debilitating, but much of the disability is excessive — that is, epiphenomenal — to the syndrome itself. The same is true of dementia. Excess disability relates to malignant social psychology in that one leads into the other.

For Sabat, the problem with standard approaches is that they simply cannot see such excess disability. They aren't designed to recognize it. Consequently, excess disability becomes invisibly grafted into the standard paradigm and seemingly "disappears." Sabat notes,

> We may be in the midst of a tragic irony here: however objective and useful the standard approach may be in certain venues, it is relatively in-

30. E. M. Brody, "Excess Disabilities of Mentally Impaired Aged: Impact of Individualized Treatment," *The Gerontologist* 25 (1971): 124-33.

31. Steven R. Sabat, *The Experience of Alzheimer's Disease: Life through a Tangled Veil* (Oxford: Blackwell, 2001), p. 93.

32. For an expanded discussion on this point in relation to schizophrenia, see John Swinton, *Resurrecting the Person: Friendship and the Care of People with Severe Mental Health Problems* (Nashville: Abingdon Press, 2000).

sensitive to the varied contexts of the social world in which all of us, including the afflicted, live our lives. Yet, on the basis of the results of research using the standard paradigm, we have painted a mosaic, created a narrative, about the afflicted person's abilities in the very social world which is not studied through that research. In other words, on the basis of the standard approach, incorrect negative assumptions can be made by those who interact with AD sufferers in the everyday social world.[33]

The place where Sabat notices such negative assumptions is in the language that we use about and around people with dementia.

A central concept which Sabat uses to capture the dynamics of this process is the idea of "malignant social positioning." Here he draws on Kitwood's idea of malignant social psychology, adding to it the theory of social positioning:

The effects of dementia derive from a great deal more than the documented neuropathological changes in the brain of the person thus diagnosed and can be exacerbated or ameliorated to some degree by the way the person is positioned by others in the everyday social world. By analyzing the nature of their social interactions with others, we can readily come to appreciate how the ways in which the person with dementia is treated by others can have a profoundly positive or profoundly negative effect on (1) the subjective experience of the person with dementia; (2) the degree to which the person can display remaining intact cognitive abilities; (3) the ability of the person to meet the demands of everyday life; and (4) the quality of the person's social life and the meaning found in each day.[34]

Sabat draws on the thinking of psychologist Rom Harré and his revision of traditional role theory, what he calls positioning theory.[35] Positioning theory provides a way to read and understand the dynamics of human role relationships as they are expressed through language. Harré criticizes standard notions of roles as being overly static, disembodied, and paying

33. Sabat, *The Experience of Alzheimer's Disease*, p. 94.

34. Steven R. Sabat, "Mind, Meaning, and Personhood in Dementia: The Effects of Positioning," in *Dementia: Mind, Meaning, and the Person*, ed. Julian C. Hughes, Stephen J. Louw, and Steven R. Sabat (Oxford: Oxford University Press, 2006), p. 287.

35. Rom Harré and L. van Langenhove, *Positioning Theory* (Oxford: Blackwell, 1999).

little attention to specific contexts. Roles describe typical social positions — wife, mother, banker, teacher, student — but fail to identify the *particular* experience of someone who is ascribed such a role. Positioning theory thus offers a more dynamic perspective than role theory, focusing on the special position of an individual within an encounter. The way in which we position a person within a relationship will determine how we respond to her and will also reveal what we think of her even if such things are unspoken. A person's position in any encounter is communicated through language. Malignant social positioning occurs when a person is positioned in such a way within a social encounter that his/her personhood is threatened.[36]

Imagine for a moment that you're walking down the street and a woman comes up to you and says, "Hello, my name is Martha. This is my husband, John. He has dementia." You can see how the husband is positioned in a very particular way. Given all of the roles that he has in his life, why does his wife choose to position him as a dementia sufferer? Normally the role of husband would be considered equal with the role of wife and would have attached to it particular duties and responsibilities and a particular sense of self-identity. It would be sufficient for Martha to say, "Hi. This is John, my husband." However, the way that Martha has linguistically positioned John means that his normal role as a husband is significantly weakened and negatively transformed. He has lost his multifaceted role as a functioning husband and has acquired a primary identity as someone who has dementia. It is in this depersonalizing sense that such positioning is malignant, according to Sabat:

> Positions help to define, strengthen, or weaken a person's moral and personal attributes and help to create story-lines about persons. Through the process of positioning, people explain their own behavior as well as that of others, so that to explain someone's actions in ways that emphasize the individual's negative attributes is to position that person in a potentially malignant way.[37]

36. Steven R. Sabat, "Positioning and Conflict Involving a Person with Dementia: A Case Study," in Fathali M. Moghaddam, Rom Harré, and Naomi Lee, *Global Conflict Resolution Through Positioning Analysis* (New York: Springer, 2008), p. 81.

37. Sabat, "Mind, Meaning, and Personhood in Dementia," p. 289.

Drawing on Lisa Snyder's ethnographic work in a home for people with dementia,[38] Sabat offers a powerful example of this process of malignant positioning:

> Betty, a retired social worker and former faculty member at San Diego State University, said about health care professionals who she encountered during the process of being diagnosed, "They're busy wanting to climb up the next rung of the ladder. That's very human. I don't blame them. But they don't really accept the significance of illness for people. They know the diagnosis, but they don't take time to know what that truly means for that person. The casualness with which professionals deal with Alzheimer's is so painful to see. . . . You have to really be willing to be present with the person who has Alzheimer's. But there are some people who don't want to learn, and it's the looking down on and being demeaning of people with Alzheimer's that is hard to watch."[39]

To position Betty as a "dementia patient" is to take away from her other formerly primary roles such as mother, sister, wife, and friend and to replace these roles with a psychiatric category. This category may make some sense, because it does its work within the health care system, but it makes little sense when Betty is at home, or as she tries to make sense of her world within a care home or sheltered accommodation. If a person becomes her illness, her very humanness is threatened. As Betty poignantly commented, "A person with Alzheimer's disease is many more things than just their diagnosis. Each person is a whole human being."[40]

Sabat offers this strong denunciation of malignant positioning of people like Betty:

> Once persons are positioned socially as nothing more than instantiations of a diagnostic category, their essential humanity, including their intellectual and emotional characteristics, needs, and their social personae beyond that of "demented, burdensome patient" become more and more obscured and can ultimately become erased.[41]

38. Lisa Snyder, *Speaking Our Minds: Personal Reflections from Individuals with Alzheimer's* (New York: Freeman, 1999).

39. Sabat, "Positioning and Conflict Involving a Person with Dementia," p. 82; Snyder, *Speaking Our Minds*, pp. 123-24.

40. Snyder, *Speaking Our Minds*, pp. 123-24.

41. Sabat, "Positioning and Conflict Involving a Person with Dementia," p. 84.

In introducing the idea of malignant positioning, Sabat draws our attention to the fact that the language people use reflects the stories they are utilizing to make sense of the person with dementia. In doing so, Sabat expands on Kitwood's suggestion of a general malignant social psychology and focuses us on the particular ways in which this positioning is manifested — in subliminal attitudes expressed through the language we use, which malignantly positions people in ways that threaten their very humanness.

Examining What It Means to Be "Your-Self"

Positioning, then, has to do with how an observer perceives and responds to a person with dementia. Of course, perception and reality are not always the same thing. Perception emerges from presumptions and presuppositions, which develop through the various stories that we learn to tell about the experience of dementia. Key among the presumptions often made about someone with dementia is that somehow the person has gone, that he or she has lost his or her "self." In other words, the subjective self becomes eroded to such an extent that it eventually disappears due to the person's gradually failing neurology. The literature is full of research and reflection wrestling with the question of whether the self is present or destroyed in dementia.[42] Writers use the term "self" in a variety of ways, but in essence the general issue seems to be whether or not that which is essential for the person to be aware of selfhood still remains in the context of advanced dementia. Put slightly more philosophically, am "I" still "me" when "I" have forgotten who "I" am? Presumptions about the loss of self lie behind a good deal of malignant social psychology and negative social positioning. If you don't believe the person before you is "really there" in the same way that you assume yourself to be "really there," then you're liable to position that person in ways that are negative, depersonalizing, and, I will argue, inaccurate.

The "Inner" Self?   In exploring the nature of the self, it will be helpful to begin by reflecting on precisely what we mean when we talk about an "in-

---

42. For a useful review of this literature, see L. S. Caddell and L. Clare, "The Impact of Dementia on Self and Identity: A Systematic Review," *Clinical Psychology Review,* 30 February 2010, pp. 113-26.

ner self" that has somehow "gone." Hans Reinders somewhat poetically describes the self as "that part of me where I am with myself."[43] The implication here is that the self is something that is internal, an aspect of who I think I am that really only I can access. It is this sense of the inner space of "selfness" that has been deeply influential in the history of Western thought. To be myself, I have to be aware of myself, and the place where I find myself is within me, via my inner sense of who I am. It is this subjective sense of an inner space which is "me" that people with dementia are assumed to be losing. To lose myself is to lose that which makes me who I am, that which provides me with my "inner" sense of who I am. If that is so, any implicit or explicit assumptions that the self is destroyed by dementia will inevitably open up the possibility of malignant social psychology and negative positioning. There is, however, good reason to think that the self is not destroyed by the decline in neurological processes that mark dementia — not least because there are good reasons to believe that the self is not in fact as "inner" as we might assume.

To begin with, we might wish to ask precisely what it might mean for the self to be located within our "inner processes." Where exactly is the "inside"? I have previously suggested that the mind, an aspect of who we are that we would normally assume to be inside of us, does in fact have a significant external social component. Our minds are both personal and social. This observation should make us suspicious of the idea that the "self," whatever that may turn out to be, should be defined by that which is "inner." Wittgenstein drew attention to the fact that human beings experience things prior to naming them and taking them "inward" toward the development of an experience of mind/self.[44] A baby first *experiences* the world. She has a variety of primal experiences which she expresses by crying, laughing, fussing, and so forth. As she grows up, she is taught to conceptualize these primal experiences by using particular forms of language. So, for example, she is taught that certain experiences should be named as pain or pleasure. Of course, the meaning of such words and the response to them vary across contexts and cultures. So to name an experience "pain" or "pleasure" is to give the primal experience a particular cultural or con-

43. Hans S. Reinders, *Receiving the Gift of Friendship: Profound Disability, Theological Anthropology, and Ethics* (Grand Rapids: Wm. B. Eerdmans, 2008), p. 21.

44. Ludwig Wittgenstein, *Philosophical Investigations* (Oxford: Blackwell, 1995).

textual form. In other words, the language that the child learns as she constructs her "inner" world brings with it a whole series of meanings and connotations linked to traditions and communities. Thus the "inner" is much more "outer" than it first appears to be.

This language that the child learns from those around her thus forms the structures of the experience of her "inner life," an experience that she is *later* taught to name and understand as "her mind" and/or her "sense of self." The nature and meaning of the language she learns from others provide the conceptual structure and shape of her mind. The apparently "inner" structures of the "individual" mind are actually found to be the product of "outer" experiences that are drawn "inward" and become experiences that we later define as mind. The "inner" experience of the mind turns out to be a thoroughly "outer" and social entity.

What is true for the mind is also true for the "self." In what sense can the self be "inner" when most of what we know about ourselves actually emerges from our relational encounters, our outer experiences? Surely the self is inevitably outer and social even if it does *feel* inner. Owen Thomas points out that the sense of interiority — the feeling or belief that the mind and the self are somehow interior to the body and separated from the wider community — is in fact

> a spatial metaphor for something that is non-spatial. It is a metaphor; it makes no sense to say that the self, consciousness, mind, or spirit is literally inside the body. But the referent of interiority, while non-spatial, is localized. It is somehow related to the body and not entirely apart from the body, although the theological and philosophical traditions are divided on this issue.[45]

Thus the idea of the mind being individual and separated from other minds and the self being something that is only "inner" is at least open to challenge. The mind and the self emerge from relationships and are formed and sustained by and in relationships.[46] That being so, neurologi-

45. Owen C. Thomas, "Interiority and Christian Spirituality," *The Journal of Religion* 80, no. 1 (January 2000): 41-60; quotation on 56.

46. The social nature of the mind is implicit even within Descartes's dictum "I think; therefore I am." Who is the "I" that is thinking, and where is she? Thought, it appears, is necessarily and inseparably connected to an "I." Presumably the "I" resides in the world of persons and is open to the types of context and influences that I have highlighted. We have no

cal damage may alter certain perceptions (in self and others) of one's "inner self," but it does not destroy the self, as the self always belongs to a broader community.

A Social Model of the Self   This brief but important philosophical reflection on some of the problems with seeing the "inner self" as definitive of the nature of the self serves as background for understanding the way in which Sabat's ideas about excess disability and malignant social positioning fit in with his broader agenda, which is to show that people with dementia do not experience a loss of self. Sabat advocates strongly that dementia does not destroy a person's sense of self. The self, he argues, can be sustained through appropriate relational encounters. Drawing on qualitative research with people who have dementia, including those in the advanced stages of the condition, Sabat shows that even in the later stages of the disease, the self remains intact and can be encountered if carers can find the means and the insight to see it and to recognize its presence and stay with it effectively.

Sabat's conception of the self is quite different from those models of self that focus on interiority as a defining criterion. For him, the self is something that is constructed within the relational dialectic that goes on between the individual and his/her communities. The self has three aspects which Sabat describes as Self 1, Self 2, and Self 3.

SELF 1 relates to personal identity:

> [This self finds its expression in] the use of personal pronouns such as "me, myself, my, mine, our" (which denotes "mine and yours"), for example. One could also point to oneself as in the use of mime to accomplish the same end of expressing one's personal identity. We experience this aspect of selfhood in that each of us has one single point of view in the world, one continuous experience of events that forms the narrative of our lives. Through the use of first-person pronouns we take responsibility for our actions, index (locate for others) feelings and experiences as being our own, and tell autobiographical stories. In principle, a person could suffer a form of amnesia which prevents him or her from re-

---

knowledge of any other world or any other way of being in the world. If the "I" is in the world, then the mind cannot simply be within the "I."

trieving information concerning name, place, and year of birth, education, and the like, and still have an intact self of personal identity as
demonstrated in conversational discourse.[47]

Self 1 relates to the person's experience of himself/herself in the present
moment. Self 1 occurs whenever a person refers to himself/herself either
through the language of "you," "mine," or "me," or by gestures that indicate a sense of being present in the world. Thus a person can forget who he
is and forget who those around him are but still have a sense of "self-in-
the-present." Unless a person is terminally unconscious, Self 1 remains
throughout the experience of dementia. That being so, the suggestion that
someone with dementia loses his sense of self is seriously mistaken.

SELF 2, according to Sabat, relates to "a person's physical and mental attributes and beliefs about those attributes":

> One's height and weight, eye pigmentation, one's sense of humor, reli-
> gious and political convictions, educational achievements, and voca-
> tional pursuits would be examples of physical and mental attributes,
> respectively. Likewise, a person may have beliefs about his or her at-
> tributes, such that pride is taken in some and disdain is the reaction to
> others. Some Self 2 attributes have long histories (being a college grad-
> uate); some may be more recent in their existence (being diagnosed
> with AD).[48]

Self 2 contains a person's physical characteristics and their biography cou-
pled with their awareness, interpretation, and valuing of such characteristics and experiences. Self 2 can shift and change over time, sometimes
quite quickly. For example, if a person becomes a Christian, many of his
assumptions about his Self 2 can change quickly and radically. Within Self
2, the ascription of the name "dementia" is an undesirable, late-onset ac-
cretion which the person may well resist by countering certain assumptions with more positive stories about his/her experience. So a person may
lose the keys to her car. Those around her might ascribe this loss to demen-

47. Sabat, *The Experience of Alzheimer's Disease*, p. 277.
48. Steven R. Sabat, "Surviving Manifestations of Selfhood in Alzheimer's Disease," *Dementia* 1, no. 1 (2002): 25-36; quotation on 27.

tia. She may counter such an ascription by pointing out that in fact her sister is sitting on them! The point is that the experience was read by others through the lens of dementia, and the explanation that might be most obvious under normal circumstances was overlooked. The problem with the Self 2 is that particular negative identities can become prominent and can overcome other, more positive ones, as Sabat points out:

> People who suffer from AD often find themselves in social situations in which the problems caused by the disease (new Self 2 attributes) increasingly become the focus of attention, thereby rendering their own more highly valued Self 2 attributes more and more invisible. . . . Few of us wish to have relationships with others in which our shortcomings are constantly the main focus of interaction.[49]

A person whose Self 2 remains intact and available retains the possibility of addressing misperceptions and false stories. However, once a diagnosis of dementia is made and ideas relating to excess disability come into play, it becomes more and more difficult for the person to sustain a positive Self 2. It is here, within the tensions of negotiating Self 2, that malignant social psychology and malignant social positioning come firmly into play.

Such negativization doesn't relate only to those who are around a person with dementia. The stigmatic nature of dementia means that the person himself can begin to position himself negatively as he interacts with the negative positioning of others. This means that such "symptoms" as withdrawal, depression, anger, non-cooperation, and "deterioration in emotional control, social behavior, or motivation" may not actually be indicative of a fragmentation of the self or of failing neurology. Instead, they may relate to a manifestation of the frustrations of trying to maintain a positive Self 2 when all those around seem to see only the worst.

The important thing to notice about Self 1 and Self 2 is that they are, to a degree, under the control of the individual. Self 3 is different. The attainment of Self 3 is almost wholly dependent on the cooperation of others.

SELF 3 has to do with the way in which a person presents or is represented to the world, as Sabat explains:

---

49. Sabat, "Surviving Manifestations of Selfhood in Alzheimer's Disease," p. 30.

Self 3 is comprised of the various different social personae which we construct in the variety of situations in which we live our lives, and each persona involves a specific pattern of behavior which is in many ways distinct from the others. One and the same person may display patterns of behavior which are quite different from one another, such as the dedicated teacher, fun-loving friend, deferential child, romantic spouse, [and] nurturing parent. Each of these different social personae requires for its existence the cooperation of at least one other person in our social world.[50]

The key thing about Self 3 is that it is wholly dependent on some form of relationship and/or community. One cannot attain or sustain Self 3 without the assistance of others. It isn't possible to be a teacher unless your pupils grant you that status. It isn't possible to be a loyal friend if you have no friends. It isn't possible to be a loving husband without having or having had a wife. It isn't possible to be a caring parent if you have no children.

Similarly, it's not possible for dementia to have a positive public profile unless people respond positively to it. Sabat explains,

[If people within the person's social world] . . . view him or her as being "defective," "burdensome," and the like, the only Self 3 persona which the afflicted person will be able to construct will be that of the "dysfunctional Alzheimer's patient." Under these conditions, there could be, potentially, a loss of Self 3 personae, but such a loss would hardly be due to the neuropathology of the disease, but rather to the lack of cooperation that the afflicted person is given by others in his or her attempts to construct healthy, more admirable social personae.[51]

Self 3 requires others. If malignant social psychology does in fact occur in the ways that Sabat and Kitwood suggest, then the chances of a person with dementia achieving and sustaining a positive Self 3 are pretty slim. Put in terms of the argument of Chapter One, if we limit the stories that we tell about dementia only to the negative ones, and if, implicitly or ex-

---

50. Sabat, "Surviving Manifestations of Selfhood in Alzheimer's Disease," p. 27.
51. Sabat, "Surviving Manifestations of Selfhood in Alzheimer's Disease," p. 28. For a fuller description of this process of "selfing," see Sabat, *The Experience of Alzheimer's Disease,*" Chapter 1.

plicitly, we prevent or curtail the person's ability to tell her own story well or prevent it from being told effectively on her behalf, then attaining and maintaining Self 3 will be impossible. The key point is this: The neurology of dementia doesn't destroy the self. *Any dissolution of the self reflects a dissolution of community.*

My Friend Gordon's Dilemma: Losing and Finding One's Self

So, what might all of this look like in "real life"? To answer this question, I will offer a personal reflection on the experience of a good friend of mine, Gordon, who was diagnosed with Alzheimer's disease and has lived with it for five years. Looking back, those of us who know him can see that the symptoms were there long before that, but five years ago he received a formal diagnosis, and Alzheimer's came formally into existence in his life. Gordon lived at home for the first three years after his diagnosis. But things were never easy. I remember a meal we had with Gordon not long after he had received the news. My wife and I got together with Gordon, his wife, Elaine, and some of his close friends to enjoy some time together and some good food. As the meal went on, I watched as Gordon gradually withdrew from the conversation. He just couldn't keep up with the flow and exchange of words and the mass of information that the conversation involved. Sometimes we forget how much information is shared in the average social gathering. If you can't remember the beginning of a long conversation that's constantly being shifted by the interjections of others, it's difficult to remain motivated to participate. As the evening moved on, I noticed that the conversation was flowing all around Gordon; people were talking around him and about him, but not to him. Gordon was somewhere else. He was surrounded by his closest friends, and yet he was deeply alone. We could have slowed down, taken time to include him, but we didn't — partly because we didn't really notice what was going on, but partly also because in the back of our minds we were all probably thinking, "It's just his Alzheimer's disease. That's what happens, isn't it?" I often wonder about that evening. If his closest friends couldn't take the time to slow down, notice what was going on, and really try to be with him, who would? The image of Gordon alone in a crowd of friends still worries me.

Life wasn't easy for Gordon's wife. Gordon was retired, and Elaine was still working. As his memory began to fail, he would call her at work twenty to thirty times a day, trying desperately to find out where she was. He couldn't remember where she had gone, and he couldn't remember that he had just called her five minutes earlier. His personality also began to shift and change. His moods were unpredictable, and occasionally he would become aggressive and violent. Elaine was lonely. The person she was living with was in many ways quite different from the person she had married. She was faithful, but she was lonely. Elaine looked after Gordon well, but eventually it became impossible for her to cope on her own at home. Last year Gordon was taken into full-time care and is now looked after in a local care home owned by an independent social care company. He is now cared for by strangers.

Gordon has a fully developed Self 2. Gordon is a highly educated man. He was a teacher by profession, and for many years he was a head teacher running taxing and complicated schools for younger children. He is a man who's used to having responsibility and being in control; he's someone who has always thrived on such responsibility and has been highly re-spected by his community. He is a person who's used to telling other peo-ple what to do rather than being told what to do himself. He is the father of two daughters and the stepfather of two sons. Gordon is also a Christian who has always adhered to deeply held moral values and beliefs. In terms of Sabat's framework of self, he has a strong, intricate, and complex Self 2 into which he's desperately trying to integrate his new experience of Alz-heimer's disease. However, while he struggles to maintain his Self 2 iden-tity, it is being overpowered more and more by the radical changes in his emerging Self 3. No matter what he does to try to avoid this, his Self 3 is be-ing created by those around him in ways that pose a serious challenge to a positive Self 2. Gradually the biographical story of his life (Self 2) is being subsumed by the new story of his life as an "Alzheimer's victim" (Selves 2 and 3), a story wherein everything he does tends to be interpreted through the lens of his "new self."

Gordon didn't like being taken into care. He has become confused, his memory loss has seemed to get worse, and at times he becomes uncharac-teristically withdrawn, unpredictable, and angry, so much so that the staff complain to his wife that the unit is "not equipped for patients with severe dementia who behave in such ways." Since this is an establishment run by a private, non-medical company, the use of the word "patient" is not insig-nificant. It's no surprise that whenever Gordon gets the opportunity, he tries to escape from the unit. He is never taken to church, although the church comes to him: it holds regular services in the establishment that has become Gordon's new home.

Understanding Gordon

So how can the framework we've developed in this chapter help us understand what's going on in Gordon's life? Consider it in this way. Gordon was taken into full-time care. When this happened, he was instantly repositioned: he went from being a husband, father, friend, and parishioner to a "client" or, as it turned out, a "patient." He knew this, and he didn't like it at all. He wanted to go home. His care and welfare have now been placed in the hands of strangers who are paid to look after him. In this case, these strangers come from all over the world: the Indian subcontinent, Eastern Europe, Africa, Asia, and England. My point is not that these people aren't good carers or that the fact that they come from a variety of cultures is in itself problematic. My point is that Gordon is an elderly man from the northeast of Scotland who has a specific history, background, colloquial language, and cultural formation, and he is being cared for by strangers who have come from many different places and whose history, traditions, and language are radically different from his own. And this cultural gap between them will inevitably lead to dissonance, miscommunication (cultural and linguistic), and a sense of alienation, fear, and anxiety for both carers and cared for. Gordon's dementia is not severe yet, but one can see exactly how and why his behavior would be interpreted in that way.

The context seems ideally set for negative positioning and malignant social psychology. Gordon is a man who has been addressed as Mr. Torrance for most of his working life. These strangers call him Gordon — this is a name that only those close to him have used before. He doesn't know his new carers, and he definitely doesn't want to be in that facility. When, in the light of all these things, he begins to assert himself and "act aggressively" (an understandable reaction to a frightening and frustrating situation?), when he tries to "run away" or "escape" (go home), when, as the staff put it, he acts in an "aloof and pompous manner" (he is a highly trained professional who is now being treated as if he knows nothing and is acting foolishly), the assumption is that these behaviors are being caused by his "severe dementia," a condition that the staff claim they haven't been taught how to cope with. It may in fact be that the staff haven't been taught how to *understand* people rather than how to "cope" with them.

And the church hasn't been much different, really. It's true that once a month the minister does a service in the home where Gordon lives, and he enjoys that. But few people visit. Gordon does get visits from friends and acquaintances, but not many people from the church spend time with him. On Sunday morning his church regularly prays for "the sick." I have heard prayers for individuals who are encountering cancer, bronchitis, and a variety of other ailments. But I have heard only one public prayer for Gordon in five years. It would appear that cancer, pneumonia, and accidents are worthy of regular prayer, but dementia is different. It seems that Gordon's forgetfulness has led to his being forgotten.

One of his friends said to me the other day, "I doubt if he would even recognize me, so there's probably no benefit in my going to see him." As this friend has never been to see Gordon, it's difficult to know how he came to such a conclusion. And this seems to be the key. People assume that because Gordon might not recognize them and won't remember that they have visited, there's probably no real point in visiting. Why? Presumably because people assume that the old Gordon has gone? It makes one wonder for whose benefit people think a visit would be. Is visiting one's sick friend a matter of charity, benevolence, and friendship, or simply a disguised form of self-interest? "If I'm not getting anything out of it, and he's not getting anything out of it, why should *I* bother?" I suspect Gordon is lonely.

Understanding the Loneliness of Dementia

This aspect of Gordon's experience and the responses of his friends are worth exploring further. Janelle S. Taylor has written a fascinating anthropological reflection on her experiences with her mother, who had dementia. She noticed the regularity with which friends, family, and others asked her the same question: "Does she recognize you?"[52] Taylor was struck by the apparent significance that this question seems to have for other people. For her the question of whether or not her mother recognized her was not

52. Janelle S. Taylor, "On Recognition, Caring, and Dementia," *Medical Anthropology Quarterly* 22, no. 4 (2004): 313-35.

particularly significant, but for others it seems to be vital. In her essay, following the thinking of the philosopher Paul Ricoeur,[53] Taylor highlights a dialectic between three meanings of the term "recognition":

(1) recognition as identification (of things);
(2) recognition of self;
(3) recognition by an Other.[54]

Recognition of things assumes that there is a correlation between what we see and what we are able to name. So, when we see a chair, we recognize it as a chair and act accordingly. At this level, recognition is simply something that we do as we try to make sense of the world and locate ourselves within it. Recognition of self is the ability to know who we are, to use that knowledge to assess and negotiate the world, and to hold and sustain our identity and our sense of self-in-the-world. According to these two aspects of recognition, the question "Does she recognize you?" is simply getting at whether or not Taylor's mother knows who her daughter is. It entails no real politics and appears relatively straightforward.

The third aspect of recognition makes things more complex. Recognition by an Other requires relationship and community and inevitably takes us into the realm of the social and the political. While the first two modes of recognition are something that we do for ourselves, the third movement of recognition is a social process. It is in this third dimension that Taylor realizes what she considers to be the *real* meaning of the question "Does she recognize you?" and the potential problem for her mother that such a question highlights:

> When a friend or acquaintance or co-worker asks me, "Does she recognize you?" he or she is, in Ricoeur's terms, giving voice to the first of the three distinct "moments" in the "course of recognition": the question concerns my mother's ability, as a sovereign self, to actively draw intellectual distinctions among the objects and people around her. I have come to think, however, that also at stake here is Ricoeur's third and final "moment," when the subject is granted social and political recognition by

---

53. Paul Ricoeur, *The Course of Recognition* (Cambridge: Harvard University Press, 2005).

54. Taylor, "On Recognition, Caring, and Dementia," p. 314.

others. The question concerns my mother's ability, as a sovereign self, to actively draw intellectual distinctions amongst the objects and people around her. I have come to think, however, that also at stake . . . is whether or not she is granted social and political recognition by others.[55]

Taylor's point and her deep concern is that in asking the question "Does she recognize you?" people are not simply moving between the first two understandings of the term "recognition." Rather, they are actually exploring the third aspect. When Taylor answers, "No, she does not," something will change in the way in which her mother is recognized within the social and political realms. Taylor's implication is that her answer will actually be a social marker, that her mother will shift from being perceived as a person to being perceived as a non-person, or at least a lesser person whose social and political recognition is about to be withdrawn.

Tied in with this point and important to our understanding of it is Taylor's noticing how almost all of her mother's friends have simply drifted away following her diagnosis and her subsequent journey into dementia:

> It appears that middle-class U.S. friendships are not generally expected to bear the weight of deep and diffuse obligations to care. More like pleasure crafts than life rafts, they are not built to brave the really rough waters — and these are rough, corrosive, bitter waters indeed. Dementia seems to act as a very powerful solvent on many kinds of social ties. I doubt that many friendships survive its onset.[56]

Taylor is on to something important. What she says about the United States could just as easily be said about the United Kingdom and Europe. I have always been struck by the ways in which people with dementia lose their social networks, sometimes gradually but sometimes very quickly. I well remember doing the funeral service of an old woman, Margaret, who had had severe Alzheimer's disease. I had never met her. She died in the hospital, and I was the chaplain who was called in to do her funeral. The service took place in the chapel of a local funeral home. The only two people there were me and Margaret's solicitor. I don't know where her friends were.

55. Taylor, "On Recognition, Caring, and Dementia," p. 314.
56. Taylor, "On Recognition, Caring, and Dementia," p. 319.

Gordon's experience is a good example of this process of "unfriending," to use a Facebook metaphor. Before he was diagnosed with Alzheimer's disease and went into a care facility, he had a wide and engaged circle of friends. Once he went into care — that is, once friends had to visit him without the social stimulation of his wife — his social circle shrank to primarily his wife, his daughters, and one or two individuals who chose to make time for him. Others were busy, had other priorities, and so on, and so on. If Gordon had had terminal cancer or some other form of chronic illness that took him into care, people who knew him more than likely would have felt a moral obligation, because of friendship, to visit him. With dementia (because they know he'll forget?), it's somehow different. Dementia, it seems, is a hard condition to be around.

In his book *The Forgetting: Alzheimer's: Portrait of an Epidemic,* David Shenk offers a clear and insightful account of Alzheimer's disease and its personal and social implications for people living in the United States. At one point Shenk reflects on the experiences of former president Ronald Reagan, who developed Alzheimer's disease in his later years:

> As expected, Reagan's descent had progressed steadily. Friends and family watched his memory lapses become the rule rather than the exception. There was, for example, the day that former Secretary of State George Shultz visited his old boss. In the midst of a casual discussion about politics, Reagan left the room with a nurse. When he returned a few moments later, he took the nurse aside and pointed to Shultz. "Who is that man sitting with Nancy on the couch?" he asked quietly. "I know him. He is a very famous man." Incidents like these drove him into further isolation. Partly out of simple courtesy to Reagan and partly due to their own personal discomfort, many of his friends stopped visiting when he started having trouble recognizing them.[57]

If someone who has been one of the most powerful men in the world has difficulties holding onto his network of friendships, what hope is there for Gordon? There is no doubt that it can be difficult to be with someone you know who has forgotten who you are and, indeed, who they are. At times it takes a leap of faith to remember them as the person that you knew. But no

---

57. David Shenk, *The Forgetting: Alzheimer's: Portrait of an Epidemic* (New York: Anchor Books, 2003), pp. 116-17.

matter what, your friends remain your friends, don't they? The ease with which people with dementia can be unfriended raises a dark question: What is it that we actually love in those we claim to love? In the following chapter I will raise some of the problems with capacities-based models of personhood. However, there may be even bigger issues with capacities-based practices of love.

Who Is Gordon?

It's not that anyone in Gordon's situation is trying to be unhelpful or un-caring. They're just mis-positioning Gordon and making assumptions about him that are misinformed and self-deceiving. At the moment, Gordon's Self 1 and Self 2 are functioning reasonably well, at least within the experience of those who know him well. He clearly has a sense of who he is in the world, even though he's forgetting his name and the names of those around him. He retains an awareness of his Self 2 — his history and biography — mainly, it must be said, because those who love him work very hard to keep him located in that history (through storytelling, memory books, reminiscences, etc.). But within the public discourse that surrounds his Self 3, finding positivity is becoming more and more difficult. People have constructed Gordon in such a way that he can be perceived only as losing himself when in fact it is other people who are losing sight of him. Table 3 on page 106 outlines the ways in which Gordon is, in a sense, being "unselfed." The table indicates that Self 1 has remained intact for Gordon. This self will not change. Some of the roles which comprise Self 2 have changed, but the social value of these retain residual power in those close to him, those who know him well and continue to love and care for him. What is changing as the disease progresses is Gordon's ability to sustain these roles. As this happens, it becomes the responsibility of those around him to tell his story well and to sustain him in his Self 2. This includes telling the story of dementia well in both its positive and its negative modes. What is clearly happening is that Gordon is losing his Self 3, and there is really nothing that he can do to get it back. Because this self is constructed by other people's presuppositions, which in turn are based on the meanings they have ascribed to the category of dementia, he has no control and no ability on his own to develop positive counter-stories that might reposition him in such a way that Self 2 could continue

Table 3: Who Is Gordon?

Self 1: Sense of self in the present moment	Self 2: Temporary and enduring roles	Self 3: Recently acquired attributes
No change	Father	Burdensome
	Husband	Of little worth
	Teacher	Violent
	Friend	Awkward
	Christian	Non-compliant
	Spiritual man	No longer spiritual
	Valuable and valued man	Unattractive and becoming invisible even to old friends
	Worthwhile companion	Alienated
	Alzheimer's victim	
	Dementia patient	

to be taken seriously within the public discourse, and the emerging Self 3 could develop positively. If everything a person does is subsumed by their condition, if the significance of their Self 1 experiences is assumed to be negligible, and if the implications of what they have achieved within Self 2 are discredited by the expectations engendered by the diagnosis of dementia, then a positive Self 3 becomes very difficult, if not impossible, to establish.

Clearly, the neurological processes that comprise dementia do not destroy a person's self — other people do that. Self 1 remains; Self 2 also remains intact, if always somewhat malleable and fragile, and even if that intactness is held in the memory of others. Self 3 is the self that is clearly lost to dementia. But — and this is the key point — *Self 3 doesn't belong to the individual; it belongs to the community.* This has significant implications and helps us to understand the profound importance of recognizing the malignant social psychology and negative positioning that Kitwood and

Sabat draw our attention toward. To repeat: the important thing to see is that *any diminution of the self is first and foremost a diminution of community.* The self is an individual *and* a communal process, not an individual, inner possession or state of mind. A person does not lose her self; her community loses her. If this is so, then dementia is much more than a neurological disease which occurs within the brains of discrete individuals. Dementia is a communal and relational condition that involves but cannot be defined by neurological decline.

Redescribing Dementia

If the arguments presented in this chapter are correct, we're left with a quite different understanding of what dementia is. Dementia emerges out of a complicated dialectical interaction between neurological impairment and interpersonal processes.[58] The relationship between neurology and dementia cannot be understood in simple causal terms. Indeed, it may be misleading to say that dementia is a neurological condition if such a statement indicates that the problem lies purely within the confines of an individual's brain. Dementia relates closely to the ways in which society treats particular people and the form of the relationships that exist between these people and society. Dementia may therefore be socially constructed not only in the sense that it is a diagnostic category arising out of social interaction and discourse by the medical profession, but also insofar as it is the result of society acting upon individuals in dysfunctional ways.[59] The dysfunction and forgetfulness that mark dementia may in fact reside within the wider community rather than within any particular individual.

We can now understand the logic of the question posed at the beginning of this chapter. Dementia can be seen to be both neurological and non-neurological. Franzen's eventual belief that his father's actions were nothing more than disease processes that are repeated within millions of other dementia sufferers is true, but it's lacking in explanatory capacity in fundamental ways. *Dementia is the product of both damaged neurons and the experience of particular forms of relationship and community.* It is as

58. Trevor Adams, "Kitwood's Approach to Dementia and Dementia Care: A Critical but Appreciative Review," *Journal of Advanced Nursing* 23 (1996): 948-53.

59. Adams, "Kitwood's Approach to Dementia and Dementia Care."

these various elements interact with one another that the full nature of dementia begins to emerge.

Summary

Before moving on, it will be helpful to provide a brief summary of the arguments presented thus far. In previous chapters we have begun to offer a constructive challenge to the defectological view of dementia. We don't want to diminish the very real pain and anguish that dementia can bring with it; however, to define it in purely negative and solely neurological terms is tempting but inappropriate. We've picked up on some of the central losses that are associated with dementia and reframed them to reveal either that they don't exist, or that if they do, they exist in a form quite different than "normal" assumptions suggest:

- Dementia has to do with more than neurology and neurological decline. It is a complex psycho-socio-neurological disease that has significant linguistic and relational components.
- Dementia isn't something that is internal to an individual's neurological makeup. It is located within the interface between the individual's physicality and experience and the attitudes, values, presumptions, and relational abilities of the individual's community. Dementia belongs to and emerges from some kind of community.
- Dementia doesn't entail a loss of mind. Rather, it provokes others to presume that there is a loss of mind. This presumption is then projected back onto the individual and used as a way of making sense of his/her experiences and changes. To suggest a loss of mind is to misunderstand the person in fundamental ways.
- Dementia doesn't entail a loss of self. Understood properly, the self remains intact even in the most severe forms of dementia. Any loss of self relates to a failure of community.
- Some of the "symptoms" of dementia such as aggression, depression, withdrawal, anxiety, and deterioration in emotional control, social behavior, or motivation may not in fact be caused by failing neurological processes alone. When understood properly, they can be seen as reasonable responses to difficult, frightening, and frustrating situations. If a person's situation is misunderstood and misrepresented, if he/she

is treated according to what is presumed to be happening ("these are nothing but symptoms of a generalizable brain disease") rather than what is actually happening (the person is quite understandably angry, frustrated, and misunderstood), then communication breaks down and the possibility of a negative hermeneutic emerging between those seeking to care and those receiving care becomes a real possibility. This is not to suggest that damaged neurological functioning is not a significant aspect of the process of dementia. The point is that its role in the process of creating dementia is not as central as it at first appears to be. Neurological functioning remains a significant inhabitant of the territory of dementia, but other perspectives are now beginning to reclaim some of the territory that has been lost.

If we take these insights seriously and are prepared to give people with dementia the benefit of the doubt, dementia begins to look different. When a thing looks different, our options for positive care are expanded. Seeing things properly makes a significant difference.

In order to understand the experience of dementia, we need first to understand the person's story. When we grasp both the disease and the story, the true structure and nature of dementia begin to emerge. This is not to suggest that dementia can be cured through relationships. It is, however, to put neuropathology in its proper place and to draw attention to the deep and formative significance of the environment, the relationships, and the attitudes and values that surround a person who has been given the name of dementia. Such an understanding provides a firm and appropriate place to begin to reflect on the theological and pastoral dimensions of dementia. Our task of redefinition and redescription is not yet completed, but the proper place to begin the journey is becoming clearer.

5. The Problem with Personhood: Why It Might Not Be Such a Good Idea for People to Be Persons

First they came for the Jews, and I did not speak out because I was not a Jew. Then they came for the Communists, and I did not speak out because I was not a Communist. Then they came for the trade unionists, and I did not speak out because I was not a trade unionist. Then they came for me, and there was no one left to speak out for me.

PASTOR MARTIN NIEMÖLLER

A new command I give you: Love one another.

JESUS

The Question of Personhood

Having begun to redescribe dementia in fundamental ways, we need now to turn to a question that haunts many people: Is the person lost to the illness? How we answer that question will determine how we respond to "persons with dementia." In order to answer such a question, we need to begin by exploring what it means to be a person in the first place. The question of what it means to be a person is complex and highly disputed. Within a culture that is marked by both hypercognition (an excessive emphasis on intellect and cognition) and hypermemory (an excessive emphasis on memory), the temptation to define the nature of personhood and humanness according to such criteria is alluring and perhaps inevitable. Implicit within certain approaches to personhood is the assumption that in order to be a person (a person being something quite different from a human being), we must have certain capacities. Not to have these capacities is not to be a person; and not to be a person is to be excluded from certain moral and ethical rights and protections that are available only to those people who are deemed to be persons. Primary among such positive capacities which are presumed to comprise personhood are such things as intellect, cognition, memory, a sense of self over time, self-awareness, and an ability to value life. The potential problems that this way of understanding personhood might cause for people with dementia are obvious. By insisting that such attributes are central to what it means to be a person, such an approach implies quite plainly that, because people with dementia don't have such attributes or are losing them, they cannot be persons: *to have dementia is to lose one's personhood.* Once again we find defectology taking a front seat in our perceptions of dementia. This time it has slipped on a moral mask. It has become a form of *moral defectology.*

Better Off Dead?

Lest the reader think that such debates about personhood are obscure and purely academic (in the sense of having no relevance for day-to-day practice), it is important to begin by noticing that while the discourse about personhood is formulated and conceptualized by academics in particular ways, it is actually quite a prominent feature in the daily lay conversations that surround dementia. It has previously been suggested that one of the ways in which our understanding of dementia has been constructed is through a cluster of discourses, the dominant one being grounded in medical science. Within this interpretative framework, the person is totally subsumed by his/her neurological condition, even to the point where he/she is frequently referred to as "dead."[1]

Previously we have looked at the power of linguistic constructions in malignantly positioning people with dementia. To linguistically construct people as defective is to place them within the parameters of those disci-

---

1. For a useful argument about the linguistic "killing" of people with dementia, see Tom Kitwood, "Towards the Reconstruction of an Organic Mental Disorder," in *Worlds of Illness: Biographical and Cultural Perspectives on Health and Disease,* ed. Alan Radley (London: Routledge, 1995).

plines which are designed to seek out, fix, and mend that which is broken. To linguistically construct someone as somehow "not there" or not worthy of respect and attention is to allow the person's forgetfulness to become perceived and highlighted in society in negative and destructive ways. To linguistically construct someone as *dead* is to position him/her in a way that can evoke only responses that relate to the death of the individual. A story will help draw out the importance of this point for our understanding of personhood.

In the previous chapter I offered a brief story about the experience of my friend, Gordon, who has Alzheimer's, and I highlighted some of the issues with regard to positioning and change in his life. (The reader should probably note the way that I am positioning him![2]) Recently Gordon's wife, Elaine, sent me an e-mail: "Dear John . . . thought you might like these two quotes for your book on dementia." The first quotation came from a worker in a local care organization for people with Alzheimer's disease. In response to Elaine's expressed concerns about the changes in her relationship with Gordon, the care worker replied "You should just divorce him." This piece of "advice" is quite stark and in some ways shocking. What might be the logic here? This woman didn't know Gordon, so she was clearly working purely on the connotations of what the name "Alzheimer's" had come to mean to her through the various ways (all negative, it would appear) in which she had been taught to understand it. Presumably her logic was something like this: "You married Gordon, and you may well have been happy together. But dementia has changed him in such a way that he's no longer the man you married [no longer a person?]. So you're justified in divorcing him — then you can have the possibility of being happy again." This response assumes that Gordon no longer has the capacity for memory, recognition, self-awareness, a sense of the future, a sense of the past; he's become a non-person. Because he isn't the person Elaine married, divorce makes sense, particularly if Elaine's freedom, autonomy, and happiness are at stake. Viewed in this way, "You should just divorce him" is a perfectly logical response.

The second quotation that Elaine brought to my attention came from a care worker in a local psychiatric hospital: "Alzheimer's! Definitely time

2. "Jesus said to them, 'Surely you will quote this proverb to me: "Physician, heal yourself! Do here in your hometown what we have heard that you did in Capernaum"'" (Luke 4:23, NIV).

for a blue pill!" It was a passing comment, presumably intended to be amusing. But deeper reflection on what appears to be a simple, flippant comment reveals something much darker. A "blue pill" is a (Scottish) euphemism for a form of euthanasia. It seems that this individual assumed that being dead was preferable to being alive with dementia. Gordon isn't dead yet, but "clearly" death is perceived to be his best option.

Although the language of personhood wasn't a formal aspect of the vocabulary of these two support workers, something very similar to it was clearly at work at some level. Popular notions about dementia and about what is important in terms of what it means to be fully human were clearly at work in these carers' perceptions, even if the language in which they were expressed wasn't subtle, academic, or conceptually well-formed. Malignant social psychology and negative positioning seem to be alive and well and living in the northeast of Scotland! When certain capacities are presumed to be gone, the person with dementia is also presumed to be gone. If that's the case, then we can see exactly why dementia could be perceived as "a fate worse than death." As Elaine put it, "All the people are very nice and easy to talk to, but surely there is something terribly wrong in all of this." I think she's right. Something is terribly wrong.

Nothing but a Shell?

Elaine's interlocutors are not alone. Wayne Yuen's response to a short post on Alzheimer's disease written by the British atheist philosopher Julian Baggini on the *Talking Philosophy* blog offers them some company. Responding to the suggestion made by John Bayley — the husband of Iris Murdoch, the famous philosopher who ended her days with dementia[3] — that the person (Iris) was not destroyed by dementia, Yuen offered this reflection:

> ... I think I understand why people would continue to care for the person even if their identity is radically changed. I think it would boil down to two reasons:
>
> 1. The physical image of the person bears a close resemblance to the person that they once loved, so they continue to care for the person out

3. For a powerful and moving account of Bayley's experiences with Iris Murdoch, see John Bayley, *Iris: A Memoir of Iris Murdoch* (London: Duckworth, 1998).

of a sort of habit. . . . This is not to minimize or trivialize their care. They simply call this person the same person because they look like the person.[4] We do this ALL the time in other circumstances, like when we meet someone who bears a striking resemblance to a person we once knew, or currently know. We start investigating if they are like the other person we know. Do they have the same hobbies and interests? We want this person in a sense to be like the other person because of physical resemblance alone.

2. I think this reason is more powerful, in the case of dementia and Alzheimer's. There are occasional moments of "lucidity" in which the patient's identity returns. They remember themselves, their loved ones and such. These moments are extremely gratifying, like receiving a postcard from a friend who is constantly traveling, except the intensity is magnified by a great order. To simply abandon them as no longer themselves would be to cut off those moments of lucidity. It would be like moving without leaving a forwarding address, to keep the postcard analogy going.[5]

There is something strangely endearing about the expression "receiving a postcard from a friend who is constantly traveling." And there is something deeply troubling about the statement that "They simply call this person the same person because they look like the person." Both statements resonate deeply with the examples of linguistic annihilation of people with dementia that we explored earlier. Dementia, it would appear, destroys the inner self that others once knew and related to and leaves behind a shell that looks like the person, but which, it is assumed, is not really the person.

4. Susan Behuniak reflects on this type of "missing person" language in her exploration of the use of the metaphor of the zombie within the Alzheimer's literature in both its lay and its professional forms. She suggests that the stigma associated with dementia is of a quite particular kind, that it is "a form of dehumanization based on disgust and terror" (p. 70). She suggests that strong negative emotional responses to Alzheimer's disease are deeply tied in with the social construction of Alzheimer's disease as zombie-making. Language which utilizes zombie metaphors for people with dementia infuses a politics of revulsion and fear which serves to separate and marginalize people with dementia. For current purposes, this is a good example of malignant social psychology and particularly negative forms of positioning. See Susan Behuniak, "The Living Dead? The Construction of People with Alzheimer's Disease as Zombies," *Ageing and Society* 31 (2011): 70-92.

5. Wayne Yuen, *Talking Philosophy* blog, "Dementia and Identity"; access at http://blog.talkingphilosophy.com/?p=1289.

It's a good thing to care for someone with dementia, but it's primarily an imaginative enterprise that focuses on a person who once existed but now is only a memory represented by certain visual features of the person before us. The person has "gone traveling," and although he/she may pop back for a few seconds every now and then, for all accounts and purposes, he/she is effectively no longer here. While Yuen doesn't attempt to work out the ethical implications of his position, the message is quite clear: The person has gone; only a shell remains.

Till Death Do Us Part?

Similar malignant positioning can be found in many places within our society, even within law, which one might assume should be protective of people with dementia. For example, the High Court in Glasgow, Scotland, found that Kenneth Edge couldn't come to court to be tried because he was severely depressed. The judge took the unusual step of dealing with him in his absence. Edge had previously pled guilty to culpable homicide. He had smothered his wife, Winifred, with a pillow. Winifred was eighty-five and had severe dementia. Kenneth and Winifred had been married for fifty-five years. Both were deeply involved in the life of the Presbyterian Church of Scotland. Their marriage was long and loving. They had no children. When Winifred developed dementia, Kenneth found himself under a huge amount of pressure in his role as caregiver. He was suffering so much stress that he started to have blackouts. One night, Winifred apparently hadn't been sleeping much, and Kenneth had been trying to stay alert to make sure that she was safe. But in the end she wasn't safe: "On the night she died, Mrs. Edge woke and began waving and thrashing her arms around. Her husband put a pillow over her face, and Mrs. Edge offered little or no resistance. When he realized what he had done, Edge phoned the police and confessed."[6]

This is a tragic story. This man was left seemingly alone to care for someone he had loved deeply for a very long time. He had very little support, and no family around to ease his massive burden. Whether his depression preceded or followed his tragic actions isn't clear. Either way, he

6. BBC News, "Church Elder Smothered Sick Wife." The full transcript of this story can be found on the BBC News Web site: http://news.bbc.co.uk/1/hi/scotland/4485827.stm.

was isolated and alone in a very difficult situation. One might have expected the judge to present a ringing critique of dementia care services for their lack of support in this situation. It seemed like an ideal opportunity to highlight the plight of carers trapped in similar situations who are desperate for help, companionship, and relief. Judge Lady Smith might also have been justified in highlighting that the Church of Scotland hasn't been as faithful in its pastoral visitation and befriending as it should have been. But instead she said this: "It is perfectly plain that you have punished, and will continue to punish, yourself because you have removed from your life your lifetime partner, whom you have loved and cared for." This is a kind and compassionate observation. It must truly be awful to know that you are responsible for taking the life of someone you have known and loved for that length of time. Continuing, the judge said, "You did so in circumstances precipitated by the enormous stresses and strains you had been put under as you tried to care for *a woman who ceased to be the woman you married*, and whom you had known and loved for more than fifty years."[7] I imagine that many of us may see no real problem with the general thrust of this statement. The stress that caregivers are under is huge and must not be underestimated. The judge is quite right to highlight this. But in what way had Winifred "ceased to be the woman" Kenneth had married? If she had ceased to be the woman he had married, then precisely who was she? Who was the person he had been caring for? More importantly, why would such "ceasing to be who one previously was" be an aspect of the rationale for not taking a punitive response toward the person who killed her?

I think I know what the judge was trying to say. She was trying to say something like, "I think that the radical changes in dementia had changed the relationship Kenneth had had with his wife in such a way that some of the key aspects of their marriage no longer looked or felt like they used to. That being so, Kenneth must have a deep sense of loss which is exacerbated by the difficulties that he has had caring for Winifred." But if we think this through using Steven Sabat's ideas concerning malignant social positioning, the language that the judge uses positions both Kenneth and Winifred in quite particular ways. Kenneth is presented as a tragic hero who has tried to cope with a situation in which he has been in a sense forced, or obligated, to care for a "stranger" who looks like his wife, but who, apparently, "isn't the woman he married." Winifred is positioned as someone

7. BBC News, "Church Elder Smothered Sick Wife" (italics added).

who *was* someone, but is now someone else. The implication, then, is that while it is tragic that Kenneth killed her, it was not really her whom he killed; it was what she had become, and what she had become was not the same as what she was. That being so, her killing is heartrending but understandable, and her dementia is a completely valid reason for mitigation.

I understand the logic of this position. But my concern is this: Is Winifred really not the person Kenneth married? Is dementia really a mitigating circumstance in a case of culpable homicide? I will leave the latter question to the lawyers. But the former — *Is Winifred really not the woman Kenneth married?* — is a question that we need to think through.

In the Name of God?

Televangelist Pat Robertson recently caused a good deal of controversy by making remarks about dementia during an interview on his television program, "The 700 Club." Robertson responded to a caller who asked how Robertson would advise the caller's friend, "whose wife was deep into dementia and no longer recognized him." The caller informed Robertson that "his wife as he knows her is gone," and that the friend is "bitter at God for allowing his wife to be in that condition, and now he's started seeing another woman."[8] Robertson's reply stunned many people in the evangelical community:

> "This is a terribly hard thing," Mr. Robertson said, clearly struggling to think his way through a wrenching situation. "I hate Alzheimer's. It is one of the most awful things, because here's the loved one — this is the woman or man that you have loved for 20, 30, 40 years, and suddenly that person is gone."[9]

At this point understandable compassion and concern shift into precisely the type of malignant social positioning that we have been examining — only now it has developed a significant spiritual and theological edge:

8. Erik Eckholm, "Robertson Stirs Passions with Suggestion to Divorce an Alzheimer's Patient," *The New York Times;* access at http://www.nytimes.com/2011/09/17/us/pat-robertson-remarks-on-alzheimers-stir-passions.html.

9. Eckholm, "Robertson Stirs Passions with Suggestion to Divorce an Alzheimer's Patient."

"I know it sounds cruel," he continued, "but if he's going to do something, he should divorce her and start all over again, but to make sure she has custodial care, somebody looking after her." When Mr. Robertson's co-anchor on the program wondered if that was consistent with marriage vows, Mr. Robertson noted the pledge of "till death do us part," but added, "This is a kind of death."[10]

A kind of death? The caller's friend's wife was still with him, but in essence she was dead, and theologically should be treated as such. So, it is possible to stay within the marriage vows and still divorce your wife. Why? Presumably because "divorce" is a legal term that relates to people who are alive. Thus it would seem that, in Robertson's opinion, the term "divorce" in the context of dementia becomes a metaphor for "burying" the "dead" person within the health care system and moving on. Robertson admitted that the situation and the questions that it raised presented an ethical dilemma that was beyond his ability to answer. (One wonders, then, why he tried to answer it.) But he did have an opinion about how a Christian faced with this dilemma could respond to it:

> "I certainly wouldn't put a guilt trip on you if you decided that you had to have companionship," Mr. Robertson said, apparently suggesting divorce as a way to avoid the sin of adultery.[11]

Robertson's position provoked outrage from both inside and outside the evangelical community. At a basic level, this question arises: If dementia is a kind of death, then what does that say about the types of dementia services that are provided? Are those who care for people with dementia to perceive themselves as living undertakers who store bodies and keep them clean until they can legally put them into the ground? But why would Robertson (or anyone else who equates dementia with "living death") think that this particular condition, as opposed to other similar conditions, could be equated with death? As Kate Meyer of the Alzheimer's Association put it,

---

10. Eckholm, "Robertson Stirs Passions with Suggestion to Divorce an Alzheimer's Patient."

11. Eckholm, "Robertson Stirs Passions with Suggestion to Divorce an Alzheimer's Patient."

It is hard to imagine a religious leader condoning divorcing a spouse who has cancer, or MS, or Parkinson's, or Lou Gehrig's disease, or a severe stroke. It is hard to imagine a discussion over whether any of those diseases are essentially "death," and thus justify divorce. No one, for example, suggests Michael J. Fox's wife has a reason to leave him simply because he has a degenerative disease that may well ultimately rob him of many of his faculties.[12]

There is clearly something about dementia that evokes a particular kind of fear and a particularly malignant form of social positioning.

The main concern for evangelicals was the damage that such a position would do to the sanctity of marriage vows. If marriage is for life, then only death can break a couple apart. But Robertson equated dementia with death, and so allowed for the breaking of those vows. However, as Russell Moore points out, such a merging of dementia with death makes no sense theologically:

> A woman or a man with Alzheimer's can't do anything for you. There's no romance, no sex, no partnership, not even companionship. That's just the point. Because marriage is a Christ/church icon, a man loves his wife as his own flesh. He cannot sever her off from him simply because she isn't "useful" anymore.[13]

The importance of human contingency for how Christians should describe dementia will become clear as the book moves on. Suffice it to say here that Moore is correct in recognizing that marriage, like all human relationships, has nothing to do with what we can or cannot do, see, know, or experience. The relationship of marriage resonates with the relationship of God to human beings. God is with us in deep ways as we learn what it means to love and particularly as we learn what it means to love the vulnerable. Moore neatly sums up the key problem with triumphalist Christian positions such as Robertson's:

12. Quoted by Terry Moran, "Pat Robertson's Comments Threaten to Undermine Alzheimer's Advocates' Goals," ABC News; access at http://abcnews.go.com/blogs/health/2011/09/15/pat-robertsons-comments-threaten-to-undermine-alzheimers-advocates-goals/.

13. Russell D. Moore, "First Person: Alzheimer's, Pat Robertson, and the True Gospel"; access at http://www.bpnews.net/BPFirstPerson.asp?ID=36119.

Sadly, many of our neighbors assume that when they hear the parade of characters we allow to speak for us, they are hearing the Gospel. They assume that when they see the giggling evangelist on the television screen, they see Jesus. They assume that when they see the stadium political rallies to "take back America for Christ," they see Jesus. But Jesus tells us He is present in the weak, the vulnerable, the useless. He is there in the least of these (Matt. 25:31-46). Somewhere out there right now, a man is wiping the drool from an 85-year-old woman who flinches because she thinks he's a stranger. No television cameras are around. No politicians are seeking a meeting with them.[14]

I was encouraged by the response to Robertson's comments that I read in the media. The Christian community was clearly uncomfortable with the transference of the prosperity gospel and the quest for personal happiness at all costs into human relationships. What worried me was that, if what I have suggested thus far in this chapter is correct, Robertson's views may not be uncommon. What may be uncommon is for them to be expressed so explicitly.

A Duty to Die?

Moving on from lay perceptions of personhood into the world of academic philosophy, we see the seemingly instinctual response "Shoot me if I get like that" finds more poignant yet blunt expression. In a 2008 interview with the Presbyterian Church of Scotland's magazine *Life and Work*, Baroness Mary Warnock raised sharply the issue of personhood in people with dementia. Reflecting on why she has left instructions with her solicitor and doctor expressing a desire not to be resuscitated when she is dying, she moves on to talk about dementia with the interviewer:

"The real fear, I think shared with nearly everyone, is that I become demented. I've left instructions that if I contract pneumonia or something that I'm not to be given antibiotics, but there's not much else I can do. . . . *If you're demented, you're wasting people's lives* — your family's lives — and you're wasting the resources of the National Health Ser-

14. Moore, "First Person: Alzheimer's, Pat Robertson, and the True Gospel."

vice." I [the interviewer] point out to her that the argument for euthanasia usually revolves around pain, and that people with dementia are not normally subject to great pain. "I don't think that's the full argument," she says, shaking her head. "I'm absolutely fully in agreement that if pain is insufferable, then someone should be given help to die, but I feel there's a wider argument that if somebody absolutely, desperately wants to die because they're a burden to their family or the state, then I think they too should be allowed to die. Actually I've just written an article called 'A Duty To Die?' for a Norwegian periodical. I wrote it really suggesting that there's nothing wrong with feeling you ought to do so for the sake of others as well as yourself."[15]

Warnock makes a case for advanced directives wherein a person could appoint an advocate to ensure that his/her life was ended under certain circumstances:

I think that's the way the future will go. Putting it rather brutally, you'd be licensing people to put others down. Actually I think why not, because the real person has gone already and all that's left is just the body of a person, and nobody wants to be remembered in this condition.[16]

The negative and malignant ways in which people with dementia are positioned within Warnock's comments are far from subtle. According to her, people with dementia are a burden to their families, the National Health Service, and the state. They're wasting other people's lives and should have the decency to take their own lives. In a somewhat grotesque parody of Jesus' statement that "There is no greater love than to lay down your life for a friend," Warnock suggests that suicide is morally appropriate if one feels that it is the best thing for other people. One can only imagine how a person recently diagnosed with dementia might feel upon reading her words.

Warnock's comments provoked outrage and concern among many, with Alzheimer Scotland asking "why dementia, distinct from other illnesses, should be considered a 'burden' to the NHS and to society."[17] Why

15. Jackie Macadam, "Interview with Mary Warnock: 'A Duty to Die?'" *Life and Work*, October 2008, pp. 23-25; quotation on p. 25; italics added.

16. Warnock, "'A Duty to Die?'" p. 25.

17. "Alzheimer Scotland Response to Baroness Warnock"; access at http://www.alzscot .org/pages/media/Alzheimer_Scotland_response_to_Baroness_Warnock.htm.

indeed? The answer is quite simple: cancer, pneumonia, and appendicitis are not perceived as affecting one's personhood. The key to Warnock's position lies in her final sentence: the *real* person has gone, and the body is all that remains. Philippa Malpas sums this position up well:

> What Warnock actually seems to be suggesting is that being a person is what really matters in the context of those elderly afflicted by dementia. It is not that I have a duty to die because I have dementia and am a burden to others; rather, it is because I am no longer a person. I am just a body.[18]

According to this viewpoint, the individual diagnosed with dementia has begun making a transition from being a person to being a non-person. As a non-person, she has no right to the kinds of moral respect and protection that a person might be entitled to. That being so, to kill her is considered appropriate; if she kills herself, it's convenient.

The Problem with Personhood

In order to understand how and why ideas of personhood have been formed and why they have a tendency to drift into malignancy, we need to first examine the work that ideas about personhood is intended to do. At heart, philosophical models of personhood tend to be used as ethical devices designed to enable the separation of one group of human beings from the rest of humanity, normally in an attempt to assist practitioners or philosophers in working out how best to resolve dilemmas and deal with difficult ethical decisions. Those deemed persons are held under the banner of moral protection, and those deemed non-persons are not. So, for example, in the abortion debate, the justification for killing an unborn child is that the child is not a person, that it doesn't have certain capacities which would enable it to meet the criteria of any given definition of personhood. Thus one is killing not a person but a "fetus" — that is, a non-person. This line of thinking can be dangerous for the cognitively disabled.

18. Phillipa J. Malpas, "Do Those Afflicted with Dementia Have a Moral Duty to Die? A Response to Baroness Warnock," *New Zealand Medical Journal* (2009): 53-60.

What Is a Person?

So what then is meant by the term "person"? To begin looking at this question, it is useful to start with John Locke's influential definition of a person:

> a thinking intelligent Being that has reason and reflection, and can consider its self as its self, the same thinking thing in different times and places; which it does only by that consciousness which is inseparable from thinking, and as it seems to me essential to it.[19]

Here personhood is defined in terms of a capacity for self-awareness, identity, continuity of thinking, a sense of self over time, consciousness, and above all memory. Important for our present purposes is the observation that memory is an absolute necessity for the other capacities to be possible. The thing to note here is the inevitable way in which loss or absence of these capacities is accompanied by a loss of personhood. Viewed from this perspective, developing dementia means moving gradually and inevitably from personhood into non-personhood. This, of course, leaves us with the rather odd situation wherein certain human beings can be persons for sixty, seventy, or eighty years, living under the protection of this particular notion of personhood, only to find themselves living out their final years (or days, depending on when the assessment is made about their personhood) as non-persons who suddenly (or gradually) become less worthy of moral attention and protection. The strangeness of such a position becomes clear when one considers that, in some ways, every time we fall asleep we become non-persons! Presumably it should be legal to kill one another as long as we are not awake?

Making Difficult Decisions

It is worthwhile noting that models of personhood built on criteria similar to Locke's are primarily forensic in their intentions. They are designed to help make effective legal and ethical decisions. If persons cease to be per-

19. John Locke, *An Essay concerning Human Understanding*, ed. Peter H. Nidditch (Oxford: Clarendon Press, 1975), E II.xxvii.9, p. 335.

sons, it is easier to make hard ethical decisions about their future. If persons cease to be persons, it can be argued that it makes sense on moral, economic, and relational grounds to withhold resources or even to terminate their lives. Morally they are no longer persons, economically they are a drain on limited resources, and relationally they aren't the individuals that they once were. They remain genetically human, but that basic status isn't enough to protect them. This line of thinking opens the way for presumptions and systems of valuing that are more than a little uncomfortable for people with dementia.

English philosopher John Harris describes a person as a living creature that is capable of valuing his/her own life:

> Defining "person" as *a creature capable of valuing its own existence* makes plausible an explanation of the nature of the wrong done to such a being when it is deprived of existence. Persons who want to live are wronged by being killed because they are thereby deprived of something they value. Persons who do not want to live are not on this account harmed by having their wish to die granted — through voluntary euthanasia, for example. Nonpersons or potential persons cannot be wronged in this way because death does not deprive them of anything they can value. If they cannot wish to live, they cannot have that wish frustrated by being killed. Creatures other than persons can, of course, be harmed in other ways — by being caused gratuitous suffering, for example — but not by being painlessly killed.[20]

Harris, perhaps more subtly, echoes Warnock's position on dementia. As long as persons value their lives and are consciously in a position to make such a value judgment, they are deemed persons. If they lose that capacity, they cease to be persons:

> The life cycle of a given individual passes through a number of stages of different moral significance. The individual can be said to have come into existence when the egg is first differentiated or the sperm that will fertilize that egg is first differentiated or the sperm that will fertilize that egg is first formed. . . . This individual will gradually move from being a

20. John Harris, "The Concept of the Person and the Value of Life," *Kennedy Institute of Ethics Journal* 9, no. 4 (1999): 293-308; quotation on 303.

potential or a pre-person into an actual person when she becomes capable of valuing her own existence. And if, eventually, she permanently loses this capacity prior to death, she will have ceased to be a person.[21]

In Harris's thinking, the strange movement from non-person to person to non-person that goes on across the life cycle is clear and seems quite logical. If Harris is correct that the ability to value one's experience is what makes one a person, then Warnock is also correct in her analysis of dementia. She makes it clear that there is nothing to be valued in the experience of dementia. So she sees euthanasia and suicide carried out on or by non-persons as a logical and morally appropriate solution to the "problem of dementia."

Bert's Story

In her essay "Dementia and Personhood," Dr. Rosalie Hudson tells the story of Bert:

> Bert has remained in his nursing home bed, mute and immobile, for nine years. No longer able to recognize or to respond to his family in any meaningful way, unable to engage with friends, he is now almost totally deprived of visitors. An old photo, sitting askew on the wall beside his bed, points to a time when he served his country at war. Some faded artificial flowers are the only remnants of the last gift he received. Now, his past means little, as busy nurses clang the bedrails up and down, not infrequently tearing his frail skin in the process. Leaking urine and feces, legs contracted tight together, Bert does not exemplify wholeness or dignity, and many nurses question the value of his existence.[22]

Tom Kitwood and Steven Sabat would say that Bert's personhood is safe as long as those around him value him and offer him relationships that reveal and reinforce the practical meaning of that value. However, in Bert's situa-

---

21. Harris, "The Concept of the Person and the Value of Life," p. 307.

22. Rosalie Hudson, "Dementia and Personhood: A Living Death or Alive in God?" *Colloquium: The Australian and New Zealand Theological Review* 36, no. 2 (2004): 123-42; quotation on 124.

tion it appears that this is not the case. Those around him don't see his value, and those he used to know are no longer interested. Precisely how Bert values himself is difficult to gauge. But as most of a person's self-esteem is gained from the way in which others relate to them, one could assume that Bert's self-esteem is not high. Kitwood might point out that this is clearly a problem of community and failed relationships, not simply a problem of Bert. Harris and Warnock would, perhaps, see things quite differently. They would stand with those nurses that refuse to give Bert the benefit of the doubt. Bert cannot value himself. Indeed, he "clearly" cannot value anything at all. He is no longer a person, so, at least in Warnock's opinion, it is quite justifiable to kill him. Bert doesn't have the volition to do it himself, so the only truly compassionate thing to do is to legislate for others to kill him. One wonders what Bert thinks, or if anyone would even try to ask?

The Ethical Debate about Personhood and Dementia

From this perspective, it is easy to see how and why certain approaches to personhood make it look as if it is just fine to kill people with dementia. Perhaps more than any other philosopher, the Australian ethicist Peter Singer has been at the forefront of challenging suggestions that people with profound cognitive disabilities such as dementia are persons. Singer has become notorious for his views on the infanticide of disabled children.[23] In his view, to take the life of a severely cognitively disabled child is morally appropriate because such a child lacks the capacity for "self-awareness, self-control, a sense of the future, a sense of the past, the capacity to relate to others, concern for others, communication, and curiosity."[24] Singer's indebtedness to Locke's definition is apparent, although precisely why "curiosity" should be an aspect of personhood seems more than a lit-

23. His thinking on this can be found in a number of places, but most succinctly in Peter Singer, *Practical Ethics* (Cambridge: Cambridge University Press, 1979). See especially Chapter 7: "Taking Life: Humans." For a critique of his position in relation to people with intellectual disabilities, see John Swinton, *Raging with Compassion: Pastoral Responses to the Problem of Evil* (Grand Rapids: Wm. B. Eerdmans, 2007), Chapter 7. For a full-blown Christian critique of Singer's ethics, see Gordon R. Preece, *Rethinking Peter Singer: A Christian Critique* (Downers Grove, Ill.: InterVarsity Press, 2002).

24. Singer, *Practical Ethics*, p. 83.

tle arbitrary. Having said that, I should mention that curiosity *is* a trait that is highly valued by academics, which might explain why Singer values it above more obvious things such as love and relationships. Like Locke and Harris, Singer emphasizes the importance of consciousness and self-awareness and the importance of being able to value life:

> Only a person can want to go on living, or have plans for the future, be-cause only a person can even understand the possibility of a future existence for herself or himself. This means that to end the lives of people, against their will, is different from ending the lives of beings who are not people. Indeed, strictly speaking, in the case of those who are not peo-ple, we cannot talk of ending their lives against or in accordance with their will, because they are not capable of having a will on such a mat-ter. . . . Killing a person against her or his will is a much more serious wrong than killing a being that is not a person. If we want to put this in the language of rights, then it is reasonable to say that only a person has a right to life.[25]

It seems that Bert is in real trouble. Singer's understanding of personhood neatly excludes people with advanced dementia from the island of persons, leaving them stranded, vulnerable, and well down in the inter-species hier-archy in terms of value and worth. The dangers of such malignant philo-sophical positioning are summed up well by John Wyatt:

> Once this kind of definition is accepted, there are a number of logical implications. Firstly, it is immediately obvious that in order to be re-garded as a person, you must have an advanced level of brain function. In fact, you must have a completely developed and normally function-ing cerebral cortex. Secondly, there must be a significant group of hu-man beings who are non-persons. These include fetuses, newborn ba-bies, and infants who lack self-awareness, and a large group of children and adults with congenital brain abnormalities, severe brain injury, de-mentia, and major psychiatric illnesses. Thirdly, there are many non-human beings on the planet who meet the criteria of persons. These in-clude at least chimpanzees, gorillas, monkeys, and dolphins, but may

25. Peter Singer, *Rethinking Life and Death* (New York: St. Martin's Press, 1995), pp. 197-98.

also include dogs, pigs, and many other mammals. In fact, it has even been argued that within the foreseeable future some supercomputers may meet the criteria to be regarded as persons.[26]

From Singer's perspective, there is nothing unique about human beings. To suggest otherwise is to engage in species-ism: a form of exclusionary practice that assumes that human beings have some kind of inherent right to be perceived as more valuable than other sentient beings. The same criteria for personhood should be applied to all animals and not just humans. Once again, we come up against the strange stress on the significance of the cerebral cortex. We discussed the significance of the emphasis on the cerebral cortex when we looked at the way in which this aspect of the brain features in some key definitions of dementia. The idea that "higher cerebral functions" are important seems to be quite prevalent. One has to wonder what it is about this part of the brain that people seem to be so concerned about. Why should it be considered the biological seat of personhood — i.e., the neural correlate of the criteria that academics establish for what is and what is not a person? Is this not, as Wyatt suggests, a rather odd form of *cortextalism:*

> In effect, Singer has replaced one form of discrimination with another. Instead of discriminating on the basis of species, he is now arguing that we should discriminate on the grounds of cortical function. In fact, if we are into name-calling, we could call him a "corticalist." But why should corticalism be preferable to species-ism? Of course, Singer may wish to argue that cortical functioning is "ethically relevant," whereas species membership is not. But this is an arbitrary distinction that is hard to defend on entirely logical grounds. Why should the functioning of a 5mm layer of neurons be the central and only moral discriminating feature between beings? On purely logical grounds, species membership is a more coherent and fundamental basis for making ethical distinctions between beings.[27]

26. John Wyatt, "What Is a Person?" *Nucleus,* January 2004, pp. 10-15; quotation on p. 10. For a more fully developed argument on these points in relation to a critique of Singer's position, see John Wyatt, *Matters of Life and Death: Human Dilemmas in the Light of the Christian Faith* (Nottingham: InterVarsity Press, 2009), particularly pp. 44-46.

27. Wyatt, "What Is a Person?" p. 11; see also Wyatt, *Matters of Life and Death,* p. 47.

Wyatt's point is that a preferential option for a fully functioning cerebral cortex discriminates against people with mental impairments. There is a logical disjunction and a moral contradiction in replacing one form of discrimination with another. Why then might it be that academic philosophers like Singer choose cortextually oriented criteria to define persons and personhood? Wyatt points out that the criteria that such philosophers use are arbitrary but understandable. He highlights the example of squirrels. If they were in the position to choose which criteria might comprise special rights, they would probably choose agility and balance alongside the ability to eat nuts. Trees would focus on height or longevity. It is therefore not surprising that Singer, a human being with a fully functioning cerebral cortex who resides in a social context where the workings of this part of the brain are particularly prized, would choose to import his own values, abilities, and capacities into his understanding of what it means to be a person. It is likewise not surprising that he would exclude other things which are not important to him. The point is that the capacities that are said to comprise personhood are always worked out by those in positions of power. The powerless have nothing to say. Bert's voice is silent. The problem with capacities-based definitions of personhood is not only that they make certain people vulnerable to potentially deadly forces, but also that, when looked at critically, they actually make little sense. "I am because I am curious" is an odd way to see the world. The arbitrariness of such criteria seems mystifying at first. But when we look closer, we see that it isn't really mystifying at all — nor is it particularly subtle. Kitwood puts his finger on the issue:

> Behind such debates a vague shadow can be discerned. It is that of the liberal academic of former times: kind, considerate, honest, fair, and above all else intellectual. Emotion and feeling have only a minor part in this scheme of things; autonomy is given supremacy over relationship and commitment; passion has no place at all. Moreover, the problems seem to center on how to describe and explain, which already presupposes an existential stance of detachment.[28]

The "I-It" position seems to be the relational driving force behind capacities-based approaches to personhood. Standing back and looking in

---

28. Tom Kitwood, *Dementia Reconsidered: The Person Comes First* (Buckingham: Open University Press, 1997), p. 9.

on people's lives is the key methodological position. As in the processes of defining dementia, the focus is on "typical people." Theorists are interested in describing a generalized "Bert" who is comprised of a cluster of attributes and capacities. They have little interest in Bert-as-Bert; they're primarily interested in only Bert-as-case-study, something to be looked at and reflected on but certainly not related to.

The Problem with Individualism

Behind these types of debates about personhood lurks a particular view of what human beings are and should be and what desirable human living should look like. In other words, they are morally biased and deeply value-laden even if they hide behind the mask of logical rationality. The particular worldview that underpins and drives the goals of Western liberal democracies has deeply shaped our priorities and understandings of what is essential for our personhood. Within such a context, personhood tends to have a quite specific focus. To be a "person" means that one must be able to live one's life, develop one's potential, and develop a purposeful life-course *without any necessary reference to others*. Importantly, the capacities that comprise our constructions of personhood are not only necessary for entry into the socio-political system; they are also considered necessary for a person to live in a way which can be deemed authentically human and thus valuable.[29] Bert's life is the exact opposite of this cultural norm. To lose the capacity to function in accepted ways is to lose something of that which makes us human, or, because it is assumed that humans are no more than the other animals, that which makes us persons. Within such a context, definitions of personhood that focus on self-awareness, reason, rationality, and so forth seem to make perfect sense. Within Bert's life they make no sense whatsoever. Warnock's comments indicate the inevitable outcome of such ways of thinking for people with dementia. The constructions of personhood that often guide us in our ethical and moral perceptions and decision-making are in fact prime examples of malignant social psychology. Likewise, they exemplify and give a philosophical rationale for the type of malignant social positioning that Sabat has drawn to our attention.

29. Eva Kittay, *Love's Labor: Essays on Women, Equality, and Dependency* (New York: Routledge, 1999), pp. 2-4.

Bert and others who experience the world in the way that he does need to be protected; such definitions of personhood have no desire or ability to do that.

An Ethicist's Personal Experience with Dementia

One of the problems with the academic conversations about the lives of people with dementia — particularly advanced dementia, wherein people lose the cognitive faculties that are the cultural markers of personhood — is that they don't work well in practice. It's one thing to sit in a classroom or a university office and pontificate about who is or isn't a person. It's another thing altogether to act accordingly. "I-It" relationships function well in theoretical discussion; "I-Thou" relationships function at a different level and call for an engaged position that puts faces and names to "difficult decisions." When "difficult decisions" have names and faces, things change. This problem is illustrated well in Peter Singer's response to his mother, Cora, when she was diagnosed with Alzheimer's disease. Singer, as we have seen, is a strong and strident voice in the personhood debate and a firm advocate for the active euthanasia of people with severe intellectual disabilities and the senicide of people with dementia. He retains this position consistently throughout his academic writings. In a hypercognitive culture, Singer's position seems to make sense — until, that is, the name changes from "Alzheimer's disease" to "Cora." Within that subtle redescription of dementia which moves the conversation from "I-It" to "I-Thou," things seem to change. Dementia looks different when it has another name.

When Cora developed what was presumed to be Alzheimer's disease and was no longer able to recognize herself or her son (when she became a "non-person"), one would expect Singer to use her as an example of why euthanasia was a good thing and how awful it was that he was legally unable to put into practice what he writes about. I guess you might even expect him to kill her and accept the consequences of living out his own principles? However, his reaction was quite the opposite, as his interview with Michael Specter in the *New Yorker* reveals:

> [Singer stated that he] would never kill his mother, even if he thought it was what she wanted. He told me [Specter] that he believes in Jack Kevorkian's attempts to help people die, but he also said that such a sys-

tem works only when a patient is still able to express her wishes. Cora Singer never had that chance; like so many others, she slipped too quickly into the vague region between life and death.[30]

Singer's compromise is that, as per Warnock, if Cora had had a chance to leave a living will, then killing her might have been an option, but since she was never able to do that, no one could know her wishes, and so euthanasia is not an option. But it's interesting to note how he begins his ethical reflection by saying that he would never kill her before saying that it would be justifiable in different circumstances. Why wouldn't he kill her? Presumably because he loves her? Love and pragmatic logic are not always easy bedfellows.

When his mother became too ill to live alone, Singer — instead of pressing the authorities to allow her to die — hired a team of home health-care aides to look after her. Specter asked Singer

> how a man who has written that we ought to do what is morally right without regard to proximity or family relationships could possibly spend tens of thousands of dollars a year on private care for his mother. [Singer] replied that it was "probably not the best use you could make of my money. That is true. But it does provide employment for a number of people who find something worthwhile in what they're doing."[31]

Specter recognizes the moral basis for Singer's justification of his response, but comments,

> It hardly fits with Peter Singer's rules for living an ethical life. He once told me that he has no respect for people who donate funds for research on breast cancer or heart disease in the hope that it might indirectly save them or members of their family from illness, since they could be using that money to save the lives of the poor. ("That is not charity," he said. "It's self-interest.") Singer has responded to his mother's illness the way most caring people would. The irony is that his humane actions clash so profoundly with the chords of his utilitarian ethic.[32]

30. Michael Specter, "The Dangerous Philosopher," *The New Yorker*, 6 September 1999, p. 55.
31. Specter, "The Dangerous Philosopher," p. 55.
32. Specter, "The Dangerous Philosopher," p. 55.

So, has Singer's experience with his mother changed his perspective on his ethics of personhood? The answer seems to be, yes — and no:

> We were sitting in his living room one day, and the trolley traffic was noisy on the street outside his window. Singer has spent his career trying to lay down rules for human behavior which are divorced from emotion and intuition. His is a world that makes no provision for private aides to look after addled, dying old women. Yet he can't help himself. "I think this has made me see how the issues of someone with these kinds of problems are really very difficult," he said quietly. "Perhaps it is more difficult than I thought before, because it is different when it's your mother."[33]

"It is different when it's your mother." Indeed it is. This shouldn't really surprise us. Bernard Williams, quoted in Specter's article, puts it this way:

> "You can't make these calculations and comparisons in real life. It's bluff. . . . One of the reasons his approach is so popular is that it reduces all moral puzzlement to a formula. You remove puzzlement and doubt and conflict of values, and it's in the scientific spirit. People seem to think it will all add up, but it never does, because humans never do." Singer may be learning that.[34]

Calculations, comparisons, and neat formulae may make sense in a classroom or within the confines of a textbook, but when these decisions have faces, names, and consequences that touch us and that we have to touch physically and psychologically, things inevitably look different. Humans are much more complicated than rules and formulae can allow for. While our scientist leanings may push us to make so-called rational decisions, the "I-Thou" relationship remains primal and draws us inevitably back into forms of relationships where closeness and intimacy matter. The language of capacities gives us distance and a perception of objectivity; but as soon as we're forced to come close, we learn that such language cannot really shield us from the deep pains of committed love. Coming close changes things.

33. Specter, "The Dangerous Philosopher," p. 55.
34. Specter, "The Dangerous Philosopher," p. 55.

Singer's "no" to change is manifested in the current update of his highly influential book *Practical Ethics*,[35] within which he, among other things, lays out the moral framework required to justify killing people with dementia. None of his argument has been changed or modified in response to his experience with his mother. It seems that sometimes your reputation and history can take priority over what you really feel about a situation when it hits you in places where logic makes little sense.

It would be comforting to think that such arguments about personhood are extreme and that philosophers such as those examined in this chapter are unusual or unrepresentative. The experiences outlined at the beginning of the chapter have indicated that, sadly, they are not. All of us, it seems, can easily be tempted by models of personhood that, although often not articulated formally, are nonetheless powerful in their impact. "Alzheimer's! Definitely time for a blue pill!" is probably less of a metaphorical sentiment than we might wish it to be.

35. Peter Singer, *Practical Ethics*, 3rd ed. (Cambridge: Cambridge University Press, 2011).

6. Relational Personhood and the Vanishing Self: Is There a Person in Person-Centered Care?

Life is like an onion: You peel it off one layer at a time, and sometimes you weep. . . .

CARL SANDBURG

Despite the problems with it, the language of persons and personhood remains a significant aspect of the ongoing discussion around dementia and dementia care. It could be argued that, despite the issues raised in the previous chapter, ideas about personhood, given proper articulation, can and should retain an important place in the various conversations that go on around dementia. Such an argument has some validity. The types of person-centered models of care that have emerged from the kind of relational critique offered by Tom Kitwood, Steven Sabat, and others have, in some important ways, been among the most important innovations in the recent history of dementia care. A focus on the person as opposed to the label of "dementia" has taken understandings of dementia and dementia care into new ways of being with people with dementia and has offered fresh ways of trying to understand their experience. Nothing that I have said thus far should be read as taking away the significance of such person-centered approaches. Helping people to recognize the importance of coming close and recognizing the hidden possibilities within the person with dementia can only be a good thing. It may well be that the language of persons, properly articulated, should remain important. However, that really depends on what such language actually claims to represent.

There are three important issues that need to be raised in relation to the ways in which the ideas around person-centered approaches to dementia are currently formulated. First, and perhaps in some ways most important, is the question about whether those working within the paradigm of person-centered approaches are actually using the term "person" in the ways that have been discussed thus far. The language is similar, but is the conceptualization really about persons per se, or does it really have to do with developing particular attitudes toward people with dementia? In other words, is the term "person" really only a container for ideas about the nature of loving care rather than a philosophical statement about the status of another human being?

Second, at a more philosophical level, underpinning the various person-centered approaches to dementia care is the idea that the root of all care and deep understanding lies in authentic personal relationships. Human beings are assumed to be persons-in-relation. Thus *good care is relational care;* to treat the other as a person is to relate properly and authentically with them. Within this framework, the idea of personhood has come to be defined by relationships. However, if to be a person is to be in right relationships with others — if, in other words, persons *are* their relationships, then people with dementia have a significant problem. Most people don't want to be with them. That being so, many people with dementia *really are* non-persons even if personhood is judged according to relationality rather than capacities.

Third, and closely connected with the second point, it is not at all clear that contemporary Western liberal societies have the moral focus, desire, or strength required to create and maintain meaningful personal relationships with people who have significant cognitive and intellectual disabilities. Loving relationships and relational personhood require that people *choose* to be with people who have dementia. But why would they? In a social context marked by freedom, autonomy, and choice, the chances of anyone actually caring — other than those who feel obliged to care or who are paid to care — are not high.

Insofar as they focus attention on the uniqueness of individuals, person-centered approaches to dementia are very important. It is vital that those things which they represent remain a significant aspect of the territory of dementia and dementia care. However, their position does need to be clarified, and the territory does need to be laid out clearly in order that theology can know its proper place. This chapter takes on the task of such clarification.

Where Is the Person in Person-Centered Care?

Let's begin with the first point: What kind of "person" do we find in contemporary understandings of person-centered care? David Edvardsson and colleagues sum up the components of the person-centered approach. Proponents of this approach

- regard personhood in people with Alzheimer's disease as increasingly concealed rather than lost;
- acknowledge the personhood of people with Alzheimer's disease in all aspects of care;
- personalize care and surroundings;
- offer shared decision-making;
- interpret behavior from the person's viewpoint; and
- prioritize the relationship to the same extent as the care tasks.[1]

Person-centered approaches thus move us away from the tendency to objectify people with dementia and read their lives through the hermeneutic of their diagnosis. By coming close to the person, we can see him/her differently and interpret his/her behavior more authentically. This in turn enables the creation of effective and genuinely personal forms of care and relationship — personal in the sense of coming close, noticing, and caring. What is important here is to notice that the designator "person" doesn't relate to any kind of debate over the individual's worth, value, or general existential state. It simply refers to a way of expressing the desire of carers to come close to people, to move beyond their diagnosis and to treat them in ways that acknowledge their value and worth.

Underpinning this position is an often unarticulated adherence to some basic humanist principles, a somewhat undefined moral philosophy that considers human beings to be of particular significance and insists that treating them with respect, value, empathy, and understanding is a good and proper thing to do. This understanding of the goal of person-centered care is the embodiment of the type of values and revisions that emerge from the humanistically oriented theoretical thinking of people like Kitwood and

1. David Edvardsson, Winblad Bengt, and P. O. Sandman, "Person-Centered Care of People with Severe Alzheimer's Disease: Current Status and Ways Forward," *The Lancet: Neurology* 7, no. 4 (April 2008): 362-67; quotation on 363.

Sabat and their relational understandings of dementia. Within person-centered approaches, the deeper philosophical claim that not to care in such ways means that the individual ceases to be a person is not normally expressed. The implication in much of the person-centered literature is not that there could be a situation wherein the individual could cease to be a person — only that it is important to value human beings. The word "person" is therefore not intended as a forensic tool or as an existential designator. It is simply a form of language that expresses a desire to value human beings and to care for them respectfully. Thus Edvardsson et al. can state,

> The rationale for the use of this concept is that "person," rather than "patient," is more consistent with the underlying humanistic philosophy of person-centered care for people with severe AD that is described in the published articles. Furthermore, the terms "person-centered care" and "good-quality care" are commonly used synonymously in the literature.[2]

Edvardsson et al. further indicate terms considered equivalent with "person-centered care":

> Various descriptions of person-centered care have been proposed, and concepts such as patient-centeredness,[3] authentic consciousness,[4] skilled companionship,[5] senses framework,[6] and positive person work[7] are seemingly viewed as synonymous with person-centered care for people with severe AD.[8]

2. Edvardsson et al., "Person-Centered Care of People with Severe Alzheimer's Disease," p. 363.

3. N. Mead and P. Bower, "Patient-Centeredness: A Conceptual Framework and Review of the Empirical Literature," *Social Science and Medicine* 51 (2000): 1087-1110.

4. B. McCormack, "Person-Centeredness in Gerontological Nursing: An Overview of the Literature," *International Journal of Older People Nursing* 13 (2004): 31-38.

5. A. Titchen, "Skilled Companionship in Professional Practice," in *Practice Knowledge and Expertise in the Health Professions,* ed. J. Higgs and A. Titchen (Oxford: Butterworth-Heinemann, 2001).

6. M. R. Nolan, S. Davies, B. Brown, J. Keady, and J. Nolan, "Beyond 'Person-Centered' Care: A New Vision for Gerontological Nursing," *Journal of Clinical Nursing* 13 (2004): 45-53.

7. T. Packer, "Turning Rhetoric into Reality: Person-Centered Approaches for Community Mental Health Nursing," in *Community Mental Health Nursing and Dementia Care,* ed. J. Keady, C. Clarke, and T. Adams (Maidenhead: Open University Press, 2003), pp. 104-19.

8. Edvardsson et al., "Person-Centered Care of People with Severe Alzheimer's Disease," p. 364.

The term "person" is a designator for a general approach to caring for all people rather than a subsection of human beings. While the theoretical discourse outlined in the previous chapter assumes that it is actually possible for people to become non-persons, the discourse around person-centered care emphasizes that to treat someone as a person is to treat them with value and give them worth irrespective of the presence or absence of particular capacities. The term "person-centered care" is a synonym for good care rather than a statement about someone's moral standing. One could substitute "valued and respected individual" for "person" without doing violence to the intention of the movement. Thus, in an odd way, person-centered care in its secular humanist vein doesn't really need a person, at least not in the ways in which we have been discussing persons thus far.

Relational Personhood

Nevertheless, despite the fact that there seems to be no formal articulation of models of personhood within many of the general approaches of person-centered dementia care, a more formal notion of personhood as a particular moral standing is part of the philosophical background of some key thinkers within this approach.[9] In exploring this, it will be helpful to return to the thinking of Tom Kitwood. A formal notion of personhood does lie behind his thinking. Within his approach, the antidote to malignant social psychology is positive personal relationships. Malignant social psychology constructs the personhood of individuals with dementia in particularly negative ways. Good personal relationships reconstruct their personhood in positive ways. Such a move requires a particular understanding of the person: human beings are persons-in-relation. Personhood is primarily a *relational* concept. Here, it is not capacities that count. The thing that makes a human being a person is his/her relationships.

Persons are defined and held as persons in and through the relationships they have with others and that others have with them. The task of care providers is to learn to look at persons with dementia differently — as relational beings whose personhood is sustained in and through the relationships that people choose to have with them. When carers learn to look

---

9. See *Spirituality and Personhood in Dementia*, ed. Albert Jewell (London: Jessica Kingsley Publishers, 2011).

at people in this way, it will become possible to initiate a "new culture of care"[10] which will stand in stark opposition to dementogenic cultures[11] and in so doing act as a brake on the types of malignant social psychology that, as we have seen, are so prevalent within society. This emphasis on relational personhood has been highly influential. It is certainly a significant positive movement away from the types of capacities-based approaches to personhood that are so problematic for people with dementia. Care and caring relationships are what hold persons in their personhood, not their failing capacity to do certain things. The relational approach seems like a good place to begin to rethink the idea of personhood. There is, however, a significant problem with this approach. If our personhood is dependent on our relationships, what kind of relationships do we need to be sustained as persons, and what happens if we can't find them?

The Centrality of Relationships for Being a Person?

In what is widely recognized as his most influential book, *Dementia Reconsidered: The Person Comes First,* Kitwood describes personhood as "a standing or status that is bestowed upon one human being by others, in the context of relationships and social being. It implies *recognition, respect, and trust.*"[12] According to this understanding, personhood is not based on the presence or absence of particular capacities. It is a gift that is bestowed upon people by others, irrespective of their capabilities or capacities. Importantly, Kitwood suggests that the kind of relationships that counter malignant social psychology are *personal relationships.* If malignant relationships are marked by misunderstanding, devaluation, and mistrust, the personal relationships within Kitwood's model of personhood are marked by recognition, respect, value, and trust. Malignant social relationships move us away from the individual; relational personhood moves us toward them.

10. Tom Kitwood, "The Experience of Dementia," *Aging and Mental Health* 1, no. 1 (1997): 13-22; quotation on 16.

11. Cultures which contain the type of malignant social psychology that we have explored are deeply implicated in the formation and sustaining of the perception and experiences of dementia.

12. Tom Kitwood, *Dementia Reconsidered: The Person Comes First* (Buckingham: Open University Press, 1997), p. 8.

"I-Thou" and "I-It"

The philosophical basis of this understanding of personhood lies within the thought of Martin Buber. Buber proposes that there are two types of human relationships: "I-Thou" and "I-It."[13]

"I-It" Relationships To address the Other as an "It" requires coolness, conceptualization, detachment, and instrumentality. "I-It" relationships are analytical and conceptual; those in them are inclined to judge people and things according to their functions. Molly Haslam describes this relationship as a "bending back on oneself which develops into the attitude where the Other exists as a value-neutral object for the projects of the self."[14] The problem with I-It relationships is that they cannot reveal the wholeness of human beings. I-It relationships are turned inward and determined by criteria other than the immediacy of the present moment of meeting. One cannot see the whole being of the Other because

> the otherness that is manifest in these relations is not that of the Other as Other but as the Other-for-me, and if the Other as Other cannot be wholly manifest here, neither can the wholeness of the self. The Other is manifest as an object for the use of the self, as based on biological, sensorial, perspectival, or intellectual functions of the self.[15]

In this relationship, the Other-as-Other is lost, "being manifest as a function of the intentions of the I and not as it truly is in and of itself."[16] It is this kind of "world-dominating subjectivity"[17] that lies behind my friend Gordon losing his friends. His diagnosis has moved him from a "Thou" to an "It." In the eyes of his friends, Gordon has become another-for-me, and as his relational desirability has lessened, so also has his relational utility.

The point is not that I-It relationships are unimportant. Indeed, they're a necessary way of relating which can have positive benefits. If I

13. Martin Buber, *I and Thou* (Edinburgh: T&T Clark, 1958). In earlier chapters I have borrowed Buber's "I-Thou" language.

14. Molly C. Haslam, *A Constructive Theology of Intellectual Disability: Human Being as Mutuality and Response* (New York: Fordham University Press, 2012), p. 68.

15. Haslam, *A Constructive Theology of Intellectual Disability*, p. 68.

16. Haslam, *A Constructive Theology of Intellectual Disability*, p. 68.

17. Haslam, *A Constructive Theology of Intellectual Disability*, p. 68.

take my car to the garage, I don't expect the mechanic to be particularly polite, caring, and empathetic toward it — I just want him to fix it! In addition, the I-It relationship is necessary for us to make rational sense of the world. We need to be able to objectify the world, to conceptualize and analyze it in order to make sense of certain aspects of our perception. We saw some benefits of this previously when we explored the issue of categorization and diagnosis. A good deal of science and medicine requires that we observe and analyze from a position of perceived objectivity in order that we can clearly see what's going on within a context or a person and act accordingly. However, when the I-It is the only relationship available to human beings, it is clearly insufficient and potentially destructive.

"I-Thou" Relationships   When it comes to the lives of people with dementia, there is a tendency to treat them as "Its" (an attitude that is deeply reinforced by the type of categorization that was highlighted previously) rather than "Thous." Kitwood expresses it this way:

> Buber's starting point . . . is different from that of Western individualism. He does not assume the existence of ready-made monads, and then inquire into their attributes. His central assertion is that relationship is primary; to be a person is to be addressed as Thou. There is no implication here that there are two different kinds of objects in the world: Thous and Its. The difference lies in the manner of relating. Thus it is possible (and, sad to say, all too common) for one human being to engage with another in the I-It mode.[18]

For Buber, authentic human existence is encountered within the "I-Thou" relationship. To address the other as a "Thou" requires a nonobjectifying moving toward the Other and into the space between one's self and the Other. In this space of meeting, one does not try to conceptualize or analyze the Other or to determine what it is that makes the Other different or otherwise. It is a place of true meeting. It is a movement *toward* Others that recognizes them as meaningful beings who are worthy of respect, people who are worth spending time with, sentient beings who are worthy of a certain kind of relationship.

Buber sees the individual as a unique center of *shared* life. In our pre-

18. Kitwood, *Dementia Reconsidered,* pp. 10-11.

vious discussions on mind and self, we saw how the mind and the self are always shared experiences. Buber draws our attention to the fact that the very essence of our being is shared experience. He perceives the self as intersubjective rather than "individual."[19] Within the intersubjective self, neither the individual nor the community is given ontological primacy. Rather, it is the intersubjectivity of what occurs in the space between the "I" and the "Thou" which is the focus; the "I" and the "Thou" come together to form the "We" in the space between. Intersubjective relationships are thus seen to be both formative and dialectical. They are formative insofar as such engagement mutually forms the personhood and identity of the "Other," and also dialectic because, as the product of such encounter is greater than the sum of the parts, the developing self which emerges from the "space between" is dependent on, greater than, and constitutive of both. Within this framework, the idea of "the individual" takes on a quite particular shape. Autonomy is seen to be an illusion. All of us are deeply interconnected and dependent on one another for our very being. To be free is not to separate one's self from others but to recognize our interconnectedness and to seek to live life personally. Intersubjective connectivity, not autonomy, is the goal of the self. Thus, in Kitwood's interpretation of Buber, sustaining the personhood of someone with dementia has to do with being held in a certain form of relationship by others quite apart from any capacities or capabilities that one may or may not have.

Importantly, these relationships are marked by mutuality and immediacy of relationship. Haslam comments,

> I-Thou relations involve an immediacy of relation between I and Thou. There is no reflecting, categorization, or ordering of the Thou on the part of the I here, and there are no concepts or ideas that mediate the relation between them. In Buber's words, "The relation to the Thou is direct. No systems of ideas, no foreknowledge and no fancy . . . no aim, no lust, and no anticipation intervene between I and Thou. . . . Every means is an obstacle. Only when every means has collapsed does the meeting come about."[20]

19. For further development of this point, see Martin Buber's idea of "healing through meeting" in Martin Buber, *Pointing the Way* (New York: Harper & Row, 1963), pp. 93-97. See also John Macmurray's work on persons-in-relation: *Persons in Relation* (London: Faber & Faber International, 1991).

20. Haslam, *A Constructive Theology of Intellectual Disability*, p. 69.

We can clearly see the importance of this way of perceiving one another. It moves us beyond diagnosis and categorization and opens up the possibility of truly meeting with others in that space where we are freed to recognize them for what and who they are.

A Model of Personhood that Creates Non-Persons?

The reason that Kitwood would be drawn to such a perspective is obvious. As people with dementia begin to lose their capacities, it is the task of those around them to sustain and maintain their personhood by continuing to relate to them in particular ways, to see them and seek to be with them simply for who they are. As long as one is recognized as a person, one will remain a person. This is indeed a powerful counter both to the models of personhood discussed thus far and to the various practices of malignant social psychology and positioning encountered daily by people with dementia. The problem is that if it is our relationships that make up our personhood, then presumably if we don't have such relationships, we are no longer persons. In other words, by holding on to the idea of "personhood" as a definable ethical concept, Kitwood creates the possibility that non-persons actually do exist. It is really quite surprising that he insists on retaining the language of personhood. The humanistic values incorporated in ideas about recognition, respect, and trust would really do the work for him without his having to move into the language of personhood. Moving from these principles into a formal model of personhood seems strangely out of line with the overall intentions of his project. Jan Dewing puts this point thus:

> Kitwood's conceptualization of a person can be located within personhood theories, albeit from a revisionist perspective. This, in effect, produces a major inconsistency that goes against what his work is trying to achieve, as personhood theories ultimately are about rejecting and excluding humans based on restrictive definitions of persons and the attributes required for being a person.[21]

21. Jan Dewing, "Personhood and Dementia: Revisiting Tom Kitwood's Ideas," *International Journal of Older People Nursing* 3 (March 2008): 3-13; quotation on 10.

If, as Kitwood suggests, personhood is a standing or status, then presumably some people are included and others are excluded; otherwise, there would be no need for the category of "person" in the first place. If that is the case, then Kitwood doesn't really offer a counter-position to the personhood theories of people such as Locke, Harris, Warnock, and Singer; he ends up simply confirming that they have a point. It is, in principle, possible to be human and not be a person. People with dementia really can and really do become non-persons in certain circumstances. If malignant social psychology is real and prevalent, then the possibility of many people with dementia actually being or becoming non-persons is very real. It is true that the Buberian philosophy that underpins Kitwood's model of personhood indicates that the "I-Thou" and "I-It" distinctions don't imply that there are two different kinds of objects in the world: I's and It's. Nonetheless, in using Buber's philosophical perspective to develop a model which defines what a person is, Kitwood mobilizes Buber's relational dynamic in a way that makes it definitive of two different categories of human beings: one which is the recipient of personal relationships (persons), and the other which is not (non-persons).

The problem emerges from Kitwood's reluctance to recognize that for Buber, the I-Thou relationship is deeply tied to the necessity of the reality and presence of God: God is the ultimate Thou. In the postscript to *I and Thou,* Buber informs his reader that his central concern is the closeness of the connection between a human being's relationship to God and her relationship to other human beings.[22] The I-Thou relationship is not just a general philosophical personalism; it relates to and emerges from a specific Thou: God. Knowing God and knowing one another are deeply interconnected. Personal relationships with God are of the same basic nature as proper, authentic human relationships. As we come to know God, as we experience the Thou of God, we are enabled to know what it means to be in authentic relationship with others.

Thus there is a theological and an epistemological distinction between I-Thou and I-It relationships which, as Stuart Charmé points out, "is used to establish a parallel between relations with other people and relations with God."[23] This epistemological distinction is matched by an ethical dis-

---

22. Buber, *I and Thou,* pp. 123-24.

23. Stuart Charmé, "The Two I-Thou Relations in Martin Buber's Philosophy," *Harvard Theological Review* 70, no. 1/2 (January-April 1977): 161-75; quotation on 162.

tinction relating to how people should be treated. Charmé criticizes Buber at this ethical level, suggesting that he is simply giving an opinion on what good relationships might look like. However, to suggest this is to miss something fundamental to Buber's approach. A deeper reflection on Buber's position indicates that his perspective on the nature of I-Thou relationships is fully embedded within the Jewish religious tradition.[24] It is much more than mere personal opinion. For Buber, God is not only the God who creates and redeems; God is also a Person:

> The description of God as a person is indispensable for everyone who like myself means by "God" not a principle (although mystics like Eckhart sometimes identify him with "Being") and like myself means by "God" not an idea (although philosophers like Plato at times could hold that he was this): but who rather means by "God," as I do, him who — whatever else he may be — enters into a direct relation with us men in creative, revealing, and redeeming acts, and thus makes it possible for us to enter into a direct relation with him. This ground and meaning of our existence constitutes a mutuality, arising again and again, such as can subsist only between persons. The concept of personal being is indeed completely incapable of declaring what God's essential being is, but it is both permitted and necessary to say that God is *also* a Person.[25]

While Buber here emphasizes a perspective on the apophatic nature of all knowledge of God, his point remains clear. God is a Person, and God's way of relating with human beings is deeply personal. We may not be able to know all that there is to know about God, but we can at a minimum know the basic form in which God chooses to relate to human beings. God relates personally. More than that, God is the "absolute Person,"[26] the Person who defines persons and who cannot be limited:

> It is as the absolute Person that God enters into direct relation with us. As a Person, God gives personal life; he makes us as persons become capable of meeting with him and with one another. But no limitation can

24. For a fuller insight into the Jewishness of Buber's philosophy, see Daniel S. Breslauer, *The Chrysalis of Religion: A Guide to the Jewishness of Buber's "I and Thou"* (Nashville: Abingdon Press, 1980): 161-75; quotation on 162.

25. Buber, *I and Thou*, p. 135.

26. Buber, *I and Thou*, p. 136.

come upon him as the absolute person, either from us or from our relations with one another; the man who turns to him therefore need not turn away from any other *I-Thou* relation; but he properly brings them to him, and lets them be fulfilled "in the face of God."[27]

God, the absolute Person, enters into personal relationships with human beings; this relational movement provides the shape and form of the personal and enables us to engage in I-Thou relations. It is as we encounter God in the space between and experience God's relational movement toward us that we come to know and understand what it means to enter into analogous I-Thou relations with others.

It is, however, important to be clear about how we might understand such terms as "relational movement" and "God's movement toward us." A crucial aspect of the I-Thou relationship is that it is non-conceptual and non-mediated; it is a way of being that doesn't require explanation, analysis, or the objectification of the Other. Nor does it require the mediation of the Other through any external systems of categorization. As soon as we try to work out exactly what the Other is or precisely what it is we are experiencing, we inevitably move into the I-It mode. When we do this, we "reduce the presence of the Other to the past as its uniqueness is considered only in terms of what it has in common with others we have encountered."[28] We can recall an example from Chapter 4: When Jonathan Franzen refers to his father's Alzheimer's disease as nothing more than an instance of what millions of other people are going through, he moves his father from a Thou to an It and allows that perception to mediate his encounters. We can be in the present moment with people with dementia only when we learn how to be with one another without mediation.

The I-Thou relationship is a place of experiencing without conceptualizing, of being without knowing. In this sense there is indeed a deep apophaticism about the I-Thou relationship. What can one know about God? In what sense could one have a reciprocal relationship with God? How can one conceptualize the divine? So when we talk about recognizing God's relational movement toward us, we aren't talking about rational, analytical knowledge. Rather, we're talking about experiencing God without having to name who God is and encountering another without having to

27. Buber, *I and Thou*, p. 136.
28. Haslam, *A Constructive Theology of Intellectual Disability*, p. 69.

name that other. The I-Thou relationship in its human analogue has to do with experiencing and being with one another in the space between us, a place where we don't have to "know" who the other is in order to really be with them, and they don't need to "know" us in order to be related to. The importance of this observation will become clear later in the book. For now, the key thing to notice is that the I-Thou relationship is different from typical understandings of personal relationship that require us to conceptualize and recognize one another in cognitive ways.

It is clear, therefore, that the I-Thou relationship is not just an ethical relationship (although clearly it is that); it is deeply spiritual and profoundly theological in origin, meaning, and intent, revealing as it does some deep things about God and how God relates to human beings. To omit God from our understandings of it is to misunderstand at a deep level the profundity and theological importance of what Buber is saying.

For Buber, the I-Thou relationship is firmly rooted in God's movement toward human beings. It is not dependent on response, but it does shape the types of response that mirror the divine approach. To be a person is to be in an I-Thou relationship specifically with God. We may be wary of the non-specificity of Buber's God and the depth of the apophaticism that his God seems to reside within. Nonetheless, the important point is that the security of human personhood is wholly determined by God, the absolute Person, who unchangingly reaches toward human beings in I-Thou relationship. Even if human beings do not or cannot respond, they remain persons as God the absolute Person continues to relate with them. Buber ends his book with this statement:

> The existence of mutuality between God and man cannot be proved, just as God's existence cannot be proved. Yet he who dares to speak of it bears witness, and calls to witness him to whom he speaks — whether that witness is now or in the future.[29]

Here is the recognition that personhood has to do with God's desire to relate and that God's mode of relating is personal. Such a position cannot be proven empirically, but *it can be lived*. One who engages in I-Thou relationships bears witness to a personal relationship that transcends one's own desire to relate. As we live out that reality in our personal relations

29. Buber, *I and Thou*, p. 137.

with others, we bear witness to a different order within which human beings are shaped and defined by I-Thou relationships, which begin with the divine and find an echo in the living witness of embodied human beings.

Persons without God?

It is of course possible to work with Buber's I-Thou, I-It distinction purely on the ethical level. This is really what Kitwood and the generic person-centered approaches to dementia care strive to do. There are clear benefits in doing this if it draws attention to the importance of coming close to people with dementia and relating to them in ways that are truly personal and valuing. However, while there may be some practical utility to subsuming the epistemological and theological dimensions of the I-Thou, I-It relationships to the ethical alone, this approach actually ends up leaving people with dementia in a vulnerable position. If all that persons are is a series of temporal human relationships, there can be no real stability of personhood. While essentializing personhood within a series of capacities is dangerous, so also is embedding it in a series of relationships which have no real basis for stability or assurance. If personhood has to do with only our temporal and mundane relationships, then what we are as persons will inevitably become unraveled as our relational networks break down. Like layers of an onion, our personhood will be peeled away as the various relationships in our lives are stripped from us by malignant social psychology, disease processes, and/or the death of our friends. As we have seen, the social networks of people with dementia begin to break down as the disease progresses. If such relationships are central to personhood, then people with dementia living out their lives within person-centered cultures will have a real problem. By transposing the relational dynamic from the divine to the human, humanistic approaches to relational personhood remove the protective dimension of transcendence and leave people with dementia (and everyone else) at the mercy of human choice and temporal relational decision-making. We have already seen what that can look like.

The consequence of Kitwood's model, and indeed any other form of relational personhood that chooses to omit the transcendent dimensions of the I-Thou relationship, is that the presence or absence of personhood is completely at the discretion of others. (This is similar to the problems encountered by people with dementia within Sabat's Self 3.) If a group of individuals wish to treat people with dementia as non-persons, they can actually do that, because people who reside outside of personal relationships really aren't persons. Without the divine I-Thou, there is no protective moral dynamic (other than a vague humanism based on freedom, consensus, and choice) to ensure that recognizing someone as a person, as a Thou, and then acting accordingly is anything other than a preferable option for those who share certain personal values. If I don't want to relate personally with someone who has dementia, I'm free to make that choice. There may be prohibitions that prevent me from treating people in ways which are deemed to be legally harmful, but having an I-It relationship with a person with dementia and engaging in malignant social interactions isn't one of them. In a morally pluralistic context, I have the option to engage in an I-Thou relationship, but nothing obligates me to do so. The law can't make me love you. Rights and laws can certainly lay down a context for the development of I-Thou relationships, but that is all they can do. I-Thou relationality isn't a matter of law; it is a matter of love and imaging God. Take the "Thou" out of the I-Thou relationship, and things get much more complicated.

If personhood is a standing ascribed to someone by other human beings, then what we are as persons becomes simply a matter of the personal choices of others. If that is the case, and if malignant social psychology is as prevalent as Kitwood and Sabat indicate, then people with dementia are in trouble: *Why would anyone choose to relate to them,* particularly in the latter stages of the condition? The evidence strongly indicates that people often have no desire to relate with them. It is certainly the case that some will enter into I-Thou relationships with people who have dementia because they love them and/or feel obligated to stand by them. Others will do so because they are compassionate people and/or because they are paid to do so. But being paid to be kind to someone is not the same thing as loving them for who and what they are, which is really what a relational model of personhood calls people toward, even if it doesn't have the moral capacity to achieve such a goal.

Hans Reinders observes that there is little within the values of cultures driven by liberal philosophy that would indicate that anyone has a moral obligation toward people with cognitive disabilities like dementia:

> The question of civic and social hospitality is key, but political liberalism is not ultimately capable of engendering and fostering hospitality

towards people with overt, recalcitrant needs. The norms encircling the liberal axis of individual autonomy cannot easily accommodate lives dedicated to the care of perpetually dependent individuals, or admit the intrinsic value of these individuals.[30]

Reinders' point is important. Kitwood's understanding of personhood and the various forms of person-centered care that have emerged from this perspective is underpinned by some form of liberal humanism. Reinders' point is that societies based on liberal principles have neither the practical nor the moral capabilities or desire to protect the disabled and to ensure their future.[31] Humanistic understandings of relational personhood are wholly dependent on people being persuaded that an I-Thou relationship, understood purely at an ethical level, is the most appropriate one to offer to people with dementia. But why would people offer such forms of relationship? There is no mechanism in such models of personhood for indicating why it is that people who are free, autonomous, self-directing — who have no real obligation to any narrative other than their own and no responsibility toward others other than to ensure that their own desires do not impinge upon the freedom of others — should care for people with dementia in the ways Kitwood presses for. Certainly it might be possible to persuade a few individuals or groups that relating in this way might be a good thing, but whether they accept that has to do with choice and personal formation, that is, whether they choose to act in such ways and whether their personal formation has provided them with the appropriate character that has equipped them for the job of relating in ways which are personal rather than instrumental, oriented toward the transcendent rather than focused on the autonomous self. Such people do exist; but they may be the exception rather than the rule.

Christians are one group of people who at least *should* see the world according to the perspective of the divine Thou. The church is a place that claims to bear witness to another way of being in the world and another way of understanding personhood, both human and divine. If that is the case, then the next movement of our journey into dementia will be to ex-

30. Hans Reinders, *Receiving the Gift of Friendship: Profound Disability, Theological Anthropology, and Ethics* (Grand Rapids: Wm. B. Eerdmans, 2008), p. 14.

31. This perspective is developed more fully in Hans Reinders, *The Future of the Disabled in Liberal Society* (South Bend: University of Notre Dame Press, 2000).

plore what theology and the practices of the church have to offer to the discussion of personhood and humanness in relation to dementia. What perspective on personhood and what set of practices might this particular Person-centered community offer to our understanding of the lives of people with dementia? How might a theological redescription of humanness help develop our understanding of dementia even further?

7. Personhood and Humanness: The Importance of Being a Creature

What are human beings that you are mindful of them, mortals that you care for them?

PSALM 8:4

The earth is the LORD's, and all that is in it, the world, and those who live in it.

PSALM 24:1

The glory of human beings is not power, the power to control someone else; the glory of human beings is the ability to let what is deepest within us grow.

JEAN VANIER, BEFRIENDING THE STRANGER

It has become clear that many of the stories which are told about and around dementia are both illuminating and troubling. The various stories told by medicine, psychiatry, psychology, neurobiology, and philosophy are all in some ways helpful and necessary in terms of developing a fuller understanding of dementia and facilitating good practice and authentic caring approaches. Likewise, it is important to be aware of the relational and linguistic dimensions of dementia and how they function within social contexts. From the perspective of practical theology and pastoral care, each of these perspectives has something to offer as we try to describe and redescribe dementia with a view to enabling more faithful forms of practice. Taken together, they can point toward the places where theology and pastoral care should begin their journey into dementia. An interdisciplinary approach to dementia is fully appropriate as long as each of the participants is read critically and none is allowed to define the whole of the terrain that dementia inhabits.

Earlier in the book it was suggested that medicine, psychology, and the other disciplines that have been used to understand dementia and develop strategies for caring for people with dementia need to be recognized as practicing within a quite specific context: creation. The task of practical theology is not simply to reflect theologically on current understandings of dementia and dementia care; its task is to show the difference that it makes when we recognize that all that is known about dementia and dementia care emerges from a theological context. That context precedes and deeply shapes all of our knowledge of dementia. All understandings of dementia and dementia care are thus seen to be inherently theological, even if they are not always acknowledged as such. We seek to describe and understand dementia within the context of creation, and that context makes a difference.

In this chapter we will begin to tease out the implications and possibilities of such a suggestion for the development of a faithful redescription of dementia. When viewed from the perspective of creation, sin, and redemption — that is, from within the counter-story told in the strange new world of the Bible — dementia, like all of human experience, looks quite different. As we listen carefully to this narrative and seek to respond to its redescription, new possibilities for care and understanding emerge. It is as we listen to this powerful counter-story that the theological shape and intention of the journey into dementia will become clear.

Personhood and Humanness

In beginning to unpack the implications of describing dementia and practicing dementia care within creation, it will be helpful to pick up on our previous discussion on personhood and see what being a person might look like when it is described from the perspective of the Christian story. In his book *Persons: The Difference between "Someone" and "Something,"* Robert Spaemann presents an argument against the idea that human beings are somehow defined by their capacities. Spaemann makes an important distinction:

> Human beings have certain definite properties that license us to call them "persons"; but it is not the properties we call persons, but the human beings who possess the properties.[1]

By this Spaemann means that there may be certain things that are associated with personal existence such as the ability to communicate, to relate, to respond, and so forth. These things might be considered aspects of persons, but they emerge *from* persons rather than being definitive *of* persons. In other words, being a person is prior to any particular capacities that might be associated with personhood. So, for example, a child learns personal reciprocity from her mother or those who relate most closely to her. However, her mother doesn't wait until her daughter learns personal reciprocity before she considers her to be a person. She assumes her daughter is a person and enters into relationship with her based on that assumption. As Spaemann puts it, "Recognizing a person is not merely a response to the presence of specific personal properties, because these properties only emerge where a child experiences the attention which is paid to persons."[2] In other words, personhood precedes capacities.

For Spaemann, personhood is not a generic category that brings certain benefits to some people and prevents others from receiving them. Rather, "being a person is a *modus existendi*, there is no *genus proximum*, no more general category that the concept of 'person' could specify."[3] To be a person has to do with possessing *a way of being* rather than a set of capacities. This way of being perceives the material content of human existence (i.e., the physicality of bodily existence) not as the place where personhood is produced, but as the medium through which it is expressed and lived. Personhood is thus seen to be situated within the *life* of human beings:

> Fundamental biological functions and relations are . . . specifically personal performances and interactions. Eating and drinking are personal acts. . . . They are embedded in rituals; they provide the focus of many

---

1. Robert Spaemann, *Persons: The Difference between "Someone" and "Something,"* trans. Oliver O'Donovan (Oxford: Oxford University Press, 2006), p. 257.

2. Spaemann, *Persons*, p. 257.

3. Spaemann, *Persons*, p. 253.

forms of community life; they stand at the center of many cults. Something similar applies to sexual intercourse. Here, too, the biological function is integrated in a personal context, often as the highest form of expression of a relation between persons. The kinship-connections of mothers and fathers to sons and daughters, of grandparents to grandchildren, of siblings and cousins to one another, are not merely a biological given, but personal relations of a typical kind, relations which as a rule last for life. Human personality is not something over and above human animality. Human animality, rather, never was mere animality, but the medium of personal realization. The nearer and more distant kinship relations in which human beings stand to one another are of personal, and so of ethical, importance.[4]

Human existence is personal existence. Because it is always lived out within the human community, even that which is biological is personal. To be a person is to be a member of the human race. Liberally quoting Spaemann, Berndt Wannenwetsch summarizes Spaemann's approach on this point:

Rather than being an instantiation of a concept or a member of a class, a person is "but a participant in a community of mutual recognition." There are no "potential persons" any more than there can be only the "idea" of a person. "Person" as a concept exists only as long as there are individual persons. If "person" is not a generic term but rather the way in which individuals of the human genus exist, Spaemann proceeds, then "each of these individuals occupies an irreplaceable position in the community of persons, which we call mankind" — and it does so not by co-option but by birthright. "There can, and must, be one criterion for personality, and one only; and that is biological membership of the human race."[5]

To be a person is to be born into and to participate in the human family. Such participation is not determined by any particular capacity or set of capacities, but rather by "genealogical relations of kinship":

4. Spaemann, *Persons*, pp. 255-56.
5. Berndt Wannenwetsch, "Angels with Clipped Wings: The Disabled as Key to the Recognition of Personhood," in *Theology, Disability, and the New Genetics: Why Science Needs the Church*, ed. John Swinton and Brian Brock (London: T&T Clark, 2007), p. 187. Wannenwetsch is quoting from Spaemann's *Persons: The Difference between "Someone" and "Something."*

Members of the species *homo sapiens* are not merely exemplars of a kind; they are kindred, who stand from the outset in a personal relation to one another. "Humanity," unlike "animality," is more than an abstract concept that identifies a category; it is the name of a concrete community of persons to which one belongs not on the basis of certain precise properties objectively verified, but by a genealogical connection with the "human family." . . . Belonging to the human family cannot depend on empirically demonstrated properties. Either the human family is a community of persons from the word go, or else the very concept of a person as "someone" in his or her own right is unknown or forgotten.[6]

Within the human community, the dual and unshakable premises of birthright and mutual recognition bind together *all* of its members. Membership of that community is biological and genealogical and therefore clear and irrevocable. There is no generic category of "persons"; being a person is a statement of particularity, irreplaceability, and participation in the human community. That being so, the ideas of potential persons or non-persons make no sense.

Spaemann thus moves away from understandings of personhood that focus on particular properties within an individual and toward an understanding that insists that we value selves rather than any particular properties that those selves might contain. As members of the human race, all of us are by definition persons. Personhood thus relates to the way that human beings are in the world and relate in and to one another and the world. It is not a set of capacities, and it is not simply a standing that is bestowed upon someone by others. It is an irrevocable status that comes from being a human being.

Such an understanding of the nature of personhood has much potential for people with dementia. There is nothing that can occur to an individual that can make him less of a person. As long as he is a member of the human race (which obviously is an irrevocable status), he remains a person valued and included within that genealogically interconnected family. There is no general category called "the person" — only unique, individual persons who are bound together by their shared birthrights. Nothing can separate us from the love of God, says the apostle Paul;[7] likewise, nothing

---

6. Wannenwetsch, "Angels with Clipped Wings," p. 187.
7. Romans 8:38-39.

can alter our status as persons. Human beings are indeed persons-in-relation, but those relational ties are not constitutive of personhood; they are a consequence of a basic presupposition of personhood, an outworking of that which is already present. Relationality is fundamental to personhood, but it is not optional. It is an inevitable entailment of being human.

If we think of Spaemann's suggestion in Trinitarian terms, the theological significance of such a position becomes clearer. Elsewhere I have made a case for viewing human relationality as analogous with divine relationality.[8] Within such an understanding the inherently relational nature of human beings emerges from the nature and relational shape of the God in whose image they are created, a God who is a Trinity of persons. God is a perichoretic community of love constituted by the relationships of the three persons of the Trinity: God the Father, God the Son, and God the Holy Spirit; each person is inextricably interlinked in an eternal community of loving relationship. We should notice two things about the concept of perichoresis: it indicates a co-existence of each member with the other which is marked by both distinction and complete unity or communion; and it begins with the premise that each member of the Trinity is already a person quite apart from their mutual relations.[9] There is of course no temporal sequence or separation between their being as persons and their being persons-in-relation, but the point remains apt. It is not the relationships between the Father, the Son, and the Holy Spirit that make them persons; they are already persons. As they engage in mutual relationships of love, identity is bestowed upon one by and through the other. The Father needs the Son to be the Father; the Son needs the Father to be the Son, and the Holy Spirit needs the Father and the Son in order to be what

8. This concept of perichoresis is developed by Jürgen Moltmann as it pertains to the personhood of God within the Trinity in *The Trinity and the Kingdom of God: The Doctrine of God* (London: SCM Press Ltd., 1993), pp. 174ff., and as it applies to God's relationship with God's creation in *God in Creation: An Ecological Doctrine of Creation* (London: SCM Press Ltd., 1985).

9. While this line of thinking won't be the primary focus of this chapter, there is some degree of consensus among theologians that the notion of personhood and the various relational perspectives that have emerged in relation to this term receive their ontological support from the way in which the language of the Trinity has been developed within the Christian tradition. See John Zizioulas, *Being as Communion* (Crestwood, N.Y.: St. Vladimir's Seminary Press, 1985). See also the excellent set of essays on Trinity and personhood in *Persons: Divine and Human,* ed. Christoph Schwöbel and Colin Gunton (Edinburgh: T&T Clark, 1991).

it is. However, bestowing identity on the other is not synonymous with being persons.

Something analogous to this divine dynamic is apparent within human personhood. All human beings are irrevocably persons; to be human is to be a person. As human beings come together in community, they discover and develop their capacities and come to recognize themselves and be recognized as part of one extended human family. Tom Kitwood (à la Buber) is therefore correct in one sense when he suggests that we need one another to be who we are. Recognition and identity formation are the tasks of the human community. When people are recognized as persons, authentic personal relationships become a real possibility. However, Kitwood is incorrect in associating relationality with the essence of personhood. Persons exist independently of their relations. They are to be valued, loved, and cared for as persons simply because they are human beings. In this respect, the human family is an analogue of divine relationality — a community of persons who are called to be one family.[10] Viewed from a Trinitarian perspec-

10. Of course, a danger with this way of thinking is the matter of *projection*. Karen Kilby has serious reservations about theorists who work with models of the social trinity. Her main concern is the starting point for theological reflection on the analogical construction of human relationships which emerges from it. Which comes first — social theory or theological reflection? She points out, "The doctrine of the Trinity arose in order to affirm certain things about the divinity of Christ and, secondarily, of the Spirit, and it arose against a background assumption that God is one." (See Karen Kilby, "Perichoresis and Projection: Problems with Social Doctrines of the Trinity," *New Blackfriars* 81, no. 956 [2000]: 432-45.) It was not originally intended as a social theory or an analogical representation of ideal human community. The danger Kilby sees is that those who propose social models of the Trinity are in fact projecting previously held ideas onto God and then reflecting them back as if they provided new knowledge about God and human beings. Peter Kevern sees a similar tendency in my own work: "Although these lines of thought seem tantalizingly rich in potential, arguments from the 'social trinity' to the structure of human societies by a process of analogy neglect the fact that the 'social trinity' has already been derived analogically: we project our ideals of human society into heaven as the 'social life of the Trinity,' and then argue from that life back to human society. To put it another way, we construct our societies *in imagine dei* because we have already constructed our Trinity *in imagine hominis*. Thus it is no surprise that Swinton finds in the Trinity an image of the ideals that he (after Kitwood) espouses." (See Peter Kevern, "What Sort of a God Is to Be Found in Dementia?: A Survey of Theological Responses and an Agenda for Their Development," *Theology* 113, no. 873 [May 2010]: 174-82.) I think Kevern and Kilby have an important point to make. The issue of projection is key in terms of understanding malignant social psychology, and there is inevitably a tendency for human beings to project onto God that which they desire God to be. Nevertheless, properly understood, the relational nature of the Trinity is an important key to the

tive, Spaemann's point of view begins to open up new possibilities for our understanding of personhood which overcome some of the shortcomings in both capacities-based and relational models of persons.

What Does It Mean to Be Human?

For people with dementia, the significance of suggesting that being a person has to do with being a member of the human family pivots on the question of what it actually means to be human. What difference does it make to claim that one belongs to the genus *homo sapiens?* We have previously seen that for some people it makes no difference whatsoever. Precisely what it means to be human has become somewhat cloudy. Evolutionists inform us that being human is simply the by-product of blind natural forces working over time to produce a series of organisms whose meaning and goal are simply to produce other organisms. Humanists argue that the term "human" is nothing more than a factual designator which indicates the value of people without any need for transcendence. Ethicists and philosophers tell us that we are simply a species among other species who have no particular moral claims over monkeys, pigs, or gorillas. Creationists argue that we were created six thousand years ago and that human beings are the pinnacle of creation. Others sit somewhere in between these positions. So what it means to be a member of the biological category "homo sapiens" has become most unclear. This is not the place to try to develop a full-blown theological anthropology. But we do need to be clear about what it might mean to claim to be a human being and how that might relate to what it means to be a human being with dementia.

The basic premise of this chapter is that it is impossible to understand the full meaning of being a human person without first understanding who God is and where human beings stand in relation to God. It is only when we begin to recognize and acknowledge the position of human beings before God that the situation of people with dementia can be fully understood, their personhood authenticated, and their care effectively implemented. It

---

relational nature of human beings. The key is reflexivity and a recognition that the term "relationality" when it is applied to God may be quite different from standard romantic accounts of relationships and community. If relationality ends in crucifixion, then romantic notions of trinity and community look quite different.

is only as we come to understand what it means to be human that we can begin to understand and live out Spaemann's suggestion that to be a person is to be a participant in a community of mutual recognition and acceptance. In what follows I will offer a fivefold exploration that will help develop a perspective on what it means to be a human being, with a specific focus on those aspects that are most relevant to the questions raised by the experience of dementia. It will be suggested that to be human is to be (1) dependent and contingent, (2) embodied, (3) relational, (4) broken and deeply lost, and (5) loved and profoundly purposeful.

What follows are a series of contextual meditations on humanness that emerge from contemplation on the experience of dementia. The key underlying principle is that the experiences of people with dementia matter for the ways in which we understand humanness. In this way the insights presented will contribute to the wider conversation on theological anthropology, while at the same time retaining a specific focus on the human experience of dementia.

Dependency and Contingency

Human beings are creatures who are wholly dependent on God. *There is nothing that anyone has that has not been given to them.*[11] Mary Jo Iozzio, who wrote a reflection on her experience with her father, who had Alzheimer's disease, notes the radical dependency that marks human being:

> We are radically dependent upon our parents, families, and friends (or some other responsible persons) from the moment of our first breath and all through our formative years. . . . And we are radically dependent upon God for, among manifold graces and loves, the blessedness of everlasting life. Radical dependence challenges the ultimately isolating ends of the de rigueur absolutized autonomy of our post-modern times.[12]

Thus, in contradiction to Western cultures' prizing of freedom, autonomy, and individualism, a deeper reflection reveals dependence as the true state

---

11. Genesis 1:1: "In the beginning God created the heavens and the earth" (NIV).

12. Mary Jo Iozzio, "The Writing on the Wall . . . Alzheimer's Disease: A Daughter's Look at Mom's Faithful Care of Dad," *Journal of Religion, Disability, and Health* 9, no. 2 (2005): 49-74; quotation on 54.

of all human beings at a divine and a temporal level. At a temporal level, our dependence on families, communities, civil amenities, and other wider political relationships is seen to have an economic correlate. The recent collapse of the financial markets has indicated to all of us our radical economic interdependence as markets interweave and crisscross across the globe, leaving us dependent on people we don't know who live in worlds that are thousands of miles away from our own. We may depend on the market economically, but as human beings we depend far more fundamentally on God:

> yet for us there is but one God, the Father, from whom all things came and for whom we live; and there is but one Lord, Jesus Christ, through whom all things came and through whom we live. (1 Cor. 8:6)

Our essential state as human beings is one of radical dependence. Put slightly differently, we are *creatures*. "Creatures" is a descriptor of radical dependence and complete contingency. Without God, we literally cannot be. As Paul puts it,

> "For in him we live and move and have our being." As some of your own poets have said, "We are his offspring." (Acts 17:28)

Autonomy is a human idea that functions to separate human beings from one another and mark them out as "individuals." It is, however, an illusory idea.

Recognizing our radical dependence leads us to conclude that all that we have is gift. If this is so, then the changes that surround the experience of dementia should be viewed in a quite particular way. By that I don't mean that dementia is a gift.[13] My point is that if all that we have is gift, then the losses that occur within dementia take on a very different mean-

---

13. The idea of dementia as a gift underpins some strands of thinking. See, for example, Nader Robert Shabahangi, "Redefining Dementia: Between the World of Forgetting and Remembering." (This dissertation can be accessed at http://www.pacificinstitute.org/events/nader_dementia.pdf.) I'm not convinced that the suggestion that dementia is a gift is particularly helpful. There is a difference between saying that one can learn much from the experience of dementia and suggesting that it is a gift that God has given to persons. As we will see in the final chapter of this book, most people who have dementia or whose loved ones encounter this experience would struggle to see the giftedness of the experience.

ing. Human beings are not valued because they have certain capacities. Whatever capacities they may have are nothing more — and nothing less — than gifts. In the words of Job,

> I came naked from my mother's womb, and I will be naked when I leave. The LORD gave me what I had, and the LORD has taken it away. Praise the name of the LORD! (Job 1:21)

Human beings are gifted and valued because God loves them and continues to care for them in the midst of their joys and sufferings. To be a person is to be human; to be human is to be gifted and loved (Rom. 8:38-39). To live humanly is to learn to recognize the practical and theological significance of our natural state as contingent, dependent creatures. That being so, the movement into dependence which marks the experience of dementia in no way diminishes a person's humanness or moves someone away from personhood. Quite the opposite. The radical dependence and emerging recognition of contingency that people with dementia experience comprise a poignant and revelatory instance of what it means to be a human being, of what it means to be a creature. Such dependence doesn't downgrade one's humanity or threaten one's personhood. Nor does it strip a person of her dignity (unless those around choose for this to be the case). Rather, it reminds us all of something that we often choose to forget: We are dependent, relational creatures.

It's all too easy for us human beings to assume that we're free to write our own stories. However, in reality, we have no option other than to participate in the story that God has written into creation.[14] Stanley Hauerwas puts it this way:

---

14. According to Dietrich Bonhoeffer, "There are not two realities, but only one reality, and that is God's reality revealed in Christ in the reality of the world. Partaking in Christ, we stand at the same time in the reality of God and in the reality of the world. The reality of Christ embraces the reality of the world in itself. The world has no reality of its own independent of God's revelation in Christ. It is a denial of God's revelation in Jesus Christ to wish to be 'Christian' without being 'worldly' or [to] wish to be worldly without seeing and recognizing the world in Christ. Hence there are not two realms, but only the one realm of the Christ-reality [Christuswirklichkeit], in which the reality of God and the reality of the world are united." Quoted from DBWE 6, 58; DBW 6, 43; emphasis in original. 1986-1999 Dietrich Bonhoeffer Werke (DBW). Band 1-17. Gütersloh: Chr. Kaiser Verlag. 1995-n.d. Dietrich Bonhoeffer Works (DBWE). Volumes 1-16. Minneapolis: Fortress Press.

Long story, short: we don't get to make our lives up. We get to receive them as gifts. The story that says we should have no story except the story we chose when we had no story is a lie. To be human is to learn that we don't get to make up our lives because we're creatures. Christians are people who recognize that we have a Father whom we can thank for our existence. Christian discipleship is about learning to receive our life as gift without regret. And that has the deepest political implications. Because so much of modern political theory and practice is about creating a society where we do not have to acknowledge that our life is a gift we receive from one another.[15]

To reiterate: We are not the authors of our own stories. Our calling is to learn how to read and interpret the story of God faithfully and well. In this sense people with dementia are reminded and remind us of this fundamental fact about the world. The problem of forgetfulness is not confined to the individual with dementia. The experience of dementia brings to the fore a broader amnesia that has befallen the world which has caused it to forget where and what it is: *creation*. When the world forgets its Creator, we begin to think *we* are the creators; we begin to believe that we are self-creating beings whose task is to shape the world into our own image. In such a worldview, our capacity to do things becomes primary. Unlike God, we demand that people *have* gifts instead of recognizing that in fact *they are gifts*.

But for those who have come to recognize God as Creator, the giftedness of life is apparent, dynamic, and transformative. The declaration "I am because I am created, dependent, gifted, and loved in all circumstances and for all time" is very different from "I think; therefore I am," or "I am because of what I can do," or even "I am because others choose to relate to me." Recognizing life as God's gift challenges any temptation to try to live lives marked by autonomy and independence. Being freed from lives obsessed with a striving for freedom and the fulfillment of self-desire opens up ways of living which are humble, purposeful, patient, gentle, kind, and grateful. Such a frame allows the lives of people with dementia to be perceived quite differently. It doesn't take away the pain, suffering, and loss, but it does place dementia within a perspective wherein no

15. Stanley Hauerwas, in *Living Gently in a Violent World: The Prophetic Witness of Weakness,* ed. Stanley Hauerwas, Jean Vanier, and John Swinton (Downers Grove, Ill.: InterVarsity Press, 2008), p. 70.

matter what happens, people remain safe and loved, valued and respected, fully human and fully persons. It may not always appear that way; it will often not feel that way. But at the heart of the experience of dementia we can be assured that the God who gifts us remains active, present, and loving. We will examine precisely what such love looks like in a later chapter. For now the point to bear in mind is that the experience of dementia draws us to adopt the horizon of faith and sit, if sometimes uncomfortably, with these words of the apostle Paul:

> For I am convinced that neither death nor life, neither angels nor demons, neither the present nor the future, nor any powers, neither height nor depth, nor anything else in all creation, will be able to separate us from the love of God that is in Christ Jesus our Lord. (Rom. 8:38-39)

This seems to be a firm, necessary, and unshakable foundation for understanding the lives of people with dementia and offering care and support which are faithful and dignified. Dementia may be a story of great losses, but the fullness of the personhood of sufferers and God's faithful love for them are not among them.

Embodiment

If the first thing to notice about what it means to be human is that we are creatures who are contingent beings, gifted with life and loved for who we are, the second thing to bring to notice is that human beings are embodied creatures. Although we can't be reduced to our bodily functions, our bodies matter nonetheless. We experience the world in and through our bodies. Without them it is difficult to imagine what it might look like to know God, feel and experience love, and engage in personal relationships. The embodied nature of human being also matters for our understanding of dementia.

Breathing Life into the Earth

As Walter Brueggemann points out, contingency and embodiment are deeply interconnected:

The human person is formed of earth and is breathed upon by God, in order to become a "living being" *(nephesh)* (Gen. 2:7; Ps. 103:14). This means that the human person is, at origin and endlessly, dependent on the attentive giving of YHWH in order to have life (cf. Ps. 104:29-30). . . . The human person has vitality as a living, empowered agent and creature only in relation to the God who faithfully gives breath. Thus the human person is to be understood in relational and not essentialist terms.[16]

To be human is to be in relation with YHWH, our Creator:

YHWH as Creator of humankind and of each human person is sovereign in that relationship. Human persons are creatures who are dependent on YHWH and created for obedience to YHWH. Even before any concrete content is applied to the commands of YHWH and the obedience of human persons, the category of sovereignty and obedience is a crucial and definitional mark of human beings.[17]

To be a person-in-relationship is a status that is promised, gifted, and sustained by YHWH the Creator. The relational nature of human beings is captured in the dynamic between the sovereignty of God and the obedience of God's creatures. Human beings' natural position is one of obedience under the security of God's sovereign power. Their unnatural position is one of disobedience and the autonomous exertion of human power, capacities, and desire.

Human beings are a strange combination of the material and the immaterial.[18] Gilbert Meilaender quotes St. Augustine, who aptly described human beings as *terra animata,* "animated earth."[19] In Genesis 2:7, the author of the book talks about the way in which Adam was created:

And the LORD God formed man [of] the dust of the ground, and breathed into his nostrils the breath of life; and man became a living soul. (KJV)

16. Walter Brueggemann, *An Unsettling God: The Heart of the Hebrew Bible* (Minneapolis: Fortress Press, 2009), p. 60.

17. Brueggemann, *An Unsettling God,* p. 60.

18. Brueggemann, *An Unsettling God,* p. 61.

19. St. Augustine, quoted in Gilbert Meilaender, *"Terra es Animata:* On Having a Life," *The Hastings Center Report* 23, no. 4 (July-August 1993): 25-32; quotation on 25.

Human beings are thus created from matter, but given breath/brought into living existence by the very breath of God. Matter understood without its necessary connection with that which transcends matter is misunderstood and misnamed. We are our bodies as we are our souls. The two are one; one cannot exist without the other.

Wendell Berry, reflecting on Genesis 2:7, makes this observation:

> My mind, like most people's, has been deeply influenced by dualism, and I can see how dualistic minds deal with this verse. They conclude that the formula for man-making is: man = body + soul. But that conclusion cannot be derived, except by violence, from Genesis 2:7, which is not dualistic. The formula given in Genesis is not man = body + soul; the formula there is soul = dust + breath. According to this verse, God did not make a body and put a soul into it, like a letter into an envelope. He formed man of dust; by breathing his breath into it, he made the dust live. Insofar as it lived, it was a soul. The dust, formed as man and made to live, did not embody a soul; it became a soul. "Soul" here refers to the whole creature. Humanity is thus presented to us, in Adam, not as a creature of two discrete parts temporarily glued together, but as a single mystery.[20]

This breath that God breathes into Adam is referred to in Hebrew by the term *nephesh*. Glenn Whitlock informs us that one of the primary meanings of the word *nephesh* is ". . . the vital principle of life itself, without which a person dies. . . . [It refers to] the animal essence of life with which every creature must be endued."[21] *Nephesh* is often translated from the Hebrew by the English word "soul."[22] However, as Berry points out, the term "soul" does not relate to a discrete, immortal dimension of the human person. Rather, it refers to the in-breathing of God's Spirit into dust, which creates a living entity.[23]

20. Wendell Berry, *The Art of the Commonplace: The Agrarian Essays of Wendell Berry* (Berkeley: Counterpoint Press, 2002), p. 313.

21. Glenn E. Whitlock, "The Structure of Personality in Hebrew Psychology," *Interpretation: A Journal of Bible and Theology* 14, no. 1 (January 1960): 3-14; quotations on 8-9.

22. Ray S. Anderson, *On Being Human: Essays in Theological Anthropology* (Grand Rapids: Wm. B. Eerdmans, 1982), p. 5.

23. Walter Brueggemann points out, "The articulation of 'breathed out dust' in order to become a 'living being' precludes any dualism. It is unfortunate that 'living being'

Here, the human being is perceived as, to use H. Wheeler Robinson's phrase, "an animated body, and not an incarnated soul." John A. T. Robinson helpfully develops this point:

> Man does not *have* a body; he *is* a body. He is flesh-animated-by-soul conceived as a psycho-physical unity: "The body is the soul in its outward form." There is no suggestion that the soul is the essential personality, or that the soul *(nephesh)* is immortal, whilst the flesh *(basar)* is mortal. The soul does not survive a man — it simply goes out, draining away with the blood.[24]

Without the life-giving *nephesh,* a creature cannot exist. Human beings are thus animated souls or, perhaps better, embodied souls, whose very breath and sustenance are wholly dependent on God for their continuation. The soul, therefore, should be understood as the vitalizing, animating force which is instilled within all creatures by the Creator God when God brings that which had no life into life. It is this *nephesh* which, as Glenn Weaver correctly points out, makes us connected with God at a deep level:

> The human "nephesh" . . . refers to the continuing relationship of our identity to God. God's act did not plant some divine entity in a body which then gave persons a generic claim to eternal existence. "Nephesh" is not a divine form or force that humans have within. "Nephesh" is what happened when God brought into existence the whole of a specific person, Adam. Adam's existence, and the existence of any other specific person whom he represents, remains completely dependent on the moment-by-moment breath of God that upholds that life. As long as the breath is in us, we may live in responsibility and love with God. The description of Adam's walking before God in the Garden of Eden imme-

---

(nephesh) is commonly rendered 'soul,' which in classical thought has made a contrast to the 'body,' a distinction precluded in Israel's way of speaking. Thus the human person is a dependent, vitality-given unity, for which the term *psychosomatic entity* might be appropriate, if that phrasing did not itself reflect a legacy of dualism." See Brueggemann, *An Unsettling God,* p. 60.

24. John A. T. Robinson, *The Body: A Study in Pauline Theology* (Chicago: Alec R. Allenson, 1952), p. 14. The quotation is from J. Pedersen, *Israel: Its Life and Culture,* 2 vols. (London: Oxford University Press, 1963), p. 171.

diately follows the record of Adam's creation. It is likewise our "being" to walk with and to praise God.[25]

Human beings are animated earth which contains the very breath of God. As animated souls, our raison d'être is to be with God.

This is a very important point. As earth animated by the breath of God, human beings are seen to be "holy creatures living among other holy creatures in a world that is holy," according to Wendell Berry.[26] Creation, therefore, is not independent of the Creator. Rather, creation is, as Berry puts it,

> . . . the continuous, constant participation of all creatures in the being of God. Elihu said to Job that if God "gather unto himself his spirit and his breath, all flesh shall perish together . . ." (Job 34:15). And Psalm 104 says: "Thou sendest forth thy spirit, they are created. . . ." Creation is God's presence in creatures. The Greek Orthodox theologian Philip Sherrard has written that "Creation is nothing less than the manifestation of God's hidden being. Thus we and all other creatures live by a sanctity that is inexpressibly intimate. To every creature the gift of life is a portion of the breath and spirit of God."[27]

If this is so, then attending to God's creatures is in fact a mode of attending to God. Jesus makes a similar point when he says, "'I tell you the truth, whatever you did for one of the least of these brothers of mine, you did for me'" (Matt. 25:40). There is something of God in all human beings,[28] and something holy in all encounters between humans. The corollary of this, of course, is that depersonalizing God's creatures and treating them unjustly and malignantly positioning them is to do the same thing to God.

Animated Dust: Living in Holy Ground

Human embodiedness is thus seen to be deeply spiritual in shape and function. Our bodies are the locus of God's creative activity and the place

25. Glenn Weaver, "Senile Dementia and a Resurrection Theology," *Theology Today* 42 (1986): 444-56; quotation on 446.

26. Berry, *The Art of the Commonplace*, p. 308.

27. Berry, *The Art of the Commonplace*, p. 308.

28. John 1:4: "In him was life, and the life was the light of all people" (NRSV).

where God meets and sustains us. Our bodies are holy ground. It should be noted that talk about "our bodies" is talk about *whole* bodies. God did not take the dust and create a brain! God took the dust and created a human body within which the brain is but one component which has the same purpose and goal as the rest of the body: to enjoy God and glorify God forever. The enjoyment and glorification of God cannot be reduced to the cognitive alone. It is certainly true that in order for human beings to exercise dominion over the world, a degree of cognition and intellect is required. This is suggested in God's command in Genesis 1:

> God blessed them, and God said to them, "Be fruitful and multiply, and fill the earth and subdue it; and have dominion over the fish of the sea and over the birds of the air and over every living thing that moves upon the earth." (Gen. 1:28)

But we would be quite mistaken to presume from this that intellect and reason are definitive of human beings or even that they are required by all human beings in equal measure. Dominion was given to *all* human beings, not only to the cognitively able. If we reflect on the idea of human dominion over the earth in the light of Paul's words in 1 Corinthians 3:16-17, this point becomes clearer:

> Don't you realize that *all of you together* are the temple of God and that the Spirit of God lives in you? (italics added)

Paul highlights the fact that it is as Christians come together as a single body with different talents and gifts that we become God's temple and the Holy Spirit is able to live within us. *Together we are made holy.* In like manner, dominion occurs when human beings, created by God and inspired with God's *nephesh*, come together and recognize their responsibility to care for creation and for one another. Such care includes but is not defined by human intellect and reason. Accordingly, *all* human beings, including those with cognitive disabilities, have a contribution to make to the practice of dominion.

But what might we mean by dominion? According to the ethicist Joseph Sittler,

> the word "dominion" is a direct English effort to translate the Latin. In English "dominion" suggests domination, but that is an incorrect trans-

lation. The Hebrew statement is "and God said you are to exercise *care* over the earth and hold it in its proper place."[29] (italics added)

Thus, according to this reinterpretation of the word "dominion," humanity has been given the vocation of caring for the earth. Brueggemann makes the point in this way:

> Human persons are authorized to "have dominion" over all of creation, but that dominion, given the verbs of Gen. 2:15, is to "till" *('bd)* and "keep" *(shmr)* the earth. The verbs suggest not exploitative, self-aggrandizing use of the earth, but gentle care for and enhancement of the earth and all its creatures. In this regard the mandate of obedience issues in stewardship, the wise care for the world and its creatures, who are entrusted to human administration.[30]

Such observations have obvious ecological implications. However, there is a deeper point that should be drawn out in relation to dementia. Care lies at the very heart of the vocation given to human beings by God. This raises two key points. First, the prerogative of care is not effective cognition or an ability to reason effectively. The prerogative of care is to love. To be human is to love like God and to be loved by God. Second, if care is fundamental to what it means to be human and to act faithfully toward God's creation, then to be a recipient of care is a profound and vital aspect of that process. God calls human beings to care for creation because God loves creation; human beings as part of creation are recipients of God's desire to love and care for them and to have them care for one another. To care for others and to receive care from others are crucial aspects of human beings' dominion over the earth. That being so, to be in a position where one can only be the recipient of care is not to be in a place that is degrading or indicative of a loss of dignity; it is in fact to be in a holy place, to be part of a fundamental aspect of the human vocation to care for creation. To receive care is a deep reflection of divine love for dependent human beings. To have severe dementia is not in any sense indicative of a loss of dignity or a diminishment of humanness. It is simply a time in a person's life where the human vocation to care for creation takes on a particular form. The holiness of the hu-

---

29. Joseph Sittler, quoted by John Patton in *Pastoral Care in Context: An Introduction to Pastoral Care* (Louisville: Westminster John Knox Press, 1993), p. 16.

30. Brueggemann, *An Unsettling God,* p. 68.

man body and the sanctity of the human person do not change because some forget who they are.

Spirituality and the Brain

It could of course be argued that while the brain may not be the only aspect of the human body that matters, in terms of our spiritual lives it remains quite fundamental. Is it not the case that many if not all of the things that we associate with spirituality and knowledge of God relate to experiences that clearly have neural correlates?[31] If those parts of the brain are damaged, one's perception of one's spirituality and the things that one usually uses to actualize one's spirituality are inevitably damaged. Doesn't this indicate that while embodiment might be important, the brain remains more important than other parts of the body? Such a question is, to an extent, understandable. Our spiritual lives — that is, how we experience God and the things that we use to enable communication with God — are clearly impacted by the state of our neurology. In his autobiography titled *My Journey into Alzheimer's Disease,* Robert Davis, a Presbyterian minister who had dementia, gives a sense of what this might feel like:

> My spiritual life was still most miserable. I could not read the Bible. I could not pray as I wanted because my emotions were dead and cut off. There was no feedback from God the Holy Spirit. As I tried to fall asleep, only blackness and misery came, misery so terrifying that I could not drop off to sleep. Nighttime was horrible. My mind could not rest and grow calm but instead raced relentlessly, thinking dreadful thoughts of despair. Invariably I lay there, terrified by a darkness that I could not understand.[32]

Davis gives us a sense of the way in which failing neurology can impact feelings of spirituality and the normal spiritual practices that we use to es-

31. This is certainly the argument behind the series of essays edited by Malcolm Jeeves titled *From Cells to Souls and Beyond: Changing Portraits of Human Nature* (Grand Rapids: Wm. B. Eerdmans, 2004). These essays wrestle with the deep connection between neurology and experienced spirituality within the general framework of non-reductive physicalism.

32. Robert Davis, *My Journey into Alzheimer's Disease: Helpful Insights for Family and Friends* (Carol Stream, Ill.: Tyndale House Publishers, 1989), p. 53.

tablish and stabilize our spiritual lives. There is no denying that damage to the brain has serious consequences in this regard.

Ray Anderson acknowledges the centrality of neurology for the manifestations of spirituality:

> Physicality sets limits to our personal existence and, at the same time, produces the phenomena we recognize as manifestations of the soul. In other words, there is no manifestation of the soul that is not produced through the brain even though the brain is not the sole effective cause. Therefore we should not be surprised and should indeed expect that the firing of selective brain cells affects what we might call spiritual impulses, attitudes, and actions.[33]

Anderson uses the term "soul" not in a dualistic sense, but rather as a descriptor of those aspects of the spiritual life — prayer, faith, hope, love, meditation — that are normally attributed to the soul. His point is that as embodied souls we are deeply influenced by our biological capacities, even when it comes to those impulses and actions that we have come to call spiritual. Reading Scripture, remembering passages, praying, contemplating God — all these things require our bodies — and, in particular, our brains — to be functioning in specific ways. Malfunctions in our neurology will inevitably have a deep impact on what we previously considered to be central to our spiritual lives. At a creaturely level, we shouldn't be surprised that many of the traditional manifestations of the soul have neurological correlates which are deeply impacted by the degenerative processes of dementia. Part of being human has to do with the fragility and neurological dependency of our spiritual lives. Since we are embodied souls, it could be no other way.

However, losing spiritual practices and experiences is not indicative of God's abandonment. We have already seen the way in which God is always with us as long as he continues to sustain us through God's *nephesh*. As long as we are alive, God's *nephesh* — our fundamental source of spiritual dynamism — remains. (Hence the significance of Steven Sabat's Self 1.) Dementia cannot de-spiritualize people because God is Spirit, and unless

---

33. Ray Anderson, in *Whatever Happened to the Soul? Scientific and Theological Portraits of Human Nature,* ed. Warren S. Brown, Nancey Murphy, and H. Newton Malony (Minneapolis: Fortress Press, 1998), p. 188.

God withdraws God's spirit from us, spirituality remains (that is, spirituality understood in terms of our connectedness with God). In those who are experiencing dementia, spirituality may take a different form than it had before, but it does not disappear along with their vanishing neurons. Our inherent holiness is not affected by neurological decline, even if our previous modes of articulating it change or become unavailable. The challenge is for those around persons with dementia to explore how best this holiness can be sustained in the midst of profound changes.

Spiritual Identity

The key, of course, is to recognize that our spiritual lives, along with the rest of our existence, are contingent and dependent. Contemporary approaches to spirituality have a tendency to focus on the actualization of the self as the primary criterion for authentic spirituality. If spirituality is self-actualization, and if the spiritual self no longer has the capacity for standard ways of developing, then failing neurology will inevitably be equated with failing spirituality. However, the essence of truly Christian spirituality is not *self*-actualization. At the heart of a genuinely Christian spirituality is God's approach to human beings. God's *nephesh* brings us into existence and sustains us in that existence. The Holy Spirit comes to us in the midst of that existence and acts to sustain our spiritual existence quite apart from our ability to articulate that experience. *It is the Spirit who sustains us in our spirituality and in our identity.*[34]

Anderson, reflecting on the issue of human identity and how it is affected by the inevitability of bodily change over time, notes,

> . . . spiritual self-identity, as used theologically and on biblical grounds, is contingent upon the Spirit of God both as its formation and its growth. The existence of brain cells is a necessary but insufficient condition for the expression of the life of the soul as personal spiritual being.[35]

Brain function is clearly an aspect of our spiritual development and identity formation, but our identity is wholly contingent on the movement of

34. Romans 8:27: "And he who searches our hearts knows the mind of the Spirit, because the Spirit intercedes for the saints in accordance with God's will" (NIV).
35. Anderson, in Brown et al., *Whatever Happened to the Soul?* p. 188.

the Spirit, who is the true sustainer.[36] Anderson pushes us toward an understanding of human identity as something that is both given and sustained by the Holy Spirit.[37] The Spirit forms and names the living soul, the *nephesh*-inspired body. The brain plays a part in this process of human development, but it is not definitive or determinative of it. It is God the Holy Spirit who determines who a person is; the brain as an aspect of the body simply participates in the movement of people toward that given goal. We do not actualize ourselves; rather, in some sense or another it appears that *we are told who we are*. This point will become clear and vital when later in the book we explore the nature of God's memory.

Self-identity, like the entirety of human existence, is wholly and radically contingent. Although at one level neurology may be central for aspects of experiencing our spiritual lives, at another level both our neurology and our spiritual lives are inevitably contingent on the Spirit of God. Anderson puts it this way:

> In a Christian anthropology, human nature is not defined ultimately by tracing humanity back to its origins, or by explaining humanity in terms of its existence under the conditions of sin. Rather, human nature is life experienced as a personal body/soul unity, inspired and empowered by the Spirit of God. Self-identity is both determined by the Spirit of God within each person and acquitted by the person through experience and interaction with the physical, social, and spiritual environ-

36. Psalm 104:30: *"When you send forth your spirit, they are created; and you renew the face of the ground"* (NRSV).

37. The context of Anderson's statement relates to the suggestion that contemporary neurology has shown that many of the traditional functions attributed to the soul can now be shown to be neurological in origin and evolutionary in intent. (For a deeper reflection on this area, see Nancey Murphy, *Bodies and Souls, or Spirited Bodies?* [Cambridge: Cambridge University Press, 2006], Chapter 1.) Anderson's general argument is that human beings do not have immortal souls but that as embodied souls they are and remain totally dependent on God for all things. In this respect, his argument is very much in line with the general thrust of this chapter. His concern is that if there is such a thing as an immortal soul, this would indicate some aspect of the human being that is not contingent on God for its existence. On this point I think Anderson is correct. In Matthew 10:28 (NIV), Jesus says, "Do not be afraid of those who kill the body but cannot kill the soul. Rather, be afraid of the one who can destroy both soul and body in hell." One reading of this would argue that Jesus is speaking in dualistic terms and that this would indicate a clear separation between body and soul. However, if it is the case that God can kill the soul, then it is clearly not immortal. My sense is that Jesus is working with an idea more like the perspective on *nephesh* that has been offered in this chapter.

ment. In this sense one could say that each person has an identity that is more or less dependent upon the subjective life of the self, as well as an identity that is projected upon the person from and by the Spirit of God. Even in our mother's womb, the psalmist says (Psalm 139:13-16), we are given personal identity by God.[38]

Thus human beings are seen to have an internal identity that is deeply influenced by our physiology and our social experiences (our "dustiness"), and a divine identity that is projected upon us in and through the Spirit of God (our animated and inspired self). Both aspects are significant, but they are not equal. One is fragile, uncertain, and contingent; the other is given and eternally sustained. Our neurology, then, does not contain all that is necessary for the complete outworking of the life of our embodied souls. Words from Wendell Berry quoted earlier ring true here: ". . . we and all other creatures live by a sanctity that is inexpressibly intimate. To every creature the gift of life is a portion of the breath and spirit of God."

This perspective pushes us to recognize the significance of the active presence of the Holy Spirit as it is at work in human beings, using but transcending the natural, creaturely possibilities of bodily existence. It is not accidental that Anderson in the quotation above highlights Psalm 139:13-16:

> . . . you created my inmost being;
> you knit me together in my mother's womb.
> I praise you because I am fearfully and wonderfully made;
> your works are wonderful,
> I know that full well.
> My frame was not hidden from you
> when I was made in the secret place.
> When I was woven together in the depths of the earth,
> your eyes saw my unformed body.
> All the days ordained for me
> were written in your book
> before one of them came to be.

Here we are given an insight into the workings of the Spirit in the formation and sustenance of human beings. It is God through the Spirit who

---

38. Anderson, in Brown et al., *Whatever Happened to the Soul?* p. 189.

knits together and forms all human beings. It is God who places the boundaries on our physical capacities. It is God who sustains and guides the whole of our lives. We are all limited, but even our limits have providential significance. Thus our identity — who we *really* are — is envisioned, created, and held by God. Accordingly, there is a significant dimension of what and who human beings are that isn't determined by our neurological or biographical history. This dimension is created, sustained, and nurtured by the Spirit of God quite apart from any particular capacities that we may or may not have. In this way we can see that there is something eternal (as opposed to immortal) and given within all human beings which is wholly contingent on the Spirit of God. This eternal, Spirit-given dimension of human beings cannot be understood apart from its embodiment, and its eternality cannot be grasped apart from God's work of sustaining and redeeming.

It is clear, then, that bodies matter. It is through the body of Christ that human beings find reconciliation and redemption.[39] It is through the body that the gospel is proclaimed, prisoners are visited, the sick are consoled, lovers love, and righteousness is seen to be done. It is through the body that dualisms are broken down and meaningful care is practiced. It is through our bodies that we are able to receive others even when our abilities to articulate that experience have faded. As we care for bodies, so we care for souls. As she watches her mother care for her father, Mary Jo Iozzio notices

> how when we tend in particular to the bodily needs of another, we demonstrate a very deep respect for the person and a faithful care for the material in which a person lives, and moves, and has being. . . . Care of another's body challenges the intellectualizing tendency of dualism and the elevation of spirit over matter. Any loss of bodily or mental control does not, by itself, remove or reduce the intrinsic dignity abiding in my father or everyone else.[40]

Bodies matter, and caring for bodies is as important as caring for minds. It is true that our Cartesian predilections may make such a statement feel

---

39. Ephesians 1:7: "In him we have redemption through his blood, the forgiveness of sins, in accordance with the riches of God's grace" (NIV).

40. Iozzio, "The Writing on the Wall," p. 50.

counter-intuitive, but that is simply indicative of our enculturation in a particular dualistic way of seeing persons.

Relationality

The issue of relationality has already emerged quite prominently in the previous reflections on contingency and embodiment. Human beings are creatures who are loved into existence and marked out as special by their Creator. At one level, human creatureliness makes human beings no different from other creatures. Phenomenologically, creatureliness is a state of being which is common to all creatures that have been given *nephesh* by the Creator. As Ray Anderson puts it, creatureliness is "an undifferentiated field upon which the occasion of the human occurs. To be a creature does not necessarily imply being a human, but being a human necessarily requires creatureliness."[41]

What makes human beings different from the rest of creation is revealed in the sixth-day experience of creation in which God begins to communicate with Adam and enters, for the first time, into a *personal* relationship with him. We have reflected on Genesis 1:28 previously. It is only necessary here to highlight the unique offer of relationship that it contains. The passage highlights God's desire to relate with human beings — only human beings, not any other part of creation — on a personal level. This is not speciesism; it is an aspect of God's sovereignty and providential action toward the world. It is this dynamic, relational movement of God toward Adam that marks him out (and, by implication, all of humanity) from the rest of creation. It is important to note that it is nothing internal to Adam that makes him special or worthy of love and respect. God simply chooses to make him special. God is clearly bound to and loves all of the creation to which he has given breath, but human beings are somehow different. We're just not given any explanation about why this is so.

It is crucial to repeat that absolutely none of this is Adam's doing. God initiates and God sustains the relationship. Even the catastrophe of the Fall and the relationally destructive power of human disobedience do not stop God from relating. Clearly, it would have been better if Adam had done what God had told him to do! Nevertheless, Adam's obedience was not the

41. Anderson, *On Being Human*, p. 21.

criterion for God's relational desire. Adam's status as a human being was defined as special for no other reason than that God chose it to be so. This primary, divinely given gift of relationship is an inalienable source of human identity,[42] value, worth, and dignity.

In Genesis 2:18 we discover that God's relationality finds an important counterpart in the desire of human beings to relate to each other: "The LORD God said, 'It is not good for the man to be alone. I will make a helper suitable for him.'" Despite the fullness and goodness of creation, and God's gift of loving relationship toward him, Adam was still in some sense incomplete. In response, God provided him with someone whom he could relate to and be with at a temporal level. The other creatures could not fulfill that function. Adam was called to care for them, but he could not love them in the way that he loved Eve. Only Eve, a fellow member of the human species who was both similar and dissimilar to himself, could fulfill his longing for human relationship. Thus Adam found his fulfillment[43] as a human being when God entered into personal relationship with him, and Adam immersed himself in a personal relationship with Eve. Without God, Adam could not exist; without Eve, Adam was in some sense incomplete. With Eve and with God, he found fulfillment.[44]

With this in mind, we can begin to understand the theological significance of the loneliness of people with dementia. Human beings have a deep and primal craving for relationships with God and with others. There is no reason to suggest that this desire, which is common to all human beings, is not just as common in people with dementia. However, people with dementia find themselves caught up in malignant processes that threaten

42. Genesis 3:9 — "Then the LORD God called to the man, and said to him, "Where are you?" — takes on an interesting poignancy with regard to this point. God doesn't name the other creatures; that is Adam's task. Naming Adam is the work and desire of God.

43. Adam found his fulfillment, as opposed to his identity, as a human being. Adam was already affirmed as fully human by God's initial entering into a personal relationship with him.

44. To draw upon the union of Adam and Eve as an example of human relationship is not to suggest that an intimate relationship is the only type of relationship necessary for fulfilled human existence. In his life, Jesus was engaged in a number of different types of relationships. What is being pointed toward here is the revelation implicit within the Genesis account, which suggests that human beings are fundamentally relational beings who require relationships at a number of levels for the fulfillment of their temporal existence. This desire to relate is a direct consequence of their being made in the image of a God who desires to relate.

to destroy both their relationships with God and with others. Not to have relationships is to enter into a state that God clearly says is "not good." Thus, relational isolation on a temporal level is a deeply spiritual and theological matter.

Loving Relationships in All Their Complexity

At the heart of human relationality is the desire to love and be loved. To be human is to be loved; to live humanly is to love. In his book *Faith, Hope, and Love*, Josef Pieper reflects on the nature of love. His answer to the question "What is the nature of love?" is helpful:

> In every conceivable case love signifies much the same as approval. This is first of all to be taken in the literal sense of the word's root: loving someone or something means finding him or her *probus*, the Latin word for "good." It is a way of turning to him or it and saying, *"It's good that you exist; it's good that you are in this world!"*[45]

Love is an act of engagement with another at a deep and personal level which states clearly in word and action that "I want you (or it) to exist! Loving is therefore a mode of willing."[46] The type of love that Pieper focuses our attention on is quite different from romantic love. Romantic love focuses on positive feelings, desires, and a longing to be with someone because you find them deeply attractive and compelling. Willful or intentional love is different. It requires determination, fidelity, and an intentional desire to be with the other and to continue to love them no matter what. Such love doesn't say, "Well, seeing as you're here, I'll put up with you." It states boldly that it wants the other to be here and, more than that, that it is *good* that he/she is here no matter what the circumstances. This is precisely the way in which God loves his creation, and it is precisely the way that human beings are called to love one another. The reason Jesus tells us to love our enemies is because not to love them is to behave in a way that is less than human. To hate the other — to suggest that it is not good that they are here and that you really wish that they didn't exist — is

45. Josef Pieper, *Faith, Hope, Love* (San Francisco: Ignatius Press, 1997), p. 164.
46. Josef Pieper, *Faith, Hope, Love*, p. 164.

to act in a way that denies the reality of love. To act in such a way is to act inhumanly. This is why malignant social psychology is so dangerous. It not only dehumanizes people with dementia; it also dehumanizes those who engage with those with dementia. Care for those with dementia that is truly person-centered in the ways described here is thus re-humanizing for all concerned.

Such intentional love is the kind of love we see God showing to his creation. God brings creation into existence as a loving act of his will. God looks at it and at humans and says, *"It's good that you exist; it's good that you are in this world."*[47] When creation rebels against God, God's intentional love persists. When human beings become amnesic about their nature and their roots, when they live lives which are intentionally loveless, God persists. When God is disappointed by what is happening, God's love still pushes onwards. To be human is to be loved persistently; to live humanly is to show persistent love toward others. Engaging in personal, loving relationships is not the product of moral obligation or choice; it is a matter of faithfulness. Learning to love people with dementia with all of the issues, disappointments, hurts, and joys that accompany such a calling brings into sharp focus our vocation as human beings: to willfully, intentionally love one another as God has loved us: "A new command I give you: Love one another. As I have loved you, so you must love one another" (John 13:34).

Of course, as we all know, love is inevitably complicated. It becomes even more complicated within the context of dementia, when personalities and behaviors can change and those whom we love can appear very different than they once did. To say "It's good that you exist; it's good that you are in this world" when the person you're claiming to love has changed so much that you hardly recognize his/her behavior or personality — this raises fundamental issues about the nature and the practice of love. My friend and colleague Anastasia Scrutton explored this matter in correspondence with me:

> There are . . . questions about there being a duty or command to love —
> is it really possible to choose to love? Or does the command to love just
> put a burden of guilt on to someone who is already suffering? And if we

---

47. Genesis 1:31: "Then God looked over all he had made, and he saw that it was very good! And evening passed and morning came, marking the sixth day" (NLT).

can't choose to love, what on earth are we doing when we make marriage vows? If it is possible to choose to love, aren't there situations in which it becomes more healthy and helpful to everyone involved to stop loving someone (to let the person go, or to escape an abusive partner), or to stop loving in a certain way?

These are important questions. We will pick up on some of the implications of such observations in the final chapter of this book.

The point here with regard to dementia is that as the condition continues, as a person's abilities to relate change and may even seem to disappear, so the ways of understanding and practicing love will inevitably change. However, these changed modes of love, as they work themselves out in the day-to-day routines of living with and sometimes struggling with people who have dementia, are no less authentic than the modes of love that we see more often. They're just different. As a carer or family member bears witness to the changes and struggles to love the person in the way that he/she did previously, it is necessary to recognize that love changes and that relationships change. The key thing is to begin to reflect on what this "new love" looks like and to recognize the diverse and innovative ways in which we can say to the person with dementia, "It's good that you exist; it's good that you are in this world." Within the context of dementia, love might look quite different than it usually does; but love nonetheless remains love, even if it changes its shape in confusing ways. Our task is to perceive, understand, and respond to the changes.

The Tragedy of Being Human

Finally, we cannot talk about creation, the nature of human existence, and the love of God without at the same time talking about the reality of human sin and fallenness. While the basis of creation is love, and the proper status of human beings is inevitably and thoroughly contingent, the limited freedom given to human beings has challenged the potency of love. The creation story informs us that we are creatures loved by God beyond measure, creatures whom God considers to be very good (Gen. 1:31). However, the necessity of recognizing our contingent state and the centrality of God's love was pushed aside by Adam, and it is not difficult to see similar resonances in our individualized and autonomy-driven cultures. In seeking autonomy, self-sovereignty, and God-like freedom and knowledge, human beings managed — and continue to manage — to alienate themselves from their one source of life and love, to reject the sustaining love of God. It is in rejecting the recognition of the absolute necessity of human obedience, dependency, and contingency that human beings find God's loving embrace toward them loosened — not because God loves them less, but because their desire to be loved becomes distracted by their sinful desire to be free.

The importance of recognizing the fallen nature of the world for understanding dementia emerges from how we read and understand the consequences of the Fall. One reading of the Genesis account suggests that human beings were created as immortal beings who, through the folly of the Fall, lost their immortality as the punishment inflicted on them by God. Within this reading, dementia can be perceived as a direct consequence of human disobedience and an unnatural consequence of God's punishment. Another interpretation of the account of the Fall is that human beings were always mortal beings.[48] They were always dependent on their life-giving, *nephesh*-filled relationship with God. They may well have lived forever, but only as a consequence of God's sustaining breath (eternal life as opposed to immortality). By choosing to turn away from their source of eternal sustenance, human beings encountered mortality, not as a potentiality, as it had been before, but now as a reality that impacted every aspect of their lives. According to this interpretation (the one we are using here), the human race *as a whole* now finds itself living mortally. We live in a world that has chosen to turn away from its primary relationship of love, and that turning away and turning inward has consequences that are manifested throughout creation. *Thus, there is no direct connection between dementia and sin.*

However tragic, such a perspective on mortality is in a strange way helpful for the development of a positive understanding of dementia and how dementia "sits" within God's creation. To be human is to be mortal, and mortality means that decay is inevitable. That being so, our humanness is not diminished by dementia or any other condition. Such conditions are simply part of what it means to be human beings who are living out their lives in a creation which is broken but in the process of being re-

---

48. See Thomas Aquinas, *Summa Theologica* (Raleigh, N.C.: Hayes Barton Press, 1925), p. 899.

deemed. When certain persons develop dementia, they do not move from being persons to being non-persons. Theologically, the suggestion that dementia destroys personhood makes no sense. It's like saying that if I get the flu, I will become a pencil! Change and decay in all of its forms is part of what it means to be human. To be human in a world that is not yet redeemed is to get old and to forget things.

Dementia, Humanness, and Life in All of Its Fullness

Throughout this chapter, a key proposition has been the suggestion that nothing exists apart from God's desire for it to exist. Strangely, this includes dementia. Wendell Berry makes an important point when he says,

> We will discover that God made not only the parts of Creation that we humans understand and approve, but all of it: "all things were made by him; and without him was not anything made that was made" (John 1:3). And so we must credit God with the making of biting and dangerous beasts, and disease-causing micro-organisms. That we may disapprove of these things does not mean that God is in error, or that the creator ceded some of the work of Creation to Satan; it means that we are deficient in wholeness, harmony, and understanding — that is, we are "fallen."[49]

To take up Berry's point is not to suggest that God is indifferent to the suffering that dementia brings. It is, however, to emphasize that dementia has meaning. It is not punishment; it is not the work of the devil. It is a mystery which is firmly rooted in God's creative and redemptive actions in and for the world. It may not be understandable. It may make us angry, distressed, even outraged. But it is not without meaning. In this sense, people with dementia are part of the flux of fallen humanity, but their condition does not alter their meaningfulness and their lovableness. Put slightly more poignantly, despite the fallenness of our condition, everything we have and everyone we know exists because of God and is deeply loved by God. This is the beginning point for understanding the importance of people with dementia: *They are loved.* It is true that the practices of love

49. Berry, *The Art of the Commonplace*, p. 307.

that surround people with dementia are difficult and complex. Nevertheless, this fundamental truth remains irrevocable. Human beings are both wanted and loved irrespective of their physical or psychological condition. It is not any capacity within them that gives them value. Nor is it the value that those around them bestow upon them (a value that could be rescinded at any moment). Human beings' value and their identity are held and assured by the God who created them, who inspired them with God's *nephesh*, who sustains them in the power of the Holy Spirit, and who continues to offer the gift of life and relationship to all of humanity. It is this powerful counter-story that has the potential to provide a firm foundation for dementia care that is authentically person-centered and truly faithful.

8. Living in the Memories of God: Memory and Divine Embrace

I will not forget you! See, I have engraved you on the palms of my hands.

ISAIAH 49:15-16

God is not unjust; he will not forget your work and the love you have shown him as you have helped his people and continue to help them.

HEBREWS 6:10

Thus far I have presented an argument indicating that there is nothing about dementia that can destroy the personhood or humanness of the individual with dementia, nor is there anything that can taint a person's unending lovableness. This is not to try to romanticize dementia; it is simply to offer a different description that will frame it in such a way that we can see people as people and recognize that dementia is but another example of the limitedness and mortality of the human condition. In this way we have retaken some of the territory that rightly belongs to theology and pastoral care. As our horizons have been expanded, so also have our options broadened. Our redescription of dementia, personhood, and humanness brings us to an important issue in relation to dementia: the issue of memory.

Previously I described the exploration of dementia as a journey. There is a real sense in which the experience of dementia itself can be viewed as a journey — that is, a profound movement from one way of being in the world to a quite different way of encountering one's self and others. Each step along that journey brings with it different needs, opportunities, and challenges. In this chapter and the next we will focus our attention on the later stages of the journey, on that time in the process of moving into dementia when people begin to lose certain things that previously they assumed to be central for their sense of identity, and primary among these things are their memories. It is the loss of memory that is perhaps the most feared aspect of dementia. Who are we when we have forgotten ourselves and those whom we once loved? Who are we before God when we have forgotten who God is? For many people, the idea of losing their memory evokes a deep fear of losing themselves. Not to remember is to cease to exist.

The Fear of Dementia

Dementia is more feared than cancer. A recent British YouGov poll of two thousand people in the United Kingdom (carried out on behalf of Alzheimer's Research UK) yielded these results:

- Thirty-one percent of respondents fear dementia the most, with 27 percent fearing cancer the most, and 18 percent fearing death the most.
- Dementia fears extend to all ages. Over half (52 percent) of UK adults aged 30 to 50 primarily fear that their parents will develop dementia, compared to 42 percent who are most afraid of cancer, and 33 percent who are most afraid of heart attacks.
- Among retirees, 34 percent worry about health the most — more than other issues such as money (33 percent). When asked specifically which conditions they worry about, 52 percent said dementia, 33 percent said cancer, and 30 percent said stroke.

Interestingly, when people were asked what forms of illness they were *concerned* about, as opposed to afraid of, cancer came to the fore. Among the respondents, 35 percent said cancer was their biggest concern; 24 percent named dementia.[1] *Cancer evokes concern; dementia evokes fear.* At the heart

1. Alzheimer's Research UK, "Alzheimer's Research UK Launches as Public Dementia

of people's fears is the fear of losing their memory, and in so doing losing themselves.

For those who believe in a different story than the one told in the previous chapter, the experience of advanced dementia seems like the end of everything — the end of identity, the end of humanness. Almost all of the things that liberal cultures assume to be valuable in a human being appear to be taken away from the person in the latter stages of dementia. If losing one's memory and one's ability to reason and respond at an intellectual level means losing one's humanness, then who wouldn't be afraid? Isn't an illness that seems to bring about death before death actually occurs worthy of fear? The fear of dementia is closely tied to our cultural worldview.

Tragedy and Possibility

Within the church, there are reasons to be hopeful. However, the bottom line is that all of us who claim to be participants in God's church are also participants in our culture. Often we fear precisely the same things that others in our culture do for precisely the same reasons. When those fears are transferred uncritically into our theology and practice, things become very difficult. In an ecclesial culture where remembering the acts of God and proclaiming the name of Jesus are often assumed to be central to a person's salvation, a loss which prevents one from engaging in such intellectually oriented propositional spiritual activities creates dissonance and uncertainty. This might not always be formally articulated, but it often runs like a silent undertow through the framing of and the responses to many experiences of advanced dementia. The deep forgetfulness of dementia and the often profound changes to personality and perceived identity that accompany it raise fundamental theological questions: "Is my mother really saved, even though she has forgotten Jesus?" "Who will she be in heaven if she has changed so drastically in the present?" "What does it mean to love God when you have forgotten who God is?" "What does it mean to be 'you' when 'you' no longer know who 'you' are?" "If our hope lies in the resurrection, which 'you' will be resurrected?" Such theological questions have crucial practical significance. How we articulate and an-

Fears Spiral"; access at: http://www.alzheimersresearchuk.org/news-detail/10183/Alzheimers -Research-UK-launch/.

swer them will determine how we conceptualize, understand, and respond to people with dementia.

In advanced dementia, a person's memory problems become severe, and dependence on others begins to increase to the extent that the person becomes totally dependent on others for most if not all of his/her needs. It is at this stage of a person's experience that many of the difficult philosophical, theological, and practical questions that we have looked at thus far come into sharp focus. To focus on advanced dementia is not to suggest that other places along the journey are less important. The fear following diagnosis, the steady decline and the gradual loss of memory, the feeling that one is losing everything that one loves and feels is worthwhile — these are terrible experiences for those with dementia and for those who love them and desire to offer care and support. As we will see in the final chapter, dementia is a special kind of affliction. Nevertheless, the experiences at the beginning of the journey into dementia (particularly if it is a progressive form such as Alzheimer's disease) are inevitably shaped not only by what is happening at the moment, but also by the fear and uncertainty of what will happen in the future.

At the beginning of this book I said that I hope that I will be loved and cared for just for who I am, even if who I am is difficult for me and for others. In this chapter and the next, we will begin to see what such a desire might actually look like. My hope is that by focusing on the later stages of the journey, it will make the traveling a little easier for those who are just beginning. The picture that will be painted should not be viewed as idealistic or romantic. I acknowledge without equivocation that dementia is an extremely difficult condition to live with, both for sufferers and for those who care for them. I use the term "suffering" quite deliberately. As we will see in the final chapter of this book, suffering is a key dimension of the experience of dementia for those who bear the weight of the condition and for those who care for them. Dementia is not a romantic disease. Nevertheless, it need not be defined only as suffering. There is room for hope.

Dementia: A Problem of Memory?

One of the most prominent features of dementia is the way in which it takes away people's memories. The standard story of dementia and its relationship with memory goes something like this. Dementia is a condition that is marked by, among other things, a profound loss of memory caused by damage to the particular areas of the brain that are responsible for memory. Because as human beings our memories are crucial to our sense of self, major memory loss inevitably leads to a crisis or even a loss of identity. If we can't remember who we are, how can we know who we are? How can we be "ourselves" when we have no idea who we are? In this understanding, *we are our memories*. The filmmaker Luis Buñuel clearly believes this:

> You have to begin to lose your memory, if only in bits and pieces, to realize that memory is what makes our lives. Life without memory is no life at all, just as an intelligence without the possibility of expression is not really an intelligence. Our memory is our coherence, our reason, our feeling, even our action. Without it, we are nothing.[2]

Buñuel's statement seems quite logical and probably represents some of the thinking that lies behind the results of the YouGov poll mentioned previously. However, Buñuel's statement that "Life without memory is no life at all" begs the question: *How does he know?* Since he has never had the experience, it is difficult to know on what basis he would come to such a firm conclusion. By definition, none of us can express what it is like to live without memory. But might not life without memory be quite different from what we anticipate it to be? Presumably, Buñuel is projecting what he imagines it would be like to have no memory. However, projection and imagination are not always accurate representations of actual experience. What we find here, as we found in our discussions of issues of personhood, are projections, presuppositions, and assumptions masquerading as facts.

Buñuel's perspective is probably understandable in the light of society's general perceptions about the nature of the self and self-identity and the general fears that surround dementia. Surprisingly similar thinking is reflected in David Keck's theological account of memory and selfhood. He describes Alzheimer's disease as "deconstruction incarnate":

> It becomes possible to say that Alzheimer's disease represents deconstruction incarnate. The instability of meaning and free play of signifiers which deconstructionists enjoy talking about become manifest most

---

2. Luis Buñuel, in Joseph Ledoux, *Synaptic Self: How Our Brains Become Who We Are* (New York: Viking Press, 2002), p. 97.

clearly in an Alzheimer's patient. Particularly in the latter stages, the slipperiness of a patient's language becomes apparent.[3]

For Keck, the idea of deconstruction seems to relate to the slipping away of the structures of meaning that sustain persons with dementia as the persons they previously were. As language slips away, so do persons as they were previously known.[4] At the heart of this deconstructive process is the loss of memory. Keck asserts,

> It is impossible to distinguish between ourselves and our memories. . . . *We are our memories,* and without them we have but a physical resemblance to that person we each suppose ourselves to be. . . . The apparent dissolution of the mnemonic capacities . . . raises most serious and profound questions about human existence.[5]

Like Buñuel, Keck seems to assume that human beings very much *are* their memories.

The perspective of Buñuel and Keck at first seems to make some sense. It seems "natural" to associate "ourselves" — what we are as unique, self-aware individuals — with what we can remember about "our selves." How-

---

3. David Keck, *Forgetting Whose We Are: Alzheimer's Disease and the Love of God* (Nashville: Abingdon Press, 1996), p. 32.

4. Such a position is in stark contrast to the findings of Steven Sabat in the various writings of his that we have looked at thus far. Key to his position is the suggestion that people with dementia are semiotic subjects — that is, people whose behavior is driven by meaning: "Many people with AD in the moderate to severe stages of the disease are semiotic subjects whose selfhood may be intact despite deficits in certain cognitive abilities as revealed by standard neuropsychological tests. Although people with AD may have problems with (i) aspects of language, such as organizing syntactically correct sentences; (ii) organizing sequences of movement; (iii) performing rudimentary calculations; and (iv) recalling recent events from memory, many retain their selfhood and act on the basis of the meaning that situations hold for them." See Steven R. Sabat, "Capacity for Decision-making in Alzheimer's Disease: Selfhood, Positioning, and Semiotic People," *Australian and New Zealand Journal of Psychiatry* 39 (2005): 1030-1035; quotation on 1030-1031. Rather than perceiving challenges in the person's linguistic abilities as a slippage in personhood or humanness, it would be better to see them as a movement from a mode of communication within which the linguistically competent are comfortable to a context where interpretation and understanding need to be recalibrated in line with the changing expression. The point is that meaning remains even if the expression of that meaning becomes difficult and complicated.

5. Keck, *Forgetting Whose We Are*, p. 43; italics added.

ever, as Martin Buber and Tom Kitwood have made very clear, the distance you stand from the object of your interest matters. Assumptions about the centrality of memory for the self become deeply problematic from the perspective of people experiencing dementia. Christine Bryden, a woman going through the experience of pre-senile dementia, makes this point well:

> Dementia has been called the "theological disease" by David Keck, who cared for his mother with Alzheimer's disease. There is prolonged mental deterioration, and no presumption of the existence of a cognitive person theologically. He says that the "loss of memory entails a loss of self" and the apparent disintegration of a human being. Perhaps Alzheimer's patients can remind us that death and loss of control belong at the heart of theological reflection. David Keck's views shock me as a person with dementia in the early stages. Can I truly regard dementia as "deconstruction incarnate," "disintegrative, non-redemptive . . . amoral . . . challenging theologically"? Certainly I challenge the view of Alzheimer's Disease International that the "mind is absent and [the] body an empty shell." The question is, where does this journey begin, and at what stage can you deny me my selfhood and my spirituality?[6]

If the medical model of dementia is difficult for people with dementia, so also — and for oddly similar reasons — are certain theological/philosophical formulations of their experiences. Bryden's concern regarding Keck's proposition is a powerful reminder that clever theological language and academic conceptualizations of human experiences, even when intended for compassionate ends, may not look quite so clever or compassionate when they're read by people who are experiencing "the concept." Such malignant spiritual positioning is inevitably unhelpful and destructive. This is another good reason for ensuring that theology begins in the right places.

For Bryden, the statement that "life without memory is no life at all" is simply wrong — it's not how she sees things:

> Is cognition the only measure of our presence amongst you as spiritual beings? Certainly my capacity for accurate communication of thought

---

6. Christine Bryden and Elizabeth MacKinlay, "Dementia: A Spiritual Journey Towards the Divine: A Personal View of Dementia," *Journal of Religious Gerontology* 13, issue 3 & 4 (2003): 69-75; quotation on 71. The interior quotation is from *Alzheimer's Disease International*, 2002; access at http://www.alz.co.uk/.

is diminishing daily. It is difficult to find the words for the pictures in my head to communicate with you. Does this mean my mind is absent? Even if these pictures may themselves one day fade, is my soul connected with this failing cognition? I do not believe this is so. I might have difficulty feeling the presence of God, or being able to speak the words of a prayer in my mind, but I can commune without words. As my cognition fades, my spirituality can flourish as an important source of identity. As I lose an identity in the world around me, which is so anxious to define me by what I do and say, rather than who I am, I can seek an identity by simply being me, a person created in the image of God. My spiritual self is reflected in the divine and given meaning as a transcendent being.[7]

Bryden pleads with her readers to recognize that there is more to being human than memory alone. The changes in her life may be profound, but the key for her is to find new ways of encountering God when the old ways have faded and disappeared:

I believe that I am much more than just my brain structure and function, which is declining daily. My creation in the divine image is as a soul capable of love, sacrifice, and hope, not as a perfect human being, in mind or body. I want you to relate to me in that way, seeing me as God sees me. I am confident that even if the continuing damage to my temporal lobe might diminish the intensity of my God-experience, there will be other ways in which I can maintain my relationship with God.[8]

Will she know God when she can no longer remember? She answers the question this way:

David Keck reflected on the importance of the memory of God's past deeds to the Israelites, and yet Christian confessions and creeds start with the words "I believe," not "I remember." Will I know God if I can no longer remember? In my book, I write "As I unfold before God, as this disease unwraps me, opens up the treasures of what lies within my multifold personality, I can feel safe as each layer is gently opened out. God's everlasting

---

7. Bryden and MacKinlay, "Dementia," p. 72.
8. Bryden and MacKinlay, "Dementia," p. 72.

arms will be beneath me, upholding me." I will trust in God, who will hold me safe in his memory, until that glorious day of Resurrection, when each facet of my personality can be expressed to the full.[9]

Such a redescription of the experience of dementia couldn't be further away from the idea of "deconstruction incarnate" or "memory is all that we are." Bryden recognizes that her memory and her cognitive faculties are slipping away. But she frames that slippage quite differently. She trusts that God will remember her. When her own memory has gone, her true self will continue to exist and ultimately even flourish in the Resurrection. Who she is is held and sustained within the memories of God. That is where she finds her hope and her strength.

Being Remembered by God

I recently had a chance conversation with Sarah Coakley, my friend and colleague who teaches theology at the University of Cambridge in England. When I mentioned that I was working on a book about dementia, she told me this story:

> When I was training for the priesthood, I was allocated to a dreadful, atypical psychotic Alzheimer's ward in a . . . hospital — frankly, the conditions were hideously abusive. I subsequently read various books and articles on the theological dimensions of dementia but wasn't very satisfied. Mainly on the wards I used my portable tape-recorder and a variety of CDs which could evoke the younger lives of the people there. But what I found was that those actively "trained" in music earlier in life were the ones most able to be assisted by musical recall: it made me wonder about the neurophysiology of musical training, specifically, and its capacity to endure after language fails. (My own mother-in-law, dying of Alzheimer's in a home, could not only still play hymns on the piano and sing them, but transpose them into various keys — the memory was somehow encoded in her hands. This was true long after she

---

9. Bryden and MacKinlay, "Dementia," p. 72. The interior quotation comes from Bryden, *Dancing with Dementia: My Story of Living Positively with Dementia* (London: Jessica Kingsley Publishers, 2005), p. 153.

had ceased to be able to form sentences.) Do you know the wonderful Anglo-Catholic hymn for Maundy Thursday: "According to Thy Gracious Word"? If not, look it up in the English Hymnal. All the verses but the last focus on our remembering Jesus because of his command to remember him Eucharistically; but the last verse lays the task of remembering back with God, on our behalf. I think that hymn was more important for me on that terrible ward than any of the other things that I read at the time.

When I looked up the hymn, I saw what she meant:

> According to Thy gracious word,
> In meek humility,
> This will I do, my dying Lord:
> I will remember Thee.
> Thy body, broken for my sake,
> My bread from Heaven shall be;
> The testamental cup I take,
> And thus remember Thee.
> Gethsemane can I forget?
> Or there Thy conflict see,
> Thine agony, and bloody sweat,
> And not remember Thee?
> When to the cross I turn mine eyes,
> And rest on Calvary,
> O Lamb of God, my sacrifice,
> I must remember Thee;
> Remember Thee, and all Thy pains
> And all Thy love to me;
> Yea, while a breath, a pulse remains,
> Will I remember Thee.
> And when these failing lips grow dumb
> And mind and memory flee,
> When Thou shalt in Thy kingdom come,
> Jesus, remember me.

There is something very powerful about the image of my friend Sarah ministering in the midst of deeply forgetful people who have clearly been forgotten, and discovering a key that unlocked aspects of their memories that were otherwise inaccessible. We will return to explore the significance of music later on. For now we need to recognize something very powerful in the hymn that calls us to remember while we can, but to trust that God will remember for us when we cannot.

The idea of being remembered by God is a frequent theme within pastoral literature, and while not uncontested,[10] it has potential for helping us to understand some vital but often hidden aspects of memory loss in dementia. The following story opens up this way of thinking quite helpfully:

> An elderly lady suffering from dementia paced the corridors of the nursing home restlessly — repeating over and over just one word. The staff were disconcerted, but no one seemed quite sure how to calm her and put her mind at rest. In fact they were at a loss to understand the reason for her distress. The word she repeated over and over again was "God" — and that was all she said. One day a nurse got alongside her and walked with her up and down the corridors until eventually in a flash of inspiration she asked the lady, "Are you afraid that you will forget God?" "Yes, Yes!" she replied emphatically. The nurse was then able to say to her, "You know even if you should forget God, He will not forget you. He has promised that." For this lady who was forgetting many things, and was aware of it, that assurance was what she needed to hear. She immediately became more peaceful, and that particular behavior ceased. She was responding positively to care which extended beyond the needs of body and mind — care of the human spirit.[11]

This story is deeply moving. Ending your days in a situation where people don't understand the deepest things that are important to you is a frightening thought. It is both touching and disturbing to know that what has always been central to your life — God — is slipping away and that you feel that you can express your distress only through bodily movements which are open to multiple interpretations. The key that unlocked this woman's

10. Peter Kevern, "Sharing the Mind of Christ: Preliminary Thoughts on Dementia and the Cross," *New Blackfriars* 91, no. 1034 (2009): 408-22.

11. Margaret G. Hutchison, "Unity and Diversity in Spiritual Care," paper originally presented at the Sydney University Nursing Society First Annual Conference for Undergraduate Nursing Students in NSW, September 1997. Access at: http://members.tripod.com/marg_hutchison/nurse-4.html.

distress came from someone who saw beyond the "obvious" interpretation of her situation based on the normal associations that come with her diagnosis, and asked a simple but profound question: "Are you afraid that you will forget God?" The deep fear of forgetting is overcome by the deeper promise of being remembered. Like the plea made by the thief who hung on the cross beside Jesus ("Remember me when you come into your kingdom"; Luke 23:42), the woman's walking incessantly up and down the ward was a way of seeking the same thing. The response came in a compassionate act of spiritual listening which reinforced God's promise: "Never will I leave you; never will I forsake you" (Heb. 13:5). When the woman was assured that she would be remembered by God, she became peaceful.

Intuitively we feel that there is something very important going on here. "I think; therefore I am" is replaced with "We are because God sustains us in God's memory." Our hope lies in the fact that we are living in the memories of God. As long as God remembers us, who we are will remain: "I will not forget you. See, I have engraved you on the palms of my hands" (Isa. 49:15-16). In some ways this resonates with Kitwood's suggestion that we are sustained and identified as persons through our relationships with others — except that here, it is God who is ultimately responsible for holding onto us and remembering us well. Kitwood wants carers to engage in memorial practices, but without the transcendent, the process is incomplete, as the quotation below suggests:

> Caregivers can be not only givers of care but bestowers of a kind of immortality by recalling for others around them what the person with Alzheimer's disease no longer can recall in order to strengthen the remembering of that person and to keep his or her role in the story of the community alive in the corporate memory . . .[12]

But we are not just what others remember about us. When others forget us, God always remembers. Stephen Sapp puts it this way:

> . . . It is also possible to speak of God's memory in this light. Whether the individual remembers, or even when the community remembers for the individual, the Western religious tradition certainly affirms that

12. Stephen Sapp, "Living with Alzheimer's: Body, Soul, and the Remembering Community," *Christian Century* 115, no. 2 (1998): 54-60; quotation on 60.

God remembers. Some comfort, therefore, can be found in the fact that God's memory is unfailing, even if that of any given human being is defective or even totally lost. God never forgets.[13]

We can, and should, mourn our personal loss of memory. But if God remembers us, we are provided with a source of deep and enduring hope. *We are not what we remember; we are remembered.* Memory is first and foremost something that is *done for us,* rather than something we achieve on our own.

The Problem with God's Memory

Useful and comforting as the idea of the memory of God may be in providing a hopeful future for people with profound memory loss, not all are convinced that such an approach can actually do the job it claims to do. Peter Kevern, following the thinking of Malcolm Goldsmith, presents a typology of four main models that theologians have used to conceptualize the role of memory in our understanding of dementia:

1. A "Traditional/historical model," in which memory is central [to] placing us in a shared tradition, and which therefore progressively excludes those whose memory is vanishing.
2. An "Open to God" model, which envisages each individual as being moved by the Spirit into an ever-richer enjoyment of God's fellowship, but which runs counter to the experience of those who are dementing.
3. A "Growth" model, which envisages the individual as continuously journeying toward full spiritual maturity; again, this seems counter to the experienced decline and diminishment attendant on dementia.
4. A "Remembered by God" model, which he [Goldsmith] takes to be "the only theological model which seems to encapsulate the 'Good News' for the person with dementia," stressing that "we are remembered by God long before and long after we make any recognizable response to God. We are unconditionally accepted by God, and we are unconditionally acceptable to God."[14]

13. Sapp, "Living with Alzheimer's," p. 60.
14. Malcolm Goldsmith, "Dementia: A Challenge to Christian Theology and Pastoral

Kevern acknowledges that the "remembered by God" approach has some pastoral utility. However, on deeper reflection he finds reason to view it with some concern:

> This simplicity may be the reason why the slogan "God Never Forgets" seems to crop up repeatedly in the literature.[15] Nevertheless, the model has its limitations both as a theological and a pastoral strategy. In the first place, there is a tendency to denial of the depth of the questions raised (since, although the person forgets, God always remembers) and a profound pessimism (in which dementia is understood only as loss and as a step towards death). There is no continuing "presence" of God in dementia, but only the eschatological and somewhat vague hope that God will make everything all right in the end. Amidst the abandonments and bereavements of dementia, the person is abandoned by and bereaved of the Living God.[16]

Kevern's concern is that in the way that the idea of being remembered by God is framed in some of the literature, there is a tendency to see that remembrance as prospective and primarily eschatological in nature. He perceives that the assumption tends to be that God *will* remember in the future, rather than that God *does* remember in the present. For now, God remains absent and impassive in a sense, waiting for the time when God's memory will come to fulfillment. In the interim, persons with dementia are left alone in their suffering and concern. They can have hope that God isn't going to forget them, but they have little to give them hope that God is with them in the present, sharing in their sufferings. Kevern concludes that the idea of being remembered by God costs more theologically than it is worth:

> We may conclude, therefore, that the proclamation of a God who always remembers, however comforting, comes at too high a theological cost: it

---

Care," in *Spirituality and Ageing,* ed. Albert Jewell (London: Jessica Kingsley Publishers, 1999), pp. 125-35, 129-31, adapted in Peter Kevern, "What Sort of a God Is to Be Found in Dementia?" *Theology* 113, no. 873 (May 2010): 174-82; quotation on 176.

15. See, for example, James W. Ellor, "Celebrating the Human Spirit," in *God Never Forgets: Faith, Hope, and Alzheimer's Disease,* ed. Donald K. McKim (Louisville: Westminster John Knox Press, 1998), p. 3, and in the same volume, Denise Dombkowski Hopkins, "Failing Brain, Faithful God," p. 37.

16. Kevern, "What Sort of a God Is to Be Found in Dementia?" p. 176.

leaves us alone in our struggle with the terrifying contingency and flux of dementia, maintaining hope only in a God who will somehow be there at the end of it all. It places God on the "outside" of the process of change and deterioration, uninvolved in the messy business of living and dying in dementia; waiting at the door, as it were, for it all to be over and the victim to be released into death.[17]

Kevern may have a point with regard to those who develop the idea of God remembering from an understanding of God that perceives God as distant and impassable.[18] Even in the more developed theological work on dementia, there is a tendency to hold onto God as, to quote Kevern again, "uncompromisingly impassable and sovereign, outside of and above the situation, not within it." If we formulate our hope for people with dementia as existing only in the future, then there is indeed a danger that we implicitly abandon them in the present. If the memory of God sustains hope only for a possible future without being active in the present, it remains hopeful, but not necessarily very helpful. Kevern goes on to develop an image of God as passable and deeply involved with the suffering of creation, a perspective which is clearly an advance on models of remembering based on God's future presence.

Kevern is correct with regard to the dangers of creating an image of God which is distant and impassable. The scriptural account of God is of a person who is deeply involved with creation and who suffers with the world rather than distancing God's self from the world. The incarnation,

---

17. Kevern, "What Sort of a God Is to Be Found in Dementia?" p. 177.

18. Kevern notes, "These limitations [of the "remembering God" approach] stand out particularly starkly in David Keck's work, *Forgetting Whose We Are: Alzheimer's Disease and the Love of God,* since this represents by far the most developed and extensive theological exploration of dementia currently in print. It is a rich book, arising out of his experience of his own mother's dementia, reflected on from a broadly postliberal perspective underpinned by a Barthian theology of the Word. Thus, it treats God's sovereignty as 'non-negotiable,' focuses on the cross, and takes what it understands to be the traditional body of church doctrine as a given. Although Keck speaks of the suffering Christ, it is as an offering of human suffering to God and not a revelation of a compassionate God. His Christ offers us an 'Alzheimer's hermeneutic' in which the displacement of self entailed in caring for someone with Alzheimer's prepares one for the same displacement of self in listening for the Word of God. Keck's God is a loving and responsive one, waiting for our openness to the Spirit, but in the final analysis uncompromisingly impassable and sovereign, outside of and above the situation, not within it." See Kevern, "What Sort of a God Is to Be Found in Dementia?" p. 176.

cross, and resurrection of Jesus indicate strongly that God is deeply implicated in both the suffering and the joy of human existence and the world. As Dietrich Bonhoeffer put it, "Only the suffering God can help."[19] If God is perceived as distant and impassive, God's memory can really function only in the future, as God's involvement in the present is limited to God's passive role as sustainer, with suffering belonging only to the experience of God's creation. It is difficult to equate such an image with the suggestion that "God is love" (1 John 4:8). Love that truly loves is inevitably open to suffering and rejection. Any theological framework that omits this crucial dynamic will fall short of perceiving the glory of God's love, and in so doing will make it possible for God to be seen as abandoning people with dementia in the present.

Still, I remain unconvinced that Kevern's quite valid concern transfers in a global fashion across the breadth of possibilities that underlie the idea that we are held and sustained by the memory of God. The problem with Kevern's position is his suggestion that the idea of being remembered by God *necessarily* places God outside of the situation of people with dementia. It may be true that some approaches do this, but those who do are overlooking the significance of Jesus' words in Matthew 28:20: "And surely I will be with you always, to the very end of the age." Jesus doesn't say that he will be with his people only or even primarily at some point in the future. His clear statement is that he will be with his people now as well as in the future. What is true of Jesus, who is God, will necessarily be true of God and God's memory. If God is truly with us, then God's memory cannot simply be something that becomes active in or is even primarily oriented toward the future. God may remember the future (an apparent paradox that will become clearer when we look at the nature of time), but God remembers the past and the future in the present. The point is that to reject the idea of God's remembering on the grounds that it ignores the present is to misunderstand the nature of memory in general and God's memory in particular. To misunderstand the nature and purpose of God's memory is to misunderstand the practices of God in the lives of people with dementia.

19. Dietrich Bonhoeffer, *Letters and Papers from Prison*, ed. Eberhard Bethge, trans. Reginald H. Fuller (London: Macmillan, 1953), p. 361.

What Does It Mean to Remember?

To understand the importance of God's memory for our understanding of dementia, we need to begin by reflecting on what it actually means to remember anything at all. Of course, human memory is not the same as God's memory. Nevertheless, in order to understand something of God's memory, we need to understand the way in which human memory functions. It is only as we come to understand the strangeness and complexity of human memory that we can understand the significance of being remembered by God.

On the surface, human memory seems to be quite straightforward. It has to do with the ways in which the brain captures, records, processes, and retains information that it gathers through experience. When we see or experience something, the brain records it, and we can "play it back" later when the memory is required. Short-term memory refers to the experiences and information that we have encountered in our recent experiences. Long-term memory refers to things that have occurred in the more distant past. The past informs our sense of the present, the present informs our understandings of the past, and the past and the present together inform our perceptions of what the future might look like. It is in the constant, ongoing movement between our short-term and our long-term memories that we are able to orient ourselves in ways that allow us to gain a sense of continuity and flow through time.

This is the kind of understanding of memory that we encounter in St. Augustine's formulation of memory in Book 10 of his *Confessions*. For Augustine, memory is basically an archive of images and experiences that a person accumulates over time. It is "like a great field or a spacious palace," a "storehouse for countless images."[20] This storehouse is a private place that resides within the individual: "an inner place."[21] Augustine also sees memory as a capacity that humans use to store and retrieve information. He also equates memory with the mind and the self:

> But the mind and the memory are one and the same. We even call the memory the mind, for when we tell another to remember something we say "See that you bear this in mind," and when we forget something we

20. St. Augustine, *Confessions,* trans. R. S. Pine-Coffin (London: Penguin Classics, 2002), X.8.
21. St. Augustine, *Confessions,* X.9.

say "It was not in my mind," or "It slipped my mind." . . . Yet I do not understand the power of memory that is in myself, although without it I could not even speak of myself. . . . The power of memory is great, O Lord. It is awe-inspiring in its profound and incalculable complexity. Yet it is my mind: it is my self.[22]

In this understanding, memory is a cognitive and intellectual capacity that resides purely within the mind of an individual. In fact, memory is mind, and inevitably, memory is also the self. Our essential selves, our personal identities are tied to what we can remember. If this is the case, then the suggestion that "Life without memory is no life at all" makes perfect sense. But this isn't the way in which memory functions.

What Do We Actually Remember?

Memory is much more complex than a simple see-record-store-playback model. It is more than simply "retrieving different kinds of information: there is also a conviction that this episode is part of your personal history, related to events that came before and have occurred since."[23] Memory is the product of both biography and history. We don't simply recall things in an unedited, uninterpreted manner. We read our memories through our emotions and our ongoing biographies. The information that we gather in the past is important for us as we encounter the present; however, not all of the information that we use to form our memories emerges from direct recall. As Harvard professor of psychology Daniel Schachter observes,

> We are constantly making use of information acquired in the past. In order to type these sentences into my computer, I must retrieve words and grammatical rules that I learned long ago, yet I do not have any subjective experience of "remembering" them. Every time you start your car and begin to drive, you are calling on knowledge and skills you acquired years earlier, but you do not feel as though you are revisiting the past.[24]

22. St. Augustine, *Confessions*, X.14, 16, 17.
23. Daniel Schachter, *Searching for Memory: The Brain, the Mind, and the Past* (New York: Basic Books, 1997), p. 16.
24. Schachter, *Searching for Memory,* p. 17.

Memory works at different levels and utilizes a variety of different aspects of the brain. The brain has a series of memory systems that it uses to process the past in different ways:

1. *Semantic memory* relates to how we remember concepts and facts — that is, meanings which are not related to our personal experiences. So names, places, mathematical equations, and other impersonal concepts would be held in this aspect of memory.
2. *Procedural memory* relates to remembering how to do things. It is that aspect of memory that enables us to develop the skills and habits which allow us to engage in certain tasks and procedures. This memory can be retained even if the brain is damaged. Pianist and musicologist Clive Wearing developed a viral infection that caused severe brain damage leading to the destruction of his semantic memory system. His memory retention was reduced to seconds. But he could still play intricate melodies on the piano even if, arguably, the kind of meaning that he associated it with earlier in his life didn't appear to be present.[25]
3. *Episodic memory* relates to the "subjective experience of explicitly remembering past incidents."[26] For example, it is episodic memory that allows us to remember where our keys are or what the name of our pastor is. Episodic memory is deeply personal. "To be experienced as memory, the retrieved information must be recollected in the context of a particular time and place and with some reference to oneself as a participant in the episode."[27]

The psychologist Endel Tulving draws out the implications of this point:

The particular state of consciousness that characterizes the experience of remembering includes the rememberer's belief that the memory is a more or less true replica of the original event, even if only a fragmented and hazy one, as well as the belief that the event is part of his own past.

25. Deborah Wearing, *Forever Today: A True Story of Lost Memory and Never-Ending Love* (London: Corgi, 2007).
26. Schachter, *Searching for Memory*, p. 17.
27. Schachter, *Searching for Memory*, p. 17.

> Remembering, for the rememberer, is mental time travel, a sort of reliving of something that happened in the past.[28]

Memory in its episodic form is a creative act of fact, faith, and imagination. Our memory is the place where, in varied and diverse ways, our history is stored. Who we are and knowledge of where we have come from, where we are now and what we hope for in the future — all are inevitably tied up with our ability to remember. True, certain procedural memories will function without the memory of our history or sense of who we are, but if our episodic memory is taken from us, if we can't process the past and find meaning and understanding of who we are in the present, then it at least appears to be difficult to see in what sense we are the people we were before. This is what Buñuel and Keck are pointing toward.

Dementia in all of its different forms leads ultimately to a profound loss of episodic memory. If we assume that memory is equal to identity, then the loss of this aspect of our memory will inevitably be perceived as leading to a loss of self and self-identity. Memory understood in this way raises profound questions. What is it that gives me continuity of identity? What is the connection between what I was when I was a remembering being and what I am not now that I have forgotten what I was? These are more than just questions about personal identity in a psychological sense. Theologically such questions raise complex issues, such as "Precisely which 'me' will be resurrected? The 'me' I can remember, or the 'me' that I am now, as I live my life in what, for some, is perceived as clearly an eternal present wherein what was may have no obvious connection with what is?" The answer "God will remember you" is very powerful and attractive, given the understanding of memory currently under discussion and the significance of episodic memory in particular. If God remembers me, then my "vanishing self" will be in some sense preserved.

However, this raises the question of precisely what it is that we think we would like to be preserved. What might we mean by "preserved"? In order for something to be preserved, we need first to assume that we know and understand the thing that needs preserving — otherwise, we would never know if it was or was not preserved. Put slightly differently, if I am concerned about "myself" being in some way preserved, I need to have

---

28. Quoted in Schachter, *Searching for Memory,* p. 17.

some sense of what or who "myself" actually is. Likewise, if I'm worried about losing "myself," then I presumably think that I know who I am, which of course takes us back to Bonhoeffer's question, which opened this book: "Who am I?"

The Book of Eli

A Denzel Washington film might not be the most obvious place to begin to answer the question of whether I am who I think I am, but I ask the reader to bear with me! In *The Book of Eli*, Denzel Washington plays the part of Eli, a strange, nomadic figure in a post-apocalyptic world who hears a voice that tells him to deliver a copy of "The Book" to a location on the West Coast of the United States. The world is in turmoil following some kind of unnamed nuclear catastrophe. The entire infrastructure is gone, and violence and disorder rule the world. Eli's world is the world of Mad Max, without Mel Gibson. As the story unfolds, we're not told what the book is. But it is clearly important enough for Eli to maim, mutilate, or kill all of those who challenge him. Throughout, the viewer is treated to a dazzling display of martial arts, sharpshooting, and acts of ("defensive") violence that aren't pleasant to watch, but nonetheless skillfully performed. Eventually Eli reaches his destination and hands over the book. When it is opened, it turns out to be a copy of the Bible. Hope is reborn as this new script for the world is brought back into play. When Eli hands over the book, something else is revealed which is equally startling. Eli takes off his sunglasses, which he has worn throughout the movie. The camera goes to a close-up of his face — and his dead eyes. He's blind, a victim of radiation damage, which blinded millions of people during the nuclear event.

This is when, for me at least, things started to get interesting. With this revelation, all of the preceding story seemed to change. The way Eli fought, the way he reacted to noise, the things that occurred that he didn't respond to — these were in fact due to his being blind. His reverence and concern for the book suddenly made a different kind of sense. He was violent in the name of a greater good. Because of this last scene, everything I believed and thought I was seeing before suddenly looked very different. My eyes had deceived me; in an instant my memories of what had happened were changed and reshaped.

What Memories Are Made of

So, what does my movie experience have to do with dementia and memory? We have already hinted at the fact that memory isn't quite as straightforward as it appears to be. What I encountered in *The Book of Eli* is an example of the ways in which our memories are formed according to what we *think* we see and sometimes according to what we *want* to and expect to see and remember. Throughout the movie, I was forming memories and impressions that helped me make sense of what was going on. Until the last scene, I assumed I had the situation pretty well assessed. Then, suddenly, something shifted, and all of my memories of the movie shifted and changed in rhythm. A similar thing occurs when people are converted to Christianity. When we're converted, suddenly we see that what we thought about ourselves and the world was quite different from what was actually happening. We thought we were pretty good people. But it turns out that we were sinners all along,[29] and that even our best efforts were meaningless without God.[30] We thought we were nothing more than random events in an unseeing process of evolution. It turns out that we were created, loved, and placed in this world for a specific purpose. All of our previous memories are realigned in the light of what we now know through the revelation of the gospel. Nothing has changed in our history, but now we remember everything differently. I suspect that this is precisely what will happen on Judgment Day when God shows us what our lives were *really* like, rather than what we remember them to be. The remembered past is much more fragile, deceptive, and mysterious than we presume.

Memory, then, is not simply a straightforward recollection of what has happened in the past. We are deeply involved in the creation of our memories. Memory doesn't function the way that computer retrieval systems or tape recorders do. With both, what you put in is what you get out. The quality may vary, but the content and meaning are more or less the same. Memory is different. Memory is as subjective as it is objective. Memories are constructed not only out of what we think we remember in a historical sense, but also in accordance with our current needs, desires, and the ways

29. Romans 3:23: "For all have sinned and fall short of the glory of God."
30. Isaiah 64:6: "All of us have become like one who is unclean, and all our righteous acts are like filthy rags."

we see the world and expect it to be. Memories are also saturated with feelings and emotions. When we remember something, we often feel it emotionally. But the emotion we attach to a memory isn't necessarily representative of the emotion we felt when we originally created that memory. It will more than likely relate very closely to our current emotional state and the way in which that memory has gathered meaning and feeling over time. Memories are also intertwined not only with other memories, but also with the rememberer's memories of the memories. In other words, when we remember something, we don't simply go back to the original memory; we remember the memory as it came to us the last time we remembered it. So if, for example, in 2011 I'm struggling to remember what happened at a party I attended in 2005 and suddenly the memory comes to me, the next time I try to remember the party, I won't go back to the original memory. I'll go back to the last time I remembered it and re-remember the memory and how I felt about it when I remembered it in 2011. So I remember the last time I remember the event rather than simply remembering the original event. This is one reason why the feelings and experiences around memories can shift and change.

Another example will help clarify the point. When I remember my father's death, I'm not going back to the original moment when I heard that he was dead. I'm constantly re-remembering his death, and as time passes, the emotional content of the memory shifts and changes. Now I can remember him without the level of sadness I had when his death was fresh. And every time I remember him now, it becomes less painful, presumably because I'm remembering more recent remembering, which has a different emotional content from the original experience. Sometimes remembering him can be quite painful; at other times it's relatively easy. Presumably that has at least partly to do with how I'm feeling at the moment of remembrance. This, I presume, is one reason why time heals.

Schachter suggests that memories might be better framed as collages or jigsaw puzzles rather than pictures or tape recordings.[31] Our memories don't record everything, and they don't simply present straightforward historical pictures. Instead, they present us with a selective and highly constructed perspective on what we believe happened. Memory, then, is a highly complex process which cannot be fully explained by reflecting only on the technicalities of neural involvement. Memories are always and inev-

31. Schachter, *Searching for Memory*, p. 93.

itably constructions and reconstructions of the past that deeply involve biography, experience, and emotion.

Because of this creative and emotional dimension to memory, the meaning and interpretation of memories can change quite quickly as something occurs which makes us rethink and reconstruct the past. My experience with *The Book of Eli* is an example of this. It's obvious that within such a process there is a good deal of room for misrepresentation and distortion. Such distortions can relate to attitudes, moods, or emotional states which deeply affect the ways in which we interpret and understand a memory. Distortion may relate to the content of a memory: you can assume that something happened that didn't actually occur, or you can put a different interpretation on an event, the meaning of which you assumed was previously settled. The often used phrase "I feel much better about things today" indicates such a change in the meaning of memories. More seriously, a child might not remember that he has been abused until later in life, when certain things are pointed out which make it obvious that his original interpretation of the memory was flawed and/or that the way he perceived the experience was misinterpreted. Again, if a woman witnesses a crime, a policeman might show her a picture of the primary suspect. She might say that it isn't the person she saw — but when it comes to the "identity parade," she ends up picking out the man in the picture she was previously shown. He is in fact not the man she saw, but her memory has been primed by the previous information she's been given.[32]

My point in outlining this perspective on memory is not to try to suggest that we don't know anything at all about our past, or that it's impossible to remember anything accurately. Clearly, we do know some things and remember them quite well. Nonetheless, the discussion does indicate the ways in which our past and our memories of that past are much more mysterious, fragile, and unclear and much less accurate than we often assume them to be. Indeed, we have forgotten most of what has happened to us in the past. And that's how it should be. To remember everything would be a most unhealthy state. Sometimes we need to forget to survive.[33]

32. Schachter, *Searching for Memory,* p. 99.

33. For a fascinating and somewhat disturbing account of what it might be like to live without being able to forget, see A. R. Luria, *The Mind of a Mnemonist: A Little Book about a Vast Memory,* trans. Lynn Solotaroff (Cambridge, Mass.: Harvard University Press, 1986). The book tells the story of Solomon Shereshevskii, who had a rare medical condition called synaesthesia. This meant that it was impossible for him to forget anything. *All* of his experi-

My essential point is that to claim that people with dementia have lost their identity because they've forgotten certain things about themselves and the world isn't a straightforward claim. None of us are clear about who we are if who we are is determined by the accuracy of what we can remember. How, then, can we be sure of who we are? Is Bonhoeffer's answer to the question "Who am I?" plausible?

Living in the Memories of God: A Theology of Memory

At the beginning of the book I offered a quotation from the book of Jeremiah. At this stage it will be worthwhile returning to it. In Jeremiah 17:7-10 the prophet gives us a statement that offers us a clue:

> But blessed is the man who trusts in the LORD, whose confidence is in him. He will be like a tree planted by the water that sends out its roots by the stream. It does not fear when heat comes; its leaves are always green. It has no worries in a year of drought and never fails to bear fruit.
>
> The heart is deceitful above all things and beyond cure. Who can understand it? I the LORD search the heart and examine the mind, to reward a man according to his conduct, according to what his deeds deserve.

Who can understand the human heart? Only God. Human memory is inevitably flawed and open to deception and distortion. This, combined with our inherent fallenness, means that there is a real sense in which we can never know who we really are. This self-amnesia is a fact that Freud brought to our attention many years ago in his reflections on the human unconscious. It reaches another dimension when perceived theologically. We may be uncertain about who we are, but God is not. God remembers us properly. God remembers us because God knows us. So the psalmist can claim,

---

ences became vivid and unforgettable memories. He had no process for discerning what was a useful memory and what was not. Consequently, he became more and more incapacitated, because he was unable to work or function effectively within relationships. This story shows us that without the ability to forget, our memories cease to be uniquely important. Developing a sense of who we are in the world and what is important and not important to remember about the world are crucial for us to be able to orientate ourselves in any kind of meaningful sense. Shereshevskii's life was ruined because he couldn't forget.

You know when I sit down or stand up.
You know my thoughts even when I'm far away.
You see me when I travel
and when I rest at home.
You know everything I do.
You know what I am going to say
even before I say it, LORD.
You go before me and follow me.
You place your hand of blessing on my head.
Such knowledge is too wonderful for me,
too great for me to understand!
I can never escape from your Spirit!
I can never get away from your presence!
If I go up to heaven, you are there;
if I go down to the grave, you are there.
If I ride the wings of the morning,
if I dwell by the farthest oceans,
even there your hand will guide me,
and your strength will support me.
I could ask the darkness to hide me
and the light around me to become night —
but even in darkness I cannot hide from you.
To you the night shines as bright as day.
Darkness and light are the same to you. (Ps. 139:2-12, NLT)

God's knowledge of me is "too great for me to understand"! At the heart of God's intimate knowing of human beings lies God's remembering of us. In Psalm 8:4 the psalmist asks the wistful question of what it is to be a human being: "What is man that you are mindful of him, the son of man that you care for him?" The adjective "mindful" derives from the verb "remember" (Hebrew: *zkr*). While the psalmist may not be totally clear in his mind about what a human being is, he is very clear about one thing: God is mindful of human beings. To be human is to be held in the memory of God. God watches over human beings, knows them intimately, and remembers them.

The Memories of God

Recognizing that human beings may struggle to know who they are but are held and known by God in God's memory has important implications. To begin with, it means that we need to be very careful when we say or believe that persons with advanced dementia have lost their identity (who they think they are) because they have lost their memory. Our brief reflections on the psychology of memory have indicated that an over-identification of memory with identity may be deceptive. Theologically, as I will argue in more detail below, it is not a person's memory that assures his/her identity; it is the memory of God and, by proxy, the memory of others. But, quite apart from the psychological and theological difficulties in making memory the seat of identity, such a suggestion is dangerous for the practical reasons that have been outlined previously. If we believe that people with dementia have somehow gone, or, to use Keck's phrase, if we assume that all that is left is "a physical resemblance" to those persons we once knew, then precisely who or what do we think we are dealing with in our personal encounters with people who have advanced dementia? If they are not the persons they were, then who are they? If we don't know who they are, then how and why might we desire to care for them? Wasn't Peter Singer's point just that: the sufferers have lost all sense of identity over time; they have lost their personhood, and therefore they have lost the right of moral protection?[34] As we have seen, the suggestion that the person has gone and all that is left is a physical resemblance, even in the most advanced stages of dementia, is simply wrong. Certainly the person may have changed, and aspects of what we and he thought he was will become different, sometimes quite radically so. Maybe he doesn't recognize us, and perhaps we struggle to recognize him. Nevertheless, his identity — that which holds him in his place of self and humanness — is not lost or forgotten. The tension between what we see and experience as we encounter a person who has clearly been changed by dementia and the suggestion that his identity

34. I'm not for a second suggesting that Keck is pushing in this direction. He is absolutely not doing so. However, by suggesting that all that is left is a body without a mind, he does leave open questions of identity, worth, and value, particularly if the criteria used to judge the person with severe dementia are based on the types of liberal philosophy we have looked at in previous chapters. Keck also plays into the cultural trope of zombie that was discussed in Chapter 5, footnote 4. My point in quoting Keck here is simply to suggest that I think his premise is wrong, not to directly associate his views with those of Singer.

remains held in the memory of God and the memory of others can undoubtedly be dissonant and pastorally difficult. But that doesn't make the suggestion untrue. The fact that God will remember is the key to faithful hoping and Christ-like healing practices.

Memory without Neurology

It is important to highlight the fact that God's memory is quite different from the type of memory we have been looking at in our explorations of human memory, if for no other reason than that God doesn't have a brain! As Dallas Willard once put it, "For God, everything is a no-brainer!"[35] This is a serious point. When we use the term "memory" in relation to God, it is tempting to assume that God's memory is similar to human memory. When God remembers, we might think, he draws on his remarkable skills of recall and plumbs the depths of history for facts which have been stored in the divine database: the book of life. If God's memory is similar to human memory, only more comprehensive and more powerful, and if the reflections on human memory that I have presented previously are accurate, then being remembered by God is not a particularly comforting or stable prospect for any of us, demented or otherwise. If, like humans, God unintentionally forgets more about us than God remembers, and if God has no real idea of who we are, then divine memorial hope is at best fragile and at worst hopeless.

God's memory, however, is quite different from human memory. It's different not only because it's not a neurological act, but also because God's memory holds and remembers us as we *actually* are, not simply as we think we are or have been. As the psalmist puts it, "O Lord, you have searched me and you know me" (Ps. 139:1). That being so, God's memory will be full of surprises — some of them good, some of them bad![36] The suggestions that God remembers differently and that God doesn't have a brain are not "by the ways." Like Augustine, many of us are used to the as-

---

35. Dallas Willard, "The Redemption of Reason," 1998. A transcription of an address given by Dr. Willard on 28 February 1998 at Biola University in La Mirada, California, at the academic symposium titled "The Christian University in the Next Millennium"; access at: http://www.dwillard.org/articles/artview.asp?artID=118.

36. Matthew 7:21: "Not everyone who says to me, 'Lord, Lord,' will enter the kingdom of heaven, but only the one who does the will of my Father in heaven" (NRSV).

sumption that memory is something that emerges from and is confined within the brain. However, if God doesn't have a brain but still remembers, then clearly the concept of memory is broader than our standard neurological and psychological definitions, and memory may well not reside purely and simply within individual brains. Our standard accounts of memory reflect one aspect of what the term "memory" might mean. Divine memory opens up a whole new story around the nature of memory. God's memory is the place where all other memories are held.

Divine Memory as Sustenance and Action

God's memory is not the same as human memory. It doesn't simply recall events and actions, not least because (as we will see in the next chapter) past, present, and future aren't concepts that can be applied to God. God sits outside of time, and thus there is, in a sense, no past to recall and no future to move toward. God's memory has to do with *sustenance* and *action*. To be remembered is to be sustained; to be forgotten is to cease to exist. To be remembered is to be the recipient of divine *action*.

In his book *Memory and Tradition in Israel,* Brevard Childs offers an extensive study on the Hebrew word for memory: *zkr.*[37] Childs observes,

> God remembers and forgets, and this process stands parallel to a series of psychological descriptions (Jer. 31:20; 44:21). Of course, God's remembering has not only a psychological effect but an ontological one as well. Whoever Yahweh does not remember has no existence (Ps. 88:6). When God forgets sin, he forgives (Jer. 31:34).[38]

When God forgets something, it literally no longer exists. To be remembered is to exist and to be sustained by God. There is a close connection between memory and the concept of *nephesh*, which we explored previously. To be forgotten is to have one's *nephesh* withdrawn: to cease to exist, to no longer be sustained by God. This explains why when God forgives sin

---

37. I am indebted to David Keck's work on memory — especially Chapter 2 of *Forgetting Whose We Are* — for pointing me to some of the implications of this text.

38. Brevard S. Childs, *Memory and Tradition in Israel* (Naperville, Ill.: Alec R. Allenson, 1962), p. 33.

God forgets it: it literally no longer exists.[39] Redemption and the cleansing of human sin are literal events that occur within the memory of God.

As well as having a deep connection with sustenance, memory is deeply tied to *action*. In line with the kinds of arguments presented previously, Childs observes that for the Hebrews, a human being was a whole person. The precise nature of that wholeness is very important for our understanding of the nature of divine memory:

> Man, in his total essence, is a *nephesh* (soul). The will or volition of the soul is not an independent feature, but the "tendency of the totality of the soul." The term *lebh* (heart) designates the self when it functions as operative power. As a result, the relationship between thought and action differs radically from that conceived of by the modern. Theoretical, objective thinking which is divorced from the will is unknown. The Hebrew understands as thought the process by which an image enters the heart and immediately influences the will. Thought which does not lead to action is a meaningless flash.[40]

For the Hebrews, thought and the will are not merely contemplative aspects of persons. They are attitudes or inclinations toward particular forms of action. When a person remembers something, she doesn't do so simply to conjure up a pleasant picture or a useful image to reflect upon. The reason she remembers the image is to assist in determining right *action*. Contemplative perceptions of memory divorced from action are unknown to the Hebrews. When the soul thinks, it acts. As Childs says, "The peculiarity about the Israelite is that he cannot at all imagine memory, unless at the same time an effect on the totality and its direction of will is taken for granted."[41]

Memory and action are thus seen to be thoroughly interconnected:

> The characteristic feature of Hebrew mentality is in refusing to see thought as an objective image to which volition must be added to produce action. An image must be joined to will even to be regarded as thought.[42]

---

39. Isaiah 43:25: "I, even I, am he who blots out your transgressions, for my own sake, and remembers your sins no more."
40. Childs, *Memory and Tradition in Israel*, p. 17.
41. Childs, *Memory and Tradition in Israel*, p. 17.
42. Childs, *Memory and Tradition in Israel*, p. 19.

Clearly, the emphasis is on remembrance-as-action directed toward some-one.[43] When people remember, it is to enable action. The crucial parallel here is this: *When God remembers, God acts.* More specifically, God's memory is for the purpose of re-membering. To re-member something is to bring back together that which has been fragmented. In terms of the redemption of humanity, to be re-membered by God is to be reconstituted and brought back together, moved from a state of fragmentation to one of wholeness in God: *shalom.*

To be held and remembered by God implies some form of divine action toward the object of the memory. It is not purely eschatological action; it is something that occurs in the past and in the present as well as in the future. God acts in particular ways toward people because of a previous commitment. In other words, God remembers because God promises.[44] God remembers God's *hesed:* God's great mercy and love (Ps. 25:6-7). God's remembering of God's people is always for a purpose. God remembered Noah and delivered him from the Flood (Gen. 8:1). God remembered Abraham and voided his judgment (Gen. 19:29). God remembered Rachel and allowed her to have children (Gen. 30:22). Above all, God remembers God's covenant, a covenant that existed before creation had even begun (Gen. 1:26-28).

It's important to notice that God's remembering of the covenant is not simply reflected in past history. The acts of the covenant continue to meet Israel in the present and the future (Ps. 111:5). As the psalmist puts it, "He remembers his covenant *forever,* the word he commanded, for a thousand generations" (Ps. 105:8; italics added). Childs draws out the significance of this recognition of God's memory as active in past, present, and future:

> In terms of God's memory, time-sequence plays a secondary role. How the great acts of the past relate to the present and the future is not seen as a problem which bears upon God's memory. His remembering is not conceived of as an actualization of a past event in history; rather, every event stems from the eternal purpose of God. Only from Israel's point of view is each remembrance past. God's memory is not a re-creating of

---

43. Childs, *Memory and Tradition in Israel,* p. 32.

44. Eugene H. Merrill, "Remembering: A Central Theme in Biblical Worship," *Journal of the Evangelical Theological Society* 43, no. 1 (March 2000): 27-36.

the past, but a continuation of the selfsame purpose. According to the psalmist, redemptive history does not end, because the present events which stem from God's memory are not different in quality from the former. God's memory encompasses his entire relationship with his people. His memory includes both the great deeds of the past as well as his continued concern for his people in the future.[45]

God's covenant promises are not historical in the sense that we moderns might understand the term. They are not simply past events which we remember in the way that we might remember our childhoods or the contours of a picture we once saw and enjoyed. They are moments of divine revelation that have a timeless resonance, that actualize themselves in the present just as firmly as they have in the past. This is why the writer to the Hebrews can say with confidence that "Jesus Christ is the same yesterday and today and forever" (Heb. 13:8). This is why Jesus can proclaim, "I will be with you always, to the very end of the age" (Matt. 28:20). In the Eucharist we can hear Jesus' words "Do this in remembrance of me" not simply as a retrospective glance back to the cross, but as an acknowledgment of the power and transforming impact of that memory for the present. It is a re-membering within which the church is constituted as a body, held together in, by, and through the memories of Jesus. Even though we weren't physically part of that history, we can share in these memories and be transformed by God's actions in the present. The acts and promises of God remain actualized in the "now" within God's timeless memory, which is imbued with a desire for particular forms of action. It is that memory in which Christians are called to participate. Human memory is nothing more (and nothing less) than one mode of participation in the memory of God, which is our true memory and our only real source of identity and hope.

With all of this in mind, it becomes clear that to suggest that God remembers persons with advanced dementia is not a palliative avoidance of the real truth that they have lost their identity. Neither is it an abandonment of these people by God in the present. Quite the opposite. It is a firm statement that God is with and for them and that *God is acting* with and for them in the present as they move toward God's future.

45. Childs, *Memory and Tradition in Israel,* p. 42.

217

Memory, Soul, and Resurrection

All of this helps us to get a clearer understanding of what human identity might look like and how it might be sustained even in the most severe dementia. We are who we are because God remembers us and holds us in who we are. We are who we are now and we will be who we will be in the future because God continues to remember us. Theologically, our identity relates to the "me" that God sees and remembers. This has a direct bearing not only on persons' endurance after their death and their identity when they have dementia, but on every moment that they exist. Bonhoeffer has it right when he ends the poem "Who Am I?" (which I presented in the Introduction) this way:

> Who am I? They mock me, these lonely questions of mine.
> Whoever I am, Thou knowest, O God, I am Thine!

To be remembered by God is to endure in the present and into eternity. However, this type of remembering is not a matter of looking back and holding on to what was. For God there is no "back" to look at, no "forward" to look toward. God is beyond time; for God, all is now. We will look more carefully at God and time in the following chapter. Here the important thing to bear in mind is that the movement from life to death is a movement from time into eternity, an eternity wherein our true identity is preserved in the memory of God. It is in this sense that we endure eternally.

That being so, while many things are forgotten by human beings — indeed, sometimes everything is forgotten — nothing is forgotten by God unless God chooses to forget.[46] There is no reason to think that God chooses to forget those who have advanced dementia. Thus there is no reason to suggest that a person's identity has been lost when he/she encounters advanced dementia. My friend and colleague Brian Brock makes the point this way:

---

46. Here I am not trying to suggest that memory is equivalent to soul. Suggesting that our identity is held in the memory of God is quite different from assuming that the soul is a natural entity that endures "under its own steam" into eternity. It is God's remembering of us now that sustains us, and God's memory of us in the Resurrection that redeems us. There is nothing immortal about human beings, not even their souls. Only God is eternal, and only that which is eternal can bring that which is transient into eternal life. If God remembers us, we will live. If we die and God forgets us, we will cease to exist. The Old Testament seems to express this point quite clearly.

God always knows who we are, and we are always only partially understanding who we are. On such a view, dementia is just another stage in a totally dynamic process of the God-human relationship in which God is leading us into our true selves and we are always only grasping this in bits and pieces. A common-sense observation is that you may well have a better view of me, having watched me "objectively" over a few years, than I have of myself. Who I think I am is literally made up of who people have reflected back to me that I am. And the determinative voice is God's. I am therefore never really convinced that there is a more real "me" elsewhere. I really am here. But I don't know who I am because, well, I'm a human, I have limited powers of perception, and my perception is shaped by my interests [i.e., *my* interests as opposed to God's interests]. If soul equals endurance, only God can ensure that, not any quality of my being. If soul equals my personality, I can only trust that there is some continuity between the guy who I was twenty years ago, and the guy I am now. I certainly can't observe or prove that. Might "I" be "gone" one day if I get Alzheimer's? No, because what people experience as "my" personality is a fleeting phenomenon dependent on all kinds of biological substrates. Am I still "me" when I lose my personality? Only if God is faithful to see my living human body as continuous with the life he has given me in all its rich particularity. And I trust that God is true to his children and creatures in this way.

Our identity is safe in the memory of God. If God forgets us, we will cease to exist — but God does not forget us. As noted before, God's memory is not bound by time, space, or neurology in the way that human memory is. Thus the suggestion that "being remembered by God" is a prospective idea that finds fulfillment only in the future is wrong. Similarly, the suggestion that being remembered by God doesn't require action in the present is equally misleading. Human memory may be fallible, constructed, and uncertain, but God's memory is sure and oriented toward action in the present.

Where Are Our Memories?

If memory requires action, then what kind of action does God's remembering bring about? It is all very well to talk about God remembering us in the present and in the future, but if that is to be more than a mere platitude, we need to think through what such an assertion might look like when it is embodied. If God's memory necessarily includes action, where is that action to come from? What does it look like? Taking a look at Lisa Genova's novel *Still Alice*[47] may help answer these questions.

This novel tells the story of a fifty-year-old woman's sudden descent into early onset Alzheimer's disease. Alice Howland, a famous Harvard professor of mathematics, is happily married with three children. Everything seems to be going well, and the future seems mapped out with clarity and exciting possibilities — until Alice begins to notice her forgetfulness. At first it's just small things — forgetting to pick up items from the store, forgetting dates and appointments. But gradually she begins to get more and more confused. Her thinking becomes increasingly clouded along with her worsening memory, and eventually she is diagnosed with Alzheimer's disease. Alice struggles to hold on to her sense of self and to cope with her fast-disappearing past.

This is one of the best narratives about the experience of the journey into dementia that I have read. Although fictional, it is deeply empathic and authentic. One thing that keeps Alice going in the midst of her troubles is her BlackBerry. It is the place where her appointments are kept, her cooking times are remembered, and her life is organized. It is as the various alarms go off on her BlackBerry, alerting her to do this or that, that she is able to negotiate the ever-increasing confusion of her life. Her BlackBerry becomes her memory. Alice has a secret stash of pills that she plans to use to end her life when she feels that she can no longer cope with her existence — when the BlackBerry and other aids no longer make a difference. Not surprisingly, a powerful turning point occurs in the book when Alice loses her BlackBerry. Eventually it turns up in the fridge — but the reader knows that the frozen circuits in her telephone mark the end of its function as her memory. Alice later finds the pills she had hidden away and flushes them down the toilet. At this point she can't remember what they were for.

Alice's story reveals something important. Our memories aren't simply in our heads or in our brains; they're scattered in many places. Our reflections on the nature of the memory of God indicate that our memories and our identity are not confined to the boundaries of our skulls. Memory

47. Lisa Genova, *Still Alice* (London: Simon & Schuster, 2009).

that is in a real sense ours clearly exists both inside and outside of individual brains. The memory of God is of course one place where such memory exists and is sustained. But it exists in other places — places that we hardly notice or simply take for granted. For Alice, her telephone *really was* part of her memory. It wasn't a substitute or a compromise; it was truly part of her memory. Every time we take notes at a lecture or write down a shopping list, we're grafting in external aspects of our memory. Even within our constructions of our identities, it's often the memory of others that helps us to have memories of ourselves. When I think back on my past, I remember some things about what I once was and where I've been. But my mother remembers other things, things that I don't recall. When she tells them to me, I graft them into my story, and eventually they become a part of my memory system. If I forget again, she will remind me. I'm happy to have her remember on my behalf because I trust her to remember me well. For people with dementia, finding others who can remember them well is critical.

Memory is thus seen to be both internal and external. Some of it is held by the individual; some of it is held by her community; all of it is held by God. My point is that even in normal times some of our memories are outside of ourselves and often stored and told by others around us. And when some things about ourselves are far from clear in our own minds, we are able to experience a sense of self through the memories of us held by those around us, through the stories they tell about us. Memory, like mind and personhood, is corporate through and through.

Remembering God, Remembered by Others

If what was said above is true, it gives us a strong clue about what the practice of being remembered by God might look like. If our identity is held in and by the memory of God, then we can be certain that dementia does not destroy us now or in the future. That is the promise and the basis for enduring hope. But if being remembered by God indicates and indeed necessitates some form of action in the present as well as in the future, then presumably God is doing something *right now* in the lives of people with severe dementia. That "something *right now*" has two dimensions. One dimension, as we have seen, relates to the work of the Holy Spirit, as God is with the person who has dementia in ways that we cannot know. This dimension can be grasped only by faith. We trust that God is with and for the person even if we have no real idea of what that might mean. The apostle Paul tells us,

> . . . the Holy Spirit helps us in our weakness. For example, we don't know what God wants us to pray for. But the Holy Spirit prays for us with groanings that cannot be expressed in words. And the Father who knows all hearts knows what the Spirit is saying, for the Spirit pleads for us believers in harmony with God's own will. (Rom. 8:26-27)

When we don't know what to say, the Spirit prays on our behalf. When we can no longer say what we want to say, the Holy Spirit intervenes on our behalf. When we can no longer access God through our prayers, our meditations, or the Scriptures, we can be certain that God is with us in ways which, at least right now, we don't understand. In this sense, if and when we reach the advanced stages of dementia, we can be "sure of what we hope for and certain of what we do not see," as the writer to the Hebrews so poetically puts it (11:1).

The second dimension is more observable and can be seen quite clearly through our communities. If people act toward us in ways that remind us that we are remembered, then we can see, feel, and touch God's memories in action. As we encounter others, we encounter God. If, as has been suggested, each encounter between human beings is an encounter with the Holy, then one vital dimension of God's active memory relates to the ways in which God's people encounter one another. It is as we remember the holiness of the person with dementia that we are able to act in sanctified ways. It is as we learn to meet people soul-to-soul — *nephesh*-to-*nephesh* — that the practice of remembering finds flesh and potency.

Soul to Soul: A Community of Attention

It is as the church as a living body of remembering friends learns what it means to hold onto and practice the right memories that healing, hope, and active remembrance become a practical possibility. It is true that the church is not the only community that needs to learn to remember well. Malignant social memory is present throughout society. The church, however, is the only community that exists solely to bear active witness to the living memory of Jesus. As such, it should be the place where people learn to see what God's memory looks like. These two dimensions — the work of the Spirit and the faithful embodiment of God's spirit *(nephesh)* — provide a hopeful practical theological basis for effective dementia care. We Christians are therefore called to be attentive to the presence of God in others. If God is as close to human beings as the argument of this book has suggested, then God is a God who experiences our sufferings and our joys. As we minister to one another, we minister to God; as we suffer in community, so God suffers with us. The church, then, is called to become an attentive community of memory and hope that understands what it means to remember people with dementia and to act accordingly. The memory of God creates a community of remembering that is called to learn what it means to be attentive to God in those for whom memory is no longer their defining feature or primary learning experience.

This communal dimension of memory is highlighted by Glen Weaver, who notes,

> Hebrew men and women experienced personal identity as they lived in community with other persons. God was revealed through historical events which established covenant with a people. The worship acceptable in God's sight was worship which emanated from the collective life of the people.[48]

It should be noted that Weaver is not suggesting that identity is bestowed simply through the ongoing relationships of the community, as Tom Kitwood does. His point is deeper and safer for those with dementia. The community is the place where the implications of the *nephesh* that inspires and binds human beings together are recognized and named and its Giver worshiped. Such worship recognizes the obedience of humanity, the sovereignty of God, and the memory of God's great works. It is here within the worshiping community that our identity is sustained and upheld within both human and divine memory. As we realize that we are remembered, we are freed to remember well. As we begin to forget, so others bear the weight of remembering for us, a form of remembrance that calls for quite specific forms of loving action.

48. Glenn Weaver, "Senile Dementia and Resurrection Theology," *Theology Today* 42 (1986): 447.

The Memory of the Resurrection

Before moving on to begin to think through what such mnemonic actions might look like, there is one point that needs to be clarified. There is an important difference between the community of the Hebrews and the community of the church. That difference is Jesus. For the Hebrews, God's *nephesh,* God's breath of life, could be removed or withdrawn from an individual. When that happened, the person moved into death and was separated from God with no obvious way of reconciliation. Some of the angst that we encounter in the psalms of lament relates to the recognition that a movement toward the extinction of a person's *nephesh* is a movement toward separation from God — that is, a complete loss of identity. Thus things such as illness and suffering remind the psalmist of death and separation from God and become a profound source of fear and existential angst. Psalm 88 ends with this plaintive cry:

> You have taken my companions and loved ones from me;
> the darkness is my closest friend.

Whereas many of the other psalms find resolution in the recognition of God's *hesed* — God's unchanging love — Psalm 88 concludes with utter hopelessness. There is, of course, something important to be learned from this psalm. Very often this is precisely how many people with dementia feel. Often this is precisely how many people who care for people with dementia feel. And, as we will see in the final chapter of this book, it's all right to feel this way even if staying in that pit may not be a good thing. But we need not remain in the depths. Jesus' resurrection has changed things, including the meaning of Psalm 88. It is certainly the case that people may feel that darkness is their closest friend. There is absolutely no doubt that the experience of dementia has a tendency to rip meaning, purpose, and hope from human lives. However, darkness need not be our final destination. In Jesus we discover that we need not fear that God will withdraw God's *nephesh*. It is certainly true that we will suffer and die, but neither experience is definitive of our stories. Reconciliation with God and in God has become a possibility for all people in *all* circumstances. Nothing can separate human beings from God's love. Not death, life, loneliness, dementia, forgetfulness, anxiety, confusion, wordlessness, "nor anything else in all creation will be able to separate us from the love of God that is in Christ Jesus our Lord" (Rom. 8:38-39).

The world has changed with the rising of Jesus from the dead. That living, active memory provides a deep hope for all people, including those with dementia. Importantly, the Resurrection is not an event which relates only to the past. In his words of institution of the Eucharist, Jesus said, "This is my body given for you; do this in remembrance of me" (Luke 22:19). To remember Jesus is to bring him and the sacrifices and blessings that he represents into the present and to allow the memorial presence of Jesus to change, challenge, and strengthen us. In the same vein, to remember Jesus' resurrection is not simply to look to the past or to the future, although it does of course involve these things. It is also to look to the present and the significance of this great act of God as it works out its transforming power in the here and the now of human existence. This is an aspect of God's timelessness that takes on great significance for people with dementia:

> The upholding and renewing power of God is active in this present space and time. There is a reality in life which serves to uphold human identity even as this present "nephesh" (because of deterioration of the brain) moves toward chaos. In one sense, this power is the work of the Holy Spirit in all believers which mysteriously keeps them in the life of Christ even when their experience seems very distant from God. Even the psalmists had an unclear anticipation of this truth when they confessed paradoxically that God was present even in the pit of darkness. But in another sense, this upholding, transforming power of the Spirit is revealed and exercised in the reality which now is the presence of the resurrected Christ — his body, the church. The church has the mission and the power to renew the creation. . . . In so doing, the church may bring to fulfillment the Old Testament vision that one's identity is established, redeemed, and maintained in the collective experience of a people living in covenant with their God.[49]

The memories of God are reflected and enacted in the memorial practices of the community that is gathered around the resurrected Christ. The power of the Resurrection is the binding force that underpins the community now and into the future. Even if our *nephesh* is moving toward its end or, as Weaver puts it, is returning to chaos, there are good reasons for hope in the present and for the future. It is precisely that hope we engage with in

49. Weaver, "Senile Dementia and Resurrection Theology," p. 448.

the Eucharist. God's active memory finds embodiment in the community of memory and resurrection. It is there, within that community, that we can discover what God's memory looks like.

Remembering people with dementia requires a community of attentiveness. To be attentive is to pay close attention to the other. The church is called first of all to become a community that is attentive to God, the Rememberer and Bearer and Sustainer of our true identities. It is here that the church's worship finds its focus and goal. But the members of Christ's body are also called to become attentive to one another, and in particular to those among us who may be considered weak and vulnerable (1 Cor. 12:21-31). A church that remembers well and is attentive to the needs of people with advanced dementia is a church that is remaining faithful. In the next chapter we will turn our attention to the nature and texture of such a way of remembering and being attentive to God and to people with severe dementia.

9. Becoming Friends of Time: Learning to Live in the Present Moment

The friend of time doesn't spend all day saying: "I haven't got time."
He doesn't fight with time. He accepts it and cherishes it.

JEAN VANIER

Fidelity asks this much of us, that we remain with him even as he
fails to remember us; abandonment is not an option.

MARY JO IOZZIO

Never will I leave you; never will I forsake you.

GOD

Now here is my secret, very simple: you can only see things clearly
with your heart. What is essential is invisible to the eye. . . . It is the
time you have wasted on your rose that makes your rose so important.

ANTOINE DE SAINT-EXUPÉRY, *LE PETIT PRINCE*

In 1964 the French Canadian Jean Vanier, former naval officer and Aristotelian scholar, began a movement that would change the way that people with intellectual disabilities would be cared for.[1] Vanier's "revolu-

1. The best history and perspective on the development of L'Arche is Kathryn Spinks's book titled *Jean Vanier and L'Arche: A Communion of Love* (New York: Crossroad, 1990).

tion" started with a small gesture and ended with the development of a profound sign that points the world toward aspects of care, friendship, and being human that are often hidden, but nonetheless vital. Distressed by the institutionalization, isolation, and loneliness of people with intellectual disabilities, Vanier invited three men with intellectual disabilities who had been living in a local mental institution to live with him in his small house in Trosly, France. He called the house "L'Arche," which is French for "The Ark" in the biblical story of Noah and the Flood. His intention was to invite them to come and share their life in the spirit of the Gospel and the Beatitudes of Jesus.[2] Vanier's intention was not to start a miniature institution; he wanted to live with these men not as carer and cared for, but simply as friends. Vanier's initial patterning for community and relationships established the template for the beginning of a worldwide movement that has come to be known as the International Federation of L'Arche Communities. L'Arche grew quickly and spread around the world, attracting many young people who dedicated their lives to *living with* people who have intellectual disabilities as opposed to *caring for* them. Today, there are over 130 L'Arche communities in thirty-four countries on six continents.

Vanier's interest is not in dementia, but there is an aspect of his theology and practice that holds particular relevance for the purposes of this book. At the heart of Vanier's perspective lies a rethinking of the nature, value, and use of time. In his book *Community and Growth,* he makes the following statement:

> Individual growth towards love and wisdom is slow. A community's growth is even slower. Members of a community have to be friends of time. They have to learn that many things will resolve themselves if they are given enough time. It can be a great mistake to want, in the name of clarity and truth, to push things too quickly to a resolution. Some people enjoy confrontation and highlighting divisions. This is not always healthy. *It is better to be a friend of time.* But clearly too, people should not pretend that problems don't exist by refusing to listen to the rumblings of discontent; they must be aware of the tensions.[3]

2. Tim Kearney, "Discovering the Beatitudes at L'Arche," *The Furrow* 35, no. 7 (July 1984): 460-64.

3. Jean Vanier, *Community and Growth* (London: Darton, Longman & Todd, 1979), p. 80.

Vanier's point is that in order to truly be with a person who has severe intellectual disabilities, it is necessary to re-orient one's sense of time. Within a capitalist society, it's an almost irresistible temptation to treat time as one would treat any other commodity: you spend time, buy time, waste time, use time, keep time, and lose time. Many of us spend much of our lives at war with time. Time rules us and dictates the nature and shape of our lives and our relationships. Finding time to be with one another is not always a priority in lives where time seems to be racing away from us. Vanier urges us to take time seriously. To be with someone with severe intellectual disabilities, one needs to slow down and take time to notice those small things that the world sees as unimportant, but which, when we take time, are revealed to be profound.

In *There Is a Bridge,* Stanley Hauerwas moves Vanier's ideas into the realm of dementia:

> To become a friend with someone with Alzheimer's, I think, is exactly the kind of challenge that it means to become a friend of time. We forget that our most precious gift for others is presence; just being present. . . . When there is not a lot to do other than to be present, you find out . . . what it means to be a friend of time.[4]

One profound way in which God remembers us is by being present with us.[5] A deep way of remembering a person with dementia is by being present with them. Presence means taking time seriously. Memory and presence form the basis for the profound act of being with another without doing anything for another. This is the way of being that Vanier has had to learn during his life with people who have severe intellectual disabilities. Hauerwas urges people to learn the same practice of presence as they encounter people with advanced dementia. If L'Arche is a revolutionary movement born out of small gestures, then perhaps as we reflect on the small gesture of presence as it works itself out in the lives of people with advanced dementia, a second revolution can be initiated: a revolution that comes simply from remembering and being with another person.

The basic argument of this chapter is this: *To love one another, we need to be present for one another.* To be present, we need to learn to remember

---

4. *There Is a Bridge,* DVD.

5. Matthew 1:23: "'The virgin will be with child and will give birth to a son, and they will call him Immanuel' — which means, 'God with us.'"

well and to use time differently and more faithfully. In remembering well and using time differently, we will discover that being with another is the most powerful way of ministering, not simply with and towards people with dementia, but also with and towards all people. As the community remembers and learns the rhythms of being with one another without the need for words, so healing can begin, even in the midst of deep forgetfulness. If it is the case that love means saying to the other, "It's good that you exist; it's good that you are in this world," then our task will be to discover what it means to engage in such willful love.

Understanding Time

The place to begin is with a question: *What is time for?* It's interesting to note how time and our perceptions of time are shaped by our social context. Within a social context that values the market and that is determined by the need for effective productivity and output, time is perceived as a pseudo-physical commodity to be bartered in the marketplace of temporal/spatial existence. We live with time as if it's constantly about to run out. It's valuable to us, but we can never get enough of it. And very often time becomes our enemy rather than our friend. Why does time have such a hold on us?

In Chapter 13 of his *Confessions*, St. Augustine wrestles with the question of time:

> What, then, is time? If no one asks me, I know what it is. If I wish to explain it to him who asks me, I do not know. Yet I say with confidence that I know that if nothing passed away, there would be no past time; and if nothing were still coming, there would be no future time; and if there were nothing at all, there would be no present time.[6]

Augustine is particularly concerned with the question of what God was doing before God created the world:

> How, then, shall I respond to him who asks, "What was God doing before he made heaven and earth?" I do not answer, as a certain one is reported to

6. St. Augustine, *The Confessions of St. Augustine*, trans. Albert Cook Outler (New York: Dover Publications, 2002), p. 224.

have done facetiously (shrugging off the force of the question). "He was preparing hell," he said, "for those who pry too deep." It is one thing to see the answer; it is another to laugh at the questioner, and for myself I do not answer these things thus. More willingly would I have answered, "I do not know what I do not know," than cause one who asked a deep question to be ridiculed and by such tactics gain praise for a worthless answer. . . . Rather, I say that thou, our God, art the Creator of every creature. And if in the term "heaven and earth" every creature is included, I make bold to say further: "Before God made heaven and earth, he did not make anything at all. For if he did, what did he make unless it were a creature?" I do indeed wish that I knew all that I desire to know to my profit as surely as I know that no creature was made before any creature was made.[7]

Augustine's concern is that if time existed before the creation of the world, this would involve the creator in time. For Augustine, the absolute contingency of the world is crucial. Time relates closely to non-being. If God is in time, then God is open to this possibility, which reduces the contingency of creation:

> It is the tendency towards non-being that distinguishes the temporal from the eternal because "should the present be always present, and should it not pass into time past, truly it could not be time but eternity."[8]

If God were subject to time, this would contradict the idea that God was ever-present, eternal, and unchangeable.

For Augustine, God is in a real sense timeless — that is, God stands outside of time. It is wrong-headed to ask, "What did God do with God's time before the creation of the world?" There was no time before the creation of the world. Time came into existence when the world was created; time is an aspect of creation. Creaturely ideas about time should not be attributed to God:

> Therefore since you are the maker of all times, if there was a time before you made heaven and earth, why do they say that you rested from work?

7. St. Augustine, *The Confessions of St. Augustine,* p. 346.
8. Robert Jordan, "Time and Contingency in St. Augustine," *The Review of Metaphysics* 8, no. 3 (March 1955): 394-417; quotation on 397.

You made that very time, and no times could pass by before you made those times. But if there was no time before heaven and earth, why do they ask what you did then? There was no "then," where there was no time.[9]

The implication of all of this is that time, as an aspect of creation, is inevitably fallen and in need of redemption. Thus, it isn't really surprising that we turn time into a commodity designed to enhance human wealth and productivity rather than taking time to bring glory to God the Creator or be with God's creatures. Such a perspective on time helps us understand more fully Paul's words in Ephesians 5:15-16: "See then that you walk circumspectly, not as fools but as wise, redeeming the time, because the days are evil" (NKJV).

Time is fallen. Time requires to be redeemed.

Time and Care

Our culturally constructed assumptions about time impact the ways in which we choose to frame our practices of care. Time and caring are closely linked. Take, for example, the issue of *busyness*. It's not enough just to work; we need to be seen as busy. Busyness = doing things = proper work. If you're not busy, then you're probably not working hard enough or caring effectively. Many years ago I worked as a mental health nurse. *Real* nurses, by which I mean general medical nurses, wouldn't take mental health nurses seriously because they tended to sit down and spend long periods of time with patients and apparently not *do* anything. (The dualism between looking after bodies and looking after minds is interesting.) General nurses, on the other hand, were busy doing the various tasks that they had to complete and record during the day. To be busy doing things *for* people was to be working; to simply be *with* people was not.[10] The problem is that we can be so busy doing things for people that we cease to be

9. St. Augustine, *The Confessions of St. Augustine,* trans. John K. Ryan (New York: Doubleday, 1988), p. 252.

10. One of the problems facing chaplaincy today is that traditionally a key aspect of the chaplain's care is simply to be with people. In an evidence-based culture where the worth of a service is determined either by randomized control trials or by economic efficiency, such an idea is understandably viewed as odd.

with people in any meaningful way. Western culture, with its secular notion of time as acquiring meaning only through human plans and purposes, views unplanned time as empty time. If we see the time spent with people who have advanced dementia as empty time, then the experience of being present will inevitably appear meaningless and purposeless, and the significance of unique moments will tragically pass us by.

The Tyranny of Clock Time

Athena McLean has observed how people with dementia are cared for in American care homes, and has noticed the significance of what she, after T. I. Reed,[11] describes as "clock time."[12] She points out that the idea of clock time has deeply impacted the ways that science and Western culture conceptualize the world and human beings residing in the world:

> Clock time imposes a uniformity and management over natural lived time by dividing it into standard measurable units. This has been beneficial in promoting scientific discoveries, synchronizing human activities, and expanding communication networks. It has also promoted a profit-driven model that divides work into uniform shifts and ties wages to hours.[13]

In this way, abstract schedules "force" uniform structures over irregularly experienced "lived time" in human events.[14] This produces negative tension between "clock time" and "lived time" — lived time being the place where all of us really reside. The problem with clock time is that it fractures human beings and forces them to overlook the significance of lived time:

> Clock time transforms the self as lived into a compartmentalized collection of functions . . . [tasks which people] have to check off as they pro-

11. T. I. Reed, "Time in Relation to Self, World, and God," in *Faith, Scholarship, and Culture in the Twenty-First Century*, ed. A. Ramos (Washington, D.C.: Catholic University of America Press, 2002), pp. 166-77.
12. Athena McLean, "Dementia Care as a Moral Enterprise: A Call for a Return to the Sanctity of Lived Time," *Alzheimer's Care Today* 8, no. 4 (October-December 2007): 360-72.
13. McLean, "Dementia Care as a Moral Enterprise," p. 367.
14. McLean, "Dementia Care as a Moral Enterprise," p. 367.

ceed on their timely rounds. Thus, it fragments the naturally lived time both of caregivers and of care receivers, fracturing the inclination for intimacy that this relation brings.[15]

Thus the simple act of being present as judged by clock time seems like a waste of time. But this is only because we have been conditioned to prioritize clock time over lived time. The danger here, of course, is that the "same naturalistic mechanical worldview which reduces lived time to clock time also reduces creatures of the living world to inert machines."[16]

Institutions and approaches that are ruled by clock time, McLean suggests, "cannot adequately handle the dilemmas of the human condition. Only in settings where lived time is permitted can fallibility, lamentation, and the tragedy of life be fully embraced."[17] McLean concludes with this observation:

> Despite this pressure to conform to clock time, there are those who somehow manage to overcome the pressure of clock time to continue to engage intersubjectively with residents. The most dedicated caregiver I ever met was able to overcome the constraints of clock time as she rendered life and nurturance through intersubjective engagement with those residents she served. She adopted an *ethic of intimacy and love* as she involved herself with residents strictly as a way of being, not with any expectation of cure or any other instrumental goal. [Because she was] a spiritual person and masterful caregiver, caring was *moral and spiritual* to her, meaningful in and of itself. Motivated by a faith in the divinity of the person that remained, she often missed meals to fulfill required tasks. She regularly came to visit residents on her day off. Care to her was not compartmentalized within the precept of commoditized work; it was part and parcel of the sanctity of life as lived. It derived from a sense of identity and belonging with the resident, and with something greater.[18]

It is clear that the carer whom McLean describes was not on clock time. Her faith had ensured that her primary orientation was toward lived time.

15. McLean, "Dementia Care as a Moral Enterprise," p. 367.
16. McLean, "Dementia Care as a Moral Enterprise," p. 367.
17. McLean, "Dementia Care as a Moral Enterprise," p. 368.
18. McLean, "Dementia Care as a Moral Enterprise," p. 369.

Or, perhaps better, providential time, a mode of time which suggests that God is redeeming time and that we now inhabit an eschatological space that has a timeline and a sense of the future which are radically different from those of the world. In providential time, things begin to look different. Time is not empty.[19] Each moment is filled with meaning, new possibilities, and eschatological hope. If time is meaningful, then taking time to be with a person with severe dementia is meaningful, purposeful, and revelatory even if it might not always feel that way at the time. If time is meaningful, we should look for the meaning in each of our encounters. Thus, when we engage with a person who has severe dementia, as we learn to be in the present with him, body and soul in the sacredness of the moment, new life and fresh possibilities are born and nurtured. Our time is used well, even if the recognition of that moment may be brief and passing. So what might such "timefulness" look like?

The Sacrament of the Present Moment

John Goldingay is a professor of Old Testament at Fuller Seminary in Pasadena, California. Recently I listened to a series of lectures that he gave on the authority of the Bible. At the beginning of one of the lectures, he gave an invitation to his students to join him and his wife, Ann, for pancakes at their home the following week. Ann (who since then, sadly, has passed away) had severe multiple sclerosis and was significantly disabled, having lost the ability to move and speak. Goldingay informed the students that Ann probably wouldn't recognize or remember them, but he urged them to take the time to speak with her just the same. He said something like this: "She probably won't remember you afterwards, but in that moment she will appreciate you." This short statement stopped me in my tracks. Goldingay's encouragement to his students was born out of his deep love for his wife and the desire to affirm to her and to others the meaningfulness of her presence. He knew that she knew how he felt because he remained present with her and insisted on giving her the benefit of the

19. Philip Kenneson, "Taking Time for the Trivial: Reflections on Yet Another Book from Hauerwas," *Asbury Theological Journal* 45, no. 1 (Spring 1990): 65-74. This is a review of Hauerwas's *Christian Existence Today: Essays on Church, World, and Living in Between* (Jamestown, N.Y.: Labyrinth Press, 1988).

doubt where others might have missed the hopeful realities that he saw. He had learned not to allow her diagnosis or her increasing difficulties to become reasons to abandon her. He had learned to meet with her in the moment, and he wanted others to share that moment. It might only be a moment, but that moment mattered. And it mattered that other people were there to witness it.

The key thing is that Goldingay had *learned* to be with Ann when others might have given up. The process of learning wasn't straightforward. In his book *Walk On* he describes in depth and beauty his journey with Ann into her multiple sclerosis. At one point Goldingay despaired, as Ann seemed to be slipping away:

> It can seem now as if Ann is almost gone — gone to be with Jesus, gone to rest in Abraham's bosom. There is so little of her here now. In her disability, Ann exercised her ministry to people, even though I have a hard time discerning the mystery of what this ministry was or how it worked. But much of the time she exercised this ministry when she could communicate a bit, at least by responding with a smile to people who said hello. She can hardly exercise it now, can she?[20]

But Goldingay was challenged by a care giver who saw Ann very differently:

> I voiced that suspicion to one of the people who comes to sit with Ann from time to time — doing so not because we need her to but because she wants to. She has known Ann for only a year and has therefore no acquaintance with Ann when she was more responsive. "No," she protested. "Ann's spirit ministers to my spirit."[21]

Soul to soul, *nephesh* to *nephesh*. As this woman came close to Ann, she learned what it meant to be with her without words. As Goldingay listened and learned, he was enabled to reach a place where he could make a powerful statement to his students and bear witness to the presence of his wife in a tender and moving way: "She probably won't remember you afterwards, but in that moment she will appreciate you."

20. John Goldingay, *Walk On: Life, Loss, Trust, and Other Realities* (Grand Rapids: Baker Academic Books, 2002), pp. 192-93.
21. Goldingay, *Walk On*, p. 193.

For me, Goldingay's comment was an epiphany, a key that helped me to articulate something that I had intuitively been thinking for a long time but couldn't quite figure out how to express. I had been wrestling with the experience that many people have when they encounter someone who has advanced dementia: the person will suddenly respond to a situation, an experience, a song, or an emotion in ways that are startlingly out of line with their normal responses — or, more often, lack of responses. As a chaplain, I had always been struck by the way in which people with severe dementia who were withdrawn and were assumed to be unable to communicate would spring to life if I prayed the Lord's Prayer or sang a familiar hymn. I guess this is, at least in part, what Tom Kitwood means by the term "rementia." My medical colleagues used to tell me that it was nothing more than procedural memory — the product of long-term memories or skills that are well-learned and ingrained in ways that more recent memories and skills are not. I was never totally convinced by this explanation, but I bought it.

I also worried about why it was that I felt so helpless in the face of helplessness. My training as a psychiatric nurse and as a chaplain had made me quite efficient with words, but I was considerably less efficient with silence and uncertainty. As I sat with people who gave absolutely no response to my words, I often wondered what exactly I was doing by just sitting there. Nurses were rushing around completing tasks. Maintenance people were busy cleaning the ward. Outside, people were racing by in their cars, heading off to their next appointments. And here I was — sitting, doing nothing, saying nothing. I'm not a particularly contemplative person. The idea that doing nothing is actually doing something never did make sense to me. But Goldingay's brief, passing comment suddenly made sense of my experiences with people who have advanced dementia. By being there, I *was* doing something. I was holding them. I knew their names. I was with them in the present moment.

Silence, Presence, Naming, Holding

Another story will help get us into a position where we can begin to see the theological and practical relevance of the assertion of the significance of time and presence. As Director of the Centre for Spirituality, Health, and Disability at the University of Aberdeen, I have had the privilege and pleasure of directing a research program that has sought to explore the spiritual and theological dimensions of the lives of people with intellectual disabilities.[22] We recently completed a study exploring the lives of people with profound and complex intellectual disabilities — people for whom language is not the first mode of communication. A story that we were told during that project will open up some interesting possibilities for understanding presence in the context of dementia.

Mary's Story

When she's out of her chair or bed, Mary lies on the floor on a massage mat which makes a musical noise. She has no speech but makes sounds. She has muscle spasms continuously. She has limited vision but excellent hearing. She cannot feed herself, and she is entirely dependent on her caretakers for all her physical needs. Mary is a Quaker, having been made a member of that community when she was a baby. Quakers understand the significance of silence. In the service, Mary sometimes shouts noisily. She shouts and sometimes lets out long, rather winsome wails. However, as the community moves into its times of silence, Mary becomes silent. As the silence of the community engulfs the room, Mary shares in the silence. Precisely what that silence means for her is unclear; but her response is regular, patterned, engaged. Several years ago, Mary was diagnosed with leukemia. Her mother told us about the moment that she told Mary the news. She was deeply upset, and said simply to Mary, "You have leukemia." Mary became deeply upset. And Mary wept.

The Communal Nature of Spirituality

What's going on in this story? It's probably unlikely that Mary understood the words "You have leukemia." But who is to say? My interpretation certainly shouldn't trump that of her mother, who assumes that Mary understood perfectly well. But, assuming for a moment that the story I'm telling about Mary contains at least some truth, it seems that she is a deeply sensitive young woman who picks up on subtleties in communication, emo-

22. Centre for Spirituality, Health, and Disability, University of Aberdeen, Scotland, United Kingdom: www.abdn.ac.uk/cshad.

tion, and mood. When her mother told her about her illness, she picked up on her mother's emotions and wept with her in response to the rhythms of her mother's sadness. Even if she didn't understand the words, she did understand the feelings and the experience of sadness. In the context of her Quaker worship, a similar thing seems to be happening; Mary is sharing in the atmosphere — the feelings, emotions, and mood of the meeting. Her spirituality is being formed and held by her participation in the community. Mary's spirituality isn't a feeling or an emotion that is simply within her. It's something she shares in, an experience that goes beyond her, an experience that happens in the space between the members of the community — the space of meeting. She is dependent on her community for her spiritual experience. Thus, Mary's spirituality is a *corporate* rather than a *personal* concept and experience. This is a slightly startling counter-story to contemporary understandings of spirituality that perceive it to be something personal that is located firmly within the desires and the control of the individual, something one has to do or develop oneself rather than something we participate in through the presence of others.

Mary's experience seems to indicate that spirituality is a corporate event within which a person is greatly dependent on the presence of others. For Mary, the actualization of her spirituality and the silent presence of others are inextricably interlinked. I imagine, now that she has helped us to notice it, that what is true for Mary is true for all of us. Presence is remembrance in action.

Naming and Holding

If it is true that presence is the space where we discover surprising things about others, and if it is also true that the simple act of presence can become the place where the other's spirituality finds silent actualization, then knowing how to be present to others is foundational for faithful dementia care. Indeed, such acts of being present may turn out to reveal precisely how all people should be with one another. As we are present with one another, we learn what it means to *hold* one another well.

Ethicist and philosopher Hilde Lindemann in her work on dementia talks about the importance of *holding* people with dementia properly. Her concern is with the way in which identity is gained and lost and how that relates to the experience of progressive dementia. Lindemann describes identity as "a representation of a self":

> It consists of a tissue of stories, constructed from not only first-person but also many third-person perspectives, depicting the more important acts, experiences, relationships, and commitments that characterize a person and so allow that person and those around her to make sense of who she is. Because we change over time, some stories in the narrative tissue cease to depict us faithfully and — ideally — recede into the background, to be replaced with newer narratives that — again, ideally — represent us more accurately.[23]

Identity is formed by backward-looking stories, which tell where the person was and who they have been, and forward-looking stories, which express how the person and others think the future will play out. It is in and through this complex matrix of stories that are constantly moving backward and forward that we find and try to sustain our identities.

Importantly, Lindemann notices that, for children, third-person stories are responsible for the creation of first-person identities. Thus, the family bears the responsibility for constructing the initial identity of the child. They are also responsible for *holding* the child in that identity in and through the stories they tell and the stories that they allow to be told about and around the child as she grows, changes, and develops:

> Identity maintenance also involves weeding out the stories that no longer fit and constructing new ones that do. It's in endorsing, testing, refining, discarding, and adding stories, and then acting on the basis of that ongoing narrative work, that families do their part to keep the child's identity going.[24]

What a child needs more than anything else is to be *held* in her identity in ways that are truthful and which allow for the creation of different stories if and when she begins to see the world differently and take charge of her

---

23. Hilde Lindemann, "Holding One Another (Well, Wrongly, Clumsily) in a Time of Dementia," in *Cognitive Disability and Its Challenge to Moral Philosophy,* ed. Eva Feder Kittay (London: Wiley-Blackwell, 2010), p. 162.

24. Lindemann, "Holding One Another (Well, Wrongly, Clumsily) in a Time of Dementia," p. 163.

life story. Some of these new stories will be true, others false. It is the task of the adults in their interactions with the child to remind her who she really is.

Holding our identity, like remembering, is both a personal and a corporate task. As with Steven Sabat's three aspects of the self that we looked at earlier, some aspects of our identities need to be held by others. I can't be a husband without being held in that role by my wife. Likewise, my identities as a father and a university professor require my children and my students respectively to hold me in these roles.

As essential as stories are, not all stories are necessarily helpful, as Lindemann explains:

> Good holding almost always requires stories that depict something actual about the person. If your stories portray her as you wish to see her rather than as she actually is, you are very likely holding her wrong.[25]

The implications of these observations for dementia care are really quite obvious. As people move on into their journey of dementia, their own ability to tell their stories effectively begins to decline. More and more they become dependent on other people to hold them in their identities through the stories that are told about them and the names that these others give to them. As we have seen, many of the stories in which people with dementia are held are profoundly negative and dangerous. People who are losing their ability to tell their own stories need others to tell their stories well. They need people who will hold and remember them properly.

Naming and Vocation

Our explorations thus far show why the apparently simple act of being in the moment with someone, of coming close and learning to see, listen, and notice, is so radical and so important. Being present with someone and learning to hear and to call her by name is a way of discovering and narrating a different story about her, a way of holding her. It is a way of caring which is, as Lindemann puts it, "a part of the work of preserving, main-

---

25. Lindemann, "Holding One Another (Well, Wrongly, Clumsily) in a Time of Dementia," p. 164.

taining, and nurturing the world. To care *for* something, you have to care *about* it, and this is particularly apparent when the care involves the maintenance of a person's identity. To care for someone by holding her in her identity is to value her for who she is, and valuing is always intentional."[26]

Valuing, like willful love, is always an intentional action that relates directly to how we perceive a person. I may forget who I am. Others may want to name me a "dementia sufferer" and act accordingly. People can ignore me and fail to see what my changing "me" looks like; they can fail to see what it feels like to communicate with me as I lose my ability (if not my desire) to communicate. But *you* can still hold me well. You can hold me in my past by remembering my story and respecting what I have been; you can hold me in the present as you take time to notice me and remember what the future really is for me. You can hold me in a possible future where at a minimum I can trust that *you* will continue to love me and not forget me. I guess, looking back, that was exactly what I was doing when I was sitting with people with dementia: trying in my awkward, embarrassed, and wordless way to hold people in their identity and to show them that I cared and that I was listening with my ears, with my eyes, and with my soul. I wish I had recognized that at the time instead of feeling guilty about my apparent lack of busyness! Holding, naming, remembering, and companioning allow us in some way to share in the sacrament of the present moment with those for whom time has begun to slow down and stand still.

Coming Out of the Fog

In *Living Gently in a Violent World*, Jean Vanier tells this story:

> I know a man who lives in Paris. His wife has Alzheimer's. He was an important businessman — his life filled with busyness. But he said that when his wife fell sick, "I just couldn't put her into an institution. . . . I fed her. I bathed her." I went to Paris to visit them, and this businessman who had been very busy all his life said, "I have changed. I have become more human." I got a letter from him recently. He said that in the mid-

26. Lindemann, "Holding One Another (Well, Wrongly, Clumsily) in a Time of Dementia," p. 162.

dle of the night his wife woke him up. She came out of the fog for a moment, and she said, "Darling, I just want to say thank you for all you're doing for me." Then she fell back into the fog. He told me, "I wept and I wept."[27]

This story moves me. It moves me because it resonates with my own experience and the experience of many others. As I prayed with people with dementia, sang with them, and shared in the sacraments, things happened and people changed. These moments of lucidity when people come out of the fog and speak with us are both precious and frustrating. How are we to understand such precious moments? What might be going on? If I believed the story which tells me that such incidents are nothing more than remnants that manifest the continuing presence of procedural memory, I could rationalize these moments as just part of the person's condition. I could hold them in that identity and, when present, simply attribute everything that's going on to that explanation. And there might be some comfort in that. Perhaps it is easier for the person not to be there at all than for him to pop in and out of existence. But I don't believe in that story. In the story I choose to believe in, *something actually happens,* something that transcends and resists reduction to procedural memory. This suggestion is not based on blind faith. There is another story to tell, a story that one would have good grounds for believing. There is another way of holding the experience of sporadic lucidity: a counter-story.

Holding Identity in Our Bodies

We've already discussed in some detail the importance of recognizing the significance of embodiedness for what it means to be human. To be human is to *be* a body that finds its life and existence in the creative and sustaining actions of God. The brain is part of that body, but it isn't the whole of it or even the most important part of it. If we assume that the self is located within the brain, then it's difficult if not impossible to understand what it might mean to suggest that the brain isn't the most important aspect of the body. However, if, as has been argued thus far, the self is in fact

27. Stanley Hauerwas and Jean Vanier, *Living Gently in a Violent World: The Prophetic Witness of Weakness* (Downers Grove, Ill.: InterVarsity Press, 2008), p. 45.

held by God and others, then the primacy of the cognitive, reflective self becomes more fragile.

What goes on in our bodies is not epiphenomenal to who and what we are. Our bodies cannot be separated from our minds even when our memories and intellectual abilities appear to be abandoning us. Our bodies remember things, and that memory is not without meaning. Those of us who are used to living with implicit and explicit dualisms might find this suggestion rather counter-intuitive. In what sense can bodies remember things in any kind of meaningful way? Is bodily memory not simply mindless memory — a vestige that might remind us of the person who was but has now gone? If that were so, then spontaneous periods of lucidity and reactions to such things as prayer and sacraments should in fact be read as nothing more than reminders of a lost life. But to think in such ways is illusory.

The philosopher Eric Matthews in his work on dementia initiates a conversation about the body by drawing on Maurice Merleau-Ponty's idea of "body-subjects."[28] Merleau-Ponty offers a powerful critique of forms of dualism that place the essence of the self in the brain and the mind. According to Matthews,

> Merleau-Ponty's view is often expressed by describing the human person as a "body-subject" (though he himself does not seem to use this expression). The term obviously has two parts: "body," referring to the fact that persons are essentially biological creatures; and "subject," indicating that they are also creatures who are capable of thought, reflection, and communication. The hyphen in the expression "body-subject" indicates that these two elements in what it is to be a person are not separate from each other: that being embodied affects the nature of human subjectivity, while being connected with human subjectivity has a bearing on the nature of the human body. A person is not a "subject" loosely attached to a "body," as in Descartes's dualistic view of mind and body as separate and distinct things, but a unified being who expresses their "subjective" thoughts, feelings, and so on in bodily form — in speech, in gesture, in behavior, in interactions with their environment, both human and natural, and so on. Subjectivity exists, on this view, not in

28. Eric Matthews, "Dementia and the Identity of the Person," in *Dementia: Mind, Meaning, and the Person*, ed. Julian C. Hughes, Stephen J. Louw, and Steven R. Sabat (New York: Oxford University Press, 2006), p. 172.

some kind of "inner world," divorced from everything physical. Subjectivity exists in these physical expressions — as, for instance, you are now reading my thoughts about persons.[29]

Thus, in line with what we have already seen, the body cannot be separated from the mind, and the self cannot be understood apart from its embodiment. The body is an expression of subjectivity. The gestures, touches, glances, and expressions that our bodies offer to the world are aspects and expressions of our subjectivity; our bodies are part of who we are as persons. Merleau-Ponty, in line with the thoughts of Wittgenstein that we examined earlier, seems to be arguing that the suggestion that the self is located within some inner dimension of the subject is misleading. Our bodily experience is our outer aspect as persons that shapes and forms our sense of what is and is not "inner." Consequently, as we have seen, that which we perceive as "inner" is best seen as a metaphorical way of relating to particular experiences rather than as a concrete location of a real inner self. Merleau-Ponty urges us to notice that our bodily gestures are manifestations of our subjectivity rather than simply the outward dynamics of an inner self. The inner and the outer are really deeply bound together. In reality, ideas about inner and outer are false dichotomies:

> If human being is "in-the-world," if human subjectivity is necessarily embodied, then my existence as a subject is not that of an "inner object," accessible only to myself, but that of an object in the world who manifests his consciousness in his observable actions.[30]

This is so even if our sense of self relates only to Steven Sabat's Self 1, which may occur in the later stages of dementia. More than that, the body is inevitably prior to the self:

> We obviously must exist first as biological organisms before we can even begin to think, so the "body" element of the "body-subject" clearly has priority in a certain sense over the "subject" element. This is what makes it inadequate to think of personhood exclusively in terms of thought or consciousness.[31]

29. Matthews, "Dementia and the Identity of the Person," pp. 172-73.
30. Matthews, "Dementia and the Identity of the Person," p. 97.
31. Matthews, "Dementia and the Identity of the Person," p. 173.

First comes the body, then comes the body-self; without the body, there can be no self. For current purposes it is important to bear in mind that when Merleau-Ponty speaks of bodies, he isn't simply speaking about brains or cognitive or intellectual faculties.

Interestingly, the body remembers. The body remembers as it gathers, processes, and takes into itself the experiences of the person-in-the-world over time. We have already seen how the brain does this and has to do this in order to develop. But the body functions in a similar way. Even that which is no longer consciously thought out or intentionally intellectualized remains available and meaningful as it is revealed in the body:

> What may originally have been the result of conscious, or at least semiconscious, thought — ways of doing things, kinds of response to situations, and so on — becomes "sedimented," in Merleau-Ponty's phrase, that is, becomes gradually embedded in our unconscious habits.[32]

Gestures, habits, and responses are deeply meaningful even if the subjective self appears to have lost awareness of the original meaning of the body's actions.

A simple example will help to make this point. Pia Kontos and Gary Naglie in their ethnographic work on embodiment and dementia offer an example from their field work. Using the perspective of ethnography, they sought to explore the nature of the embodied self in people with dementia who were living in residential accommodations. This brief vignette grounds the argument quite helpfully:

> A female resident struggles to pull out a string of pearls from underneath her bib so that they could be seen by the other residents seated at her table without the staff ever responding to her proud display of her pearls.[33]

This woman had advanced dementia, but she also had a history — a personal and deeply meaningful life story. Even though she was forgetting that history, her body continued to remember. Her simple act of pulling out

32. Eric Matthews, *The Philosophy of Merleau-Ponty* (Chesham, U.K.: Acumen, 2002), p. 97.

33. Pia C. Kontos and Gary Naglie, "Expressions of Personhood in Alzheimer's Disease: An Evaluation of Research-Based Theatre as a Pedagogical Tool," *Qualitative Health Research* 17 (2007): 802.

her pearls to show people their beauty reveals a sense of self and a desire to communicate which may well not have been clearly thought through (who really knows?), but which was clearly a meaningful gesture of her selfhood manifested in a simple bodily action. The problem was that the staff didn't notice or respond. Why? Presumably because they were focused on her dementia and were working with the underlying presumption that deterioration of the brain invalidates any meaning that may emerge from bodily action. The woman's gesture of self-expression and embodied memory remained deeply and tragically hidden from the staff.

Gestures such as this, even those that are deeply sedimented and not obviously intentional (but then again, who knows?), express both meaning and purpose. Matthews puts it this way:

> Treating our body as part of our subjectivity . . . implies that not all aspects of our subjectivity — not all ways, for instance, in which we may be purposive — need necessarily be fully "conscious" in the sense of being objects of *explicit* awareness. For our bodies may have a purposive relationship to objects even if we do not cherish any *explicit* intentions for those objects. Reflex or instinctual actions, for instance, may be purposive but not consciously so.[34]

That being so, ascribing surprising responses to things such as residual procedural memory is far too simplistic. Bodies matter, and bodily actions are often acts of memory that can be deeply meaningful. So when I say that "something *really happens*" when people seem to "spring to life" on a bodily level during worship, this is part of what I mean. It may be defined neurologically as procedural memory, but in terms of personhood, embodied memory, and the meaningfulness of people's actions and words, this isn't enough to explain the situation fully. In order to be present and to hold someone well, we need to understand the language and memory of the body as well as the language and memory that springs from our neurons.

An objection to such a suggestion might be that unless we're aware of the meanings of our actions, there seems little real point in them. What difference does it make if a woman pulls out her pearls if she can't remember why she's doing it? But such a question serves only to illustrate how future-oriented our sense of self is. If the present moment is indeed deeply

---

34. Matthews, "Dementia and the Identity of the Person," p. 156.

significant, and if the person can experience both pleasure and communication in that moment, then the future orientation of her actions is not the point. *The moment is the point.*

The Keys to Our Memories

Oliver Sacks is a neurologist who has written extensively of his experiences with people who have neurological conditions that are odd, sometimes disturbing, and always deeply challenging and illuminating. In his book *The Man Who Mistook His Wife for a Hat,* Sacks relates the story of Jimmie G., a former sailor, whose memory had been destroyed by Korsakov's syndrome. This is arguably a specific form of dementia which is the product of long-term alcohol abuse. It leads to irreversible degeneration of the brain. One of its central features is profound memory loss. The loss is so profound that most sufferers become people without any sense of a past or a future, trapped in an eternal present and bound permanently within one period of time. People with this form of dementia are in a very real sense lost and unable to establish roots. Strangely, Jimmie could remember things prior to 1945 — but nothing since then.

Sacks was deeply challenged by his encounters with Jimmie. He recalls spending time talking with Jimmie at length about his life and his memories prior to 1945. They had been talking for twenty minutes or so when Sacks left the room briefly. When he returned, Jimmie seemed surprised to see him. In a matter of seconds his conversation with Sacks had disappeared from his memory, and he was starting his encounter with Sacks all over again. Sacks described Jimmie as "de-souled." The disease had, he thought, stripped Jimmie of something essential to what he was as a human being. From a neurological perspective, Sacks felt that the person Jimmie had been had gone — his soul had gone.

But those close to Jimmie saw something different. One of the nurses said to Sacks, "Watch Jimmie in chapel and judge for yourself":

> I did, and I was moved, profoundly moved and impressed, because I saw here an intensity and steadfastness of attention and concentration that I had never seen before in him or conceived him capable of. . . . Fully, intensely, quietly, in the quietude of absolute concentration and attention, he entered and partook of the Holy Communion. He was wholly held,

absorbed, by a feeling. There was no forgetting, no Korsakov's then, nor did it seem possible or imaginable that there should be.[35]

Something *really* happened to Jimmie when he entered the holy spaces of the chapel, Sacks noticed:

> Clearly Jimmie found himself, found continuity and reality, in the abso-
> luteness of spiritual attention and act. The Sisters were right — he did
> find his soul here. And so was Luria, whose words now came back to me:
> "A man does not consist of memory alone. He has feeling, will, sensibil-
> ity, moral being. . . . It is here . . . you may touch him, and see a profound
> change." Memory, mental activity, mind alone could not hold him; but
> moral attention and action could hold him completely.[36]

From Jimmie's perspective, his spiritual encounter allowed him to enter into a familiar narrative that provided him with an anchor and a sense of self that was otherwise apparently missing from his life. The fact that he would have forgotten it soon afterwards is beside the point. The intensity and power of that unique and special moment was the transformative force that held him, made his life hopeful, and changed the perspectives of those who knew him from hopelessness to hopefulness. This change of perspective allowed others to hold Jimmie well.

And this hope was stable. Jimmie responded in similar ways to certain other phenomena, but this was different:

> There was something that endured and survived. If Jimmie was briefly
> "held" by a task or puzzle or game or calculation, held in the purely
> mental challenge of these, he would fall apart as soon as they were done,
> into the abyss of his nothingness, his amnesia. But if he was held in
> emotional and spiritual attention — in the contemplation of nature or
> art, in listening to music, in taking part in the Mass in chapel — the at-
> tention, its "mood," its quietude, would persist for a while, and there
> would be in him a pensiveness and peace we rarely, if ever, saw during
> the rest of his life at the Home. I have known Jimmie now for nine years

35. Oliver Sacks, *The Man Who Mistook His Wife for a Hat* (New York: Touchstone Books, 1998), p. 37.

36. Sacks, *The Man Who Mistook His Wife for a Hat,* p. 37.

— and neuropsychologically, he has not changed in the least. He still has the severest, most devastating Korsakov's, cannot remember isolated items for more than a few seconds, and has a dense amnesia going back to 1945. But humanly, spiritually, he is at times a different man altogether — no longer fluttering, restless, bored, and lost, but deeply attentive to the beauty and soul of the world.[37]

At one level, Jimmie's responses are understandable neurologically. The places in the brain that process art and music are close to the places where memories are stored, so the fact that such things might stimulate memory would seem to make some neurological sense.[38] However, this isn't the only story that we might choose to tell. Jimmie's experience also makes theological sense. Think of it this way. When we listen to music, or at least when we're doing so in a more concentrated and intentional manner, we don't simply hum and sing along in a neutral way. Certain songs contain our memories. As soon as we hear them, we're whisked backward in time to situations, events, and people that were deeply meaningful to us and that remind us of things we have done and people we have loved. Such memories are laden with feelings and emotions. Music is a vehicle that we use as we travel through time; it brings us back to often-forgotten destinations, some of which we remember with joy, others with sadness. Understood in this way, we can see that things such as songs, music, art, dance, and ritual actually function as modes of extended memory — that is, places where memory is stored external to its normal location in the brain. They act as keys that can unlock emotions, feelings, and recollections that would otherwise be inaccessible. People may not be able to access certain memories via the normal processes. But it may be that music, art, prayer, and so forth act as keys which allow aspects of memory to be

37. Sacks, *The Man Who Mistook His Wife for a Hat,* p. 38.

38. Sacks develops this point in some detail in his book *Musicophilia* (London: Picador, 2008), Chapter 29: "Music and Identity: Dementia and Music Therapy." Also see the fascinating paper by Vernon Pickles and Raya A. Jones, "The Person Still Comes First: The Continuing Musical Self in Dementia," *Journal of Consciousness Studies* 13, no. 3 (2006): 73-79. Pickles and Jones argue that there is a residual musical self that remains even in the midst of severe dementia. This is an "enduring fragment" of who the person used to be. They argue for the presence of a neurocognitive "musical self" system that runs alongside established perspectives on the nature of the self. Fragments of musical awareness are not meaningless; they are manifestations of a self that remains.

unlocked and accessed even if that access is only temporary and sporadic. When we watch people with dementia move to the rhythm of music, when we see them dance without words, they may well be remembering cognitively or bodily something profound and deep about themselves and their pasts.

Likewise, when a person is caught up in a familiar prayer or hymn, or when they simply clap their hands to the rhythm of a song, they may well be remembering, cognitively or bodily, experiences they have had with God — or they may be having an experience with God at that very moment. If we are to remember Jesus in the Eucharist, we must remember that remembering takes many forms. Jimmie's increased functioning in the context of worship may well have neurological explanations. But that doesn't mean what's happening is only neurological. The suggestion that Christian practices may act as keys to unlock memories takes us to a different place and allows us to tell a different story and to hold him quite differently. It enables us, like Michael Ignatieff's philosopher son, to give him the benefit of the doubt. Jimmie's experience at Mass is similar to the presence of the students for Ann Goldingay and the wordless Quaker worship for Mary; the acts of presence and worship became a vital place of reconnection with God and others. The experience of the wife of Jean Vanier's friend as she temporarily moved out of the fog is not incidental or meaningless. Even though the emergence may be fleeting, it is nonetheless real.

To be present with and for people with dementia and to fellowship and worship with them is to remember them well and to act accordingly. It is to hold them in their identities as people remembered by God and by the community of God's friends. We do people who suffer from dementia a huge disservice if we simply assume that their moments of "springing to life" are nothing but instances of meaningless procedural memory. If we fail to be with them in those moments — moments that will not be remembered and which may not return — we fail to remember them well.

Becoming Friends of Time

To be in the moment with someone means that we have to change our conceptions of time. John Goldingay's statement that "in that moment she will appreciate you," Sacks's observation that despite his profound memory loss, Jimmie remains "deeply attentive to the beauty and soul of the world," Mary's wordless participation in the silence of worship — all draw our attention to the significance of time and the present moment. We have already suggested that human beings are time travelers! Through our use of memory, we are constantly moving backward and forward in time, reflecting on our past, thinking about the present, and looking toward the future. Very rarely do we slow down and take time to consider the meaning and significance of the present moment. Mary, Ann Goldingay, and Jimmie G. had three very different experiences of disability. And yet at the heart of each was a common experience of the importance of the present moment. Jimmie's past eludes him, and because of that his future is unclear. Ann's disability meant that she could not articulate a sense of movement through history (although, of course, she may have experienced such movement). The forward thrust of time as it took her from where she was to where she hoped to be going was elusive and evasive. Mary may well perceive the ebb and flow of history, but she clearly seems to be comfortable in the present moment. Each of these people experiences a different mode of time, one that is not spatial or progressive but that is at the same time deeply intentional and profoundly revealing. For all, "the now" has particular significance.

This is why Vanier and Hauerwas's suggestion of becoming friends of time is so vital and so radical. Time provides the existential space within which we learn to love and care for one another. But time needs to be sanctified, redeemed, and drawn into the service of God. We do this by simply slowing down and reclaiming time for its proper purposes. To learn to be in the present moment is to learn what it means to redeem time. As Hauerwas rightly points out, we have all the time that we need; we just need to learn how to use it faithfully:

> Patience creates the time necessary for people to come to reconciliation and knowledge of one another in a way that we're not threatened to eliminate the other because they frighten us so deeply. We have all the time we need in a world that doesn't think it's got much time at all to draw on God's love, to enact that love, that the world might see what it means to be chosen by God.[39]

39. This quotation is taken from the original version of Stanley Hauerwas's essay "The Politics of Gentleness," which was presented at a conference featuring Hauerwas and Jean

We are called to learn what it means to be in the moment, to notice the small things that the world rejects or explains away. We need to learn to live differently with time. To do so requires that we recognize where it is that we are living. If "the world" is actually creation, then we live in God's created time, and God created time for a purpose. Time doesn't just happen; it is created by God, sustained by God, and, if we take time to listen, directed by God. Time matters. Living in God's created time means, if nothing else, that time is intentional, meaningful, and purposeful.

Calling by Name: Naming and Holding

The idea of being in the moment relates to the types of intimate experiences we have looked at thus far, but it has wider implications and deeper meanings. When we are with people in the moment, we learn what it means to name them properly and to hold them faithfully in that identity. We have previously looked in some detail at the issue of naming. To name something or someone "dementia" has quite specific and typically negative connotations — socially, theologically, and neurologically. To slow down, take time, and gently call someone's name is to hold him in his identity and make a strong statement about who you think he is and how you believe he should be treated.

It matters how we name things because naming determines what we see. In Exodus 3:4, God calls Moses by name:

> When the LORD saw that he had gone over to look [at the burning bush], God called to him from within the bush, "Moses, Moses!" And Moses said, "Here I am."

In the sacrament of the present moment, we call out the names of those whom we love and seek to offer care, and then we listen. The words "Here I am" can be spoken in a myriad of different ways — through a touch, a gesture, a fleeting look, a noise that most would consider to be meaningless.

Vanier hosted by the Centre for Spirituality, Health, and Disability at Aberdeen University. That essay was published in a slightly different form in Chapter 4 of Hauerwas and Vanier's *Living Gently in a Violent World*. I have retained the original here because I feel that it captures the meaning of Hauerwas's point more fully than the revised version.

But if we are truly with someone, we recognize and hear. To call someone's name is to give her the benefit of the doubt. To listen for an answer is to show that we are willing to love. John Goldingay says this:

> As a human being, I am a person called by name — by God, and by another human being. In addressing disabled people by name, we affirm to them that they are and who they are. We affirm our love for them, which operates despite or because neither we nor they may yet know much of who they are. Naming reflects knowing and loving, but at least as much it expresses loving and thus facilitates knowing. Somehow this has implications for people such as those with Alzheimer's disease who may be so profoundly mentally disabled that we may wonder what their "knowing" of themselves can mean. "They may no longer 'know' who they are, but the church knows who they are." . . . Oftentimes it may be apparent that addressing them by name is received as an affirmation of love which meets with a response of love and trust. The one who names thus receives in return the gift of being loved and trusted and is built up.[40]

Naming something properly is an affirmation of worth and recognition and an important way of holding and remembering. To learn someone's name takes time.

The Sacrament of the Present Moment: Soulful Companioning

To be with one another in the present moment is to allow our souls to touch. Meeting in the present moment is meeting soul to soul, *nephesh* to *nephesh*; it is a place where human souls encounter the soul of God. From this vantage point we can understand why it is that for Mary, Ann Goldingay, and Jimmie G., though perhaps in different ways, it was the present moment that formed their places of meeting with those who knew their names, remembered them, and held them in that sacramental place of remembrance. A sacrament, says M. F. Egan, "is, in the first place, a sign of

40. John Goldingay, "Being Human," in *Encounter with Mystery: Reflections on L'Arche and Living with Disability*, ed. Frances Young (London: Darton, Longman & Todd, 1997), pp. 138-39.

grace: that is to say, it is an object or an action which, in virtue of some natural quality of its own, is capable of representing the supernatural and interior power of divine grace."[41] That being so, the presence of the students with Ann Goldingay and their practice of slowing down and taking time with her could be viewed as sacramental insofar as their actions and presence represent the reality of the presence of the Spirit of God as God remembers her and seeks to minister to her in and through the practice of the presence of God's people. God is in the moment, but not in the Buberian sense that the meeting place is the intersubjective space between people (as per Tom Kitwood). God is closer than that. God is in the meeting, in the moment that God has created, and in the Spirit that brings into life and sustains two creatures as they wordlessly encounter one another.

The sacrament is also revealed in the moment of Sacks's revelation. It was only as he slowed down, moved beyond those things that he had been trained to see, and saw Jimmie in a close and intimate way that he was able to see Jimmie's soul. It was as he learned to remember Jimmie differently that love became a possibility: *"It's good that you exist; it's good that you are in this world."* It should be noted that being in the moment is not necessarily a mystical experience or some kind of unearthly revelation given from on high. Mary found the moment as she shared in the very earthly practice of being silent in community. The sacrament of the present moment simply means providing the opportunities and having the epistemological awareness to allow people to notice things that they never could have noticed before and, in noticing them, to see and respond differently. To be with someone in the moment is to be open to surprise, new possibilities, and the kind of hidden experiences that we earlier suggested were vital in understanding the experiences of people with dementia.

Learning to be in the moment is not necessarily a supernatural achievement, at least not in the ways that we usually refer to the supernatural. Thomas Merton once said, "The gate of heaven is everywhere."[42] This is an interesting proposition. In our previous anthropological discussions, we have seen that there is a real sense in which heaven and earth overlap within the earthiness of human beings. When Jesus says, "Thy will be

---

41. M. F. Egan, "The Sacrament of the Present Moment," *The Irish Monthly* 65, no. 764 (February 1937): 111-17; quotation on 111.

42. Thomas Merton, *Conjectures of a Guilty Bystander* (New York: Doubleday, 1966), p. 158.

done, on earth as it is in heaven," he isn't suggesting a picture of the world as some sort of Platonic reflection of an ideal vision. The gate of heaven is everywhere insofar as we exist in a world wherein heaven and earth constantly overlap and intersect. This is also the case in and between human beings. The people of the *nephesh* cannot be at peace without God; the supernatural is much more natural than we might sometimes assume. God is not a stranger to our world. That which may appear supernatural is really just us learning to see the natural properly. God is in every moment, but there are times when the present moment is all that there seems to be, and God's enduring attention in the present moment becomes a primary and ongoing locus for revelation and worship. Jean-Pierre de Caussade articulates the point this way:

> God still speaks today as he spoke to our forefathers in days gone by, before there were either spiritual directors or methods of direction. The spiritual life was then a matter of immediate communication with God. . . . All they knew was that each moment brought its appointed task, faithfully to be accomplished. This was enough for the spiritually minded of those days. All their attention was focused on the present, minute by minute, like the hand of a clock that marks the minutes of each hour covering the distance along which it has to travel. Constantly prompted by divine impulsion, they found themselves imperceptibly turned towards the next task that God had ready for them at each hour of the day.[43]

God is in the present moment.

43. Jean-Pierre de Caussade, *The Sacrament of the Present Moment* (San Francisco: HarperCollins, 1989), p. 1.

10. Hospitality among Strangers: Christian Communities as Places of Belonging

The stranger who dwells among you shall be to you as one born among you, and you shall love him as yourself; for you were strangers in the land of Egypt: I am the LORD your God.

LEVITICUS 19:34 (NKJV)

I was a stranger and you invited me in.

MATTHEW 25:35

So now you Gentiles are no longer strangers and foreigners. You are citizens along with all of God's holy people. You are members of God's family.

EPHESIANS 2:19 (NLT)

I began this book with a series of questions, primary among them being "Who am I?" I'm not sure if I've discovered who I am, but the question no longer troubles me. I have discovered that ultimately the answer to that question lies in the hands of God, and I am at peace with that. As I approach the end of this book, I find myself no longer afraid of dementia, at least not in the way that I was before. It may be the case that if I experience dementia later in my life, much of who I thought I was and much of what others think I am will slip away as the neurological damage shifts and changes my expressions of myself. I can and probably will be anxious, angry, and disappointed, but I don't have to be afraid as long as I am certain that God will remember me and that that memory has active power for the present and the future. I need not be afraid as long as I am certain that those whom I love — my family, my friends, my community — and the people of God's memory, the church, will continue to love me and remember me. As long as I know that I can trust in God and in those who love me to remember me well, I will be safe. I am certain of that.

But there is still one nagging question that needs to be explored. It's all very well for me to expect people to remember me, but what am I actually asking them to do when I ask that they love me for who I am even when who I am is difficult? In the Introduction I said, "To ask people to continue to love me even if who I am is difficult for me and for others is a pretty big request." That is clearly the case. To ask someone to love a person who is sick is always difficult. But to ask someone to love and care for a person who often seems so different from the person he/she originally loved sometimes seems impossible. What might it mean to love this stranger who is me?

Becoming Strangers

In trying to answer this question, we need to begin by thinking about what it is about dementia that turns us into strangers. People with dementia very quickly discover that part of their changing identity relates to their becoming strangers both to themselves and to others. In his autobiographical book *Losing My Mind: An intimate Look at Life with Alzheimer's*, Thomas DeBaggio lays out a painful, moving, and often angry account of what it's like to journey into dementia:

> Alzheimer's sends you back to an elemental world before time, a world devoid of possibility and secrets. It is a world of insecurity where the certainty of words and the memory of events is unstable. It is a world of abject insecurity and tears and frustration. I sense reality slipping away, and words become slippery sand. My life is turning into a dun-colored kaleidoscope. I think it will be only a matter of months before my life becomes a nightmare and the world becomes a freshly unknowable place where even the simplest things are difficult because they are unrecognizable.[1]

1. Thomas DeBaggio, *Losing My Mind: An Intimate Look at Life with Alzheimer's* (New York: Simon & Schuster, 2003), p. 88.

As he loses his sense of who he is and what the world is like, DeBaggio finds himself a stranger to both himself and the world. Dementia is a series of small deaths that strips the peace from his previously hopeful life, casting him adrift in a world that is rapidly vanishing:

> There is a wide emotional difference between knowing you will die one day in the future and living with the knowledge you have a disease that slowly squeezes the life from you in hundreds of unexpected ways, and you have to watch it happen while those who love you stand by unable to help you.[2]

DeBaggio is lonely and helpless. Those around him are lonely and helpless — onlookers and witnesses to the demise of the one they knew and the emergence of a stranger. Every time he goes to sleep, he realizes, "This may be my last chance to dream."[3] His fear is not that he will die. His fear is that he will no longer remember what it is like to live.

Forgetting Whose We Are

One of the most profound and moving Christian testimonies about what it's like to experience dementia is Robert Davis's autobiography, *My Journey into Alzheimer's Disease*. (You'll recall that we discussed this book briefly in Chapter 7.) Davis was a pastor in one of the largest churches in Miami, Florida. He was a powerful preacher and a thoroughly dynamic minister. However, gradually it became obvious that things weren't right. He was forgetting, becoming confused. He couldn't cope with the responsibilities that he once thrived on. When he was diagnosed with Alzheimer's disease, it shook the very foundations of his faith. His book is sometimes hopeful, sometimes dark, but taken as a whole offers both insight into what it means to have dementia and to be moving into the advanced stages, and insight into what it means to try to hold onto faith and love as all one's old certainties slowly slip away.

Davis began his journey hopefully, holding onto Jesus and feeling assured that God was in control. But soon things became increasingly difficult as the spiritual resources that carried him on his journey began to fail:

2. DeBaggio, *Losing My Mind*, p. 87.
3. DeBaggio, *Losing My Mind*, p. 7.

My spiritual life was still miserable. I could not read the Bible. I could not pray as I wanted because my emotions were dead and cut off. . . . My mind also raced about, grasping for the comfort of the Savior whom I knew and loved and for the emotional peace that he could give me, but finding nothing. I concluded that the only reason for such darkness must be spiritual. Unnamed guilt filled me. Yet the only guilt I could put a name to was failure to read my Bible. But I could not read, and would God condemn me for this? I could only lie there and cry, "Oh God, why? Why?"[4]

Davis was becoming a stranger. The things that held him in the world — his faith, his love for Jesus, his sense of identity as a Christian — were all beginning to slip away. The resources that he depended on to hold onto his faith were also not functioning because of his neurological decline. He was losing himself, and his greatest fear was that he was losing God too. The resonance between Davis's lament and the words of Psalm 88 is obvious:

I call to you, O LORD, every day;
I spread out my hands to you.
Do you show your wonders to the dead?
Do those who are dead rise up and praise you?
Is your love declared in the grave,
your faithfulness in Destruction?
Are your wonders known in the place of darkness,
or your righteous deeds in the land of oblivion?
But I cry to you for help, O LORD;
in the morning my prayer comes before you.
Why, O LORD, do you reject me
and hide your face from me? (vv. 9-14)

The process of becoming a stranger is long and painful.

Watching in Helplessness

DeBaggio's comment on the helplessness of the onlooker raises important issues. Robert Davis's autobiography is frequently quoted within the pas-

---

4. Robert Davis, *My Journey into Alzheimer's Disease* (Carol Stream, Ill.: Tyndale House, 1989), p. 53.

toral literature on dementia, and rightly so. It is a powerful story about the experience of Alzheimer's and the role of faith, Spirit, and hope. But less attention has been paid to Davis's wife, Betty. Betty wrote the book with her husband and presumably gradually took on a more prominent role as his condition progressed. Her voice is formally silent until the epilogue. At that point she explodes onto the scene as herself:

> Sometimes I feel like God's special pet — held in that special place of all those who are called to share "the fellowship of his suffering." Sometimes I feel like Jesus in the Garden, "Please, if it be your will, let this cup pass — let me wake up to learn all this is just a bad dream and all is as before — please come forth in your great healing power, God, and bring the miracle we've all been praying for and waiting for. Give the literal, physical renewed mind!" Sometimes in weakness and despair I want to give voice to that primal scream starting way down in the hidden recesses of the lungs — down where the ever-present knot that lives in my stomach resides — let it whirl through that vortex that's sucking my life and being into that black hole of never-ending pain, emptiness, and loneliness — just give it voice as it rises and explodes through the top of my head — Noooooooooooo! Anything, God, but this! Death would be better than this — to hold onto the box when the present is used up — hoping the box can bring again the joy of the reality of the gift — but the box is empty! . . . How do you prepare for the holocaust? How can you say good-night to your sweetheart and wonder — will this be the night from which reason will never again awaken? Will morning find that new person in my bed — the man who will not know who I am or why I am in his bed?[5]

Dementia evokes lament.[6]

Why, Lord?

In her extended meditation on Psalm 88, my good friend Aileen Barclay, whose husband has Alzheimer's disease, offers some insight into the role

---

5. Betty Davis, in Davis, *My Journey into Alzheimer's Disease*, p. 140.

6. For a further development of the pastoral significance of lament in the face of suffering, see John Swinton, *Raging with Compassion: Pastoral Responses to the Problem of Evil* (Grand Rapids: Wm. B. Eerdmans, 2006), Chapter 5.

that lament might play in coming to terms with the losses of dementia. Reflecting on her experience with her husband, she observes,

> In despair, confusion, and the grief of living with my husband, who once was a capable, intelligent, and gracious man, I remember the person whom I married and with whom I shared my life. I withdraw from my lively church, just unable to face people who keep telling me what a wonderful person my husband is. Nonetheless, physical withdrawal from church does not mean that God withdraws, even though it may often feel as if he has. "Your wrath lies heavily upon me" wails the psalmist, conjuring up images of those six silent hours as Jesus hung on the cross when all seemed lost, broken, fractured.
>
> > You have taken from me my closest friends
> > and have made me repulsive to them.
> > I am confined and cannot escape. . . . [v. 8]
>
> From the cross, Jesus' loneliness is a stark reminder to us. We too have become repulsive to our friends and cut off from the community suffering the terrors of the night. Darkness has indeed become our closest friend. Lacking the cognitive abilities to participate in social life or overstepping the unwritten rules of social conventions, one-time friends no longer seek our company. Invitations to dinner at our home, once eagerly accepted, are "postponed" with lame excuses. I learn that I am no longer part of a couple — that honored institution of the church that opens doors for friendship and fellowship. I learn that I am not single either, and cannot find solace among the women who complain that the church only has time for those who are married.
>
> > my eyes are dim with grief.
> > I call to you, O Lord, every day;
> > I spread out my hands to you. [v. 9][7]

Her husband's dementia has turned Aileen from a wife and a friend into a stranger. Friends no longer seem to recognize her. She is married but not married; in the community of the church but not fully of that community; single but not single. Experiencing social strangeness and caring for

---

7. Aileen Barclay, "Psalm 88: Living with Dementia," *Journal of Religion, Disability, and Health* 16, no. 1 (2012): 88-101.

someone with dementia also revealed to Aileen her own inner strangeness. That emerged as she gradually became aware that the person she thought she was wasn't the person she actually was or had become. Again she quotes from Psalm 88:

> From my youth I have been afflicted and close to death;
> I have suffered your terrors and am in despair.
> Your wrath has swept over me;
> your terrors have destroyed me.
> All day long they surround me like a flood;
> they have completely engulfed me.
> You have taken my companions and loved ones from me;
> the darkness is my closest friend. [vv. 15-18]

In the darkness of the night, I remember who I truly am, the mistakes I have made, the deliberate actions and justifications to get my own way, to remain in control. I remember the lasting consequences of my thoughts, intentions, and actions, suffering the terrors, despairing that for all the years I have claimed to be part of God's eternal kingdom, as a carer I am failing to live up to the love, joy, peace, patience, kindness, goodness, faithfulness, gentleness, and self-control that first attracted me to Jesus. I sense God's wrath weighing heavily upon me, flooding my sleeping and waking hours, engulfing me under a mighty wave of reproach. My self-centeredness, my complaints, my continued anger with my increasingly frail husband all lead to alienation from others unable to cope with my endless outpouring of grievances. The throwaway remarks remind me of how I am being reconstructed.

> "If he stays with you, you'll kill him."
> "You only speak about your own needs!"
> "This is your burden — you have to get on with it."
> "I'm not interested in your needs — your husband is my client."
> "We've all got different personalities — you don't have the right one to care for a person with Alzheimer's."

Years before the medical diagnosis of Alzheimer's was given to my husband, I knew he had the disease. The deterioration has been a slow but relentless destruction of his capacities as a competent adult. He has become a frightened child, petulant and manipulative, dependent upon me for what little order can be created around his disappearing capacities. It's like carrying around on my back a weight that is too heavy for the scales. The pendulum has swung so far that the plate, like a broken swing, has hit the ground.[8]

Aileen's reflections on a psalm of lament have ended in her own lament as she gradually begins to see that both she and her husband are strangers in the eyes of others and increasingly strangers in their own eyes. Dementia brings suffering with it, and that suffering creates strangers in many senses of the word.

Beyond Suffering

The suffering that dementia brings to both the person with the diagnosis and those who seek to offer care and support is of a quite particular kind. Social anthropologist Arthur Kleinman, who cares for his Alzheimer's-stricken wife, comments, "We have been marked by a special kind of pain."[9] Dementia is a form of *affliction*. In her book *Waiting on God,* Simone Weil offers an understanding of affliction:

> In the realm of suffering, affliction is something apart, specific, irreducible. It is quite a different thing from simple suffering. It takes possession of the soul and marks it through and through with its own particular mark, the mark of slavery.[10]

Affliction involves physical pain of a particular kind. Toothache is painful, but it passes. The pain of affliction is enduring, drawn out, and deeply impacts the whole person:

> There is not real affliction unless the event which has seized and uprooted a life attacks it, directly or indirectly, in all parts, social, psychological, and physical. The social factor is essential. There is not really af-

8. Barclay, "Psalm 88: Living with Dementia."

9. Arthur Kleinman, "Caregiving: The Odyssey of Becoming More Human," *The Lancet* 373 (January 2009): 293.

10. Simone Weil, *Waiting on God* (London: Fontana Books, 1950), p. 76.

fliction where there is not social degradation or the fear of it in some form or another.[11]

This is clearly what DeBaggio experienced:

With any untreatable, disabling malady, the victims become sensitized to every movement of their body, every breath, searching for change and studying the course of the illness until it threatens to destroy friendships and the love of those around them.[12]

Dementia may not be marked by physical pain, but it is a deeply painful experience in all of the dimensions Weil highlights.

Affliction can produce self-hatred, self-contempt, and feelings of guilt.[13] Aileen's revelations of those aspects of herself that were less than perfect emerged from and reflected her experience of affliction. Affliction also makes God appear to be absent:

Affliction makes God appear to be absent for a time, more absent than a dead man, more absent than light in the utter darkness of a cell. A kind of horror submerges the whole soul. During this absence there is nothing to love. What is terrible is that if, in this darkness where there is nothing to love, the soul ceases to love, God's absence becomes final.[14]

This was clearly Davis's experience, and the psalmist's experience as well. While some forms of affliction can be eased by a change in circumstances, the terrifying thing about the affliction that accompanies dementia is that there is no real possibility of its moving on. The psalmist's cry — "You have taken my companions and loved ones from me; the darkness is my closest friend" — has an eternal quality that is deeply disturbing. It is not a coincidence that these words from Psalm 88 end the psalm. Unlike other psalms of lament, this psalm offers no hopeful return to God — only darkness.

11. Weil, *Waiting on God*, p. 78.
12. DeBaggio, *Losing My Mind*, p. 7.
13. Alexander Nava, *The Mystical and Prophetic Thought of Simone Weil and Gustavo Gutiérrez: Reflections on the Mystery and Hiddenness of God* (New York: State University of New York Press), p. 31.
14. Weil, *Waiting on God*, p. 80.

The problem with affliction is that it is isolating and alienating. Only those who are or who have been afflicted can understand what it means. It isn't really possible to project one's self directly into the situation of the afflicted. One can only think through what it might mean for *me* to be afflicted. As Eric Springsted puts it,

> If we think of the suffering of rheumatoid arthritis as the greater evil, it is because we can only imagine it in terms of ourselves, the same selves as we are now undergoing extreme pain. Affliction, however, is much more difficult to imagine because in affliction we actually lose ourselves. This is why we also do not usually even notice the afflicted; what we think we see is a person who is in need of help, or who needs to pull himself up by his bootstraps. But in fact there is no person left there to help.[15]

Springsted (after Weil) does not mean that the person literally ceases to exist. The point he wants to make is that the affliction so overwhelms a person that she loses sight of who she is; psychologically she struggles to exist. For people with dementia, this relates to their feeling that somehow their true selves are fading away — even though, as we have seen, this is not at all the case. For carers it has to do with the way in which their role as carers subsumes every other role and every other possibility for their lives. The affliction becomes all that they are, and they become slaves to their conditions. All parties involved — carers and cared for — become strangers to themselves and to others, lost within their afflictions without the resources to pull themselves from the pit:

> You have put me in the lowest pit,
> in the darkest depths.
> Your wrath lies heavily upon me;
> you have overwhelmed me with all your waves.
> You have taken from me my closest friends
> and have made me repulsive to them.
> I am confined and cannot escape;
> my eyes are dim with grief. (Ps. 88:6-9)

15. Eric O. Springsted, *Simone Weil and the Suffering of Love* (Cambridge, Mass.: Cowley Publications), p. 31.

The affliction of dementia makes strangers of ourselves and the ones we love.

The Passion of Christ

The affliction that is experienced by those who are marked by dementia is echoed in the divine affliction revealed paradigmatically in the passion of Christ. Weil points to Jesus' passion as the place where divine affliction is most poignantly revealed. Clearly Jesus was afflicted in all of the senses that we have discussed, and yet he continued to love. Perhaps Jesus' greatest sense of affliction came when he was abandoned, or at least experienced the feeling of being abandoned. But even in the void Jesus kept on loving. It is here that we begin to see some possibilities for hope. Springsted makes an interesting observation:

> Even though he [Jesus] could neither see nor understand anything that corresponded to the good he had set out to accomplish, he still contin-ued to love in the void that was left and refused to deny that love. Jesus did not mistakenly identify that good with any earthly good, nor try to find any compensation for his sufferings, as we often try to do to remedy our sufferings. He simply remained as far removed from the Father as anyone could be and continued to love. Even though God was utterly ab-sent, Jesus still loved and remained faithful, although he had no hope.[16]

In the passion and affliction of Jesus, we can see pain, loss, abandon-ment, and deep lament, which in a very real sense mirrors the experience of dementia for carer and cared for: "My God, my God, *why have you for-saken me*"[17] is a mode of speech which comes naturally to afflicted people. And yet in and through the pain and affliction of Jesus, we encounter re-demption. Even in the apparent absence of God, Weil observes, Jesus' love is in no way diminished. The passion of Christ opens up the possibility that even though what we see does not at all correspond with what we

16. Springsted, *Simone Weil and the Suffering of Love*, p. 45.
17. Weil seems to indicate that God really does abandon the person and truly is absent in the midst of affliction. However, Scripture is filled with affirmations that God does not abandon God's people even in the midst of affliction. Nevertheless, to *feel* abandoned is not particularly different from actually being abandoned.

think we should be seeing and what we truly desire to be seeing, love remains possible, and redemption can be achieved. This could be expressed as a sharp caution: "Don't believe that which seems to be apparent!" Even as our prayers seem to scream into a silent abyss, the resurrection for which the passion was a necessity puts new meaning into Jesus' words: "You parents, if your children ask for a loaf of bread, do you give them a stone instead?" (Matt. 7:9, NLT). Even when our prayers seem not to be answered, the assurance that Jesus continues to love us provides a basis for faithful hopefulness and gives a particular shape to our sufferings. How can affliction be overcome? Through love. From whence does such love come? Jesus.

However, like other crucial aspects of the experience of dementia — memory, mind, identity — such faith in the face of affliction cannot be achieved alone. Overcoming the alienation, isolation, and enforced strangerhood that accompanies the experience of dementia cannot be done without friends and without a community that has learned to recognize the value of strangers, and that can acknowledge the reality of the experience of affliction and, in so doing, bring healing and new hope. Affliction can destroy love and force us to look at people in the wrong ways. Affliction is a breeding ground for malignant social psychology and negative positioning by self and others. What is required is a community that can offer empathic hospitality to strangers, a community that truly *sees* the experiences of dementia (for carer and cared for) for what they are (understands "dementia redescribed"), a community that has the time and the resources to move people from affliction to hope: from strangeness to belonging.

Fear of Strangers

Dementia creates strangers. Love overcomes strangeness. Love, then, is central to the creation of the types of relationships that Tom Kitwood and Steven Sabat have shown are central for understanding dementia and providing person-centered dementia care. Malignant social psychology and negative positioning tend to typify the way in which we react to strangers. We fear them, and we seek ways to distance ourselves from them. To be a stranger is to be a threat to the cohesion and safety of a group or community. To be an afflicted stranger is to be someone whom others do not and really cannot understand. We don't really understand those who choose to be with the afflicted or those who have no choice other than to be with them. This was one of Jesus' problems. Because he spent time with strangers — tax collectors, sinners, prostitutes — their stigma and alienation became his. As we read in Luke 7:34, "The Son of Man came eating and drinking, and you say, 'Here is a glutton and a drunkard, a friend of tax collectors and "sinners."'" It sometimes seems that strangeness rubs off on those who hang around with strangers.

Turning people into strangers is one way of creating distance and safety. A stranger threatens the settled agreement within a community about what is good, bad, normal, and abnormal. It is much easier to push the stranger to the margins and carry on as before than it is to answer the challenge that the stranger brings with her. It is easier to offer charity to people with dementia than it is to offer welcome. Charity can mean giving alms to strangers — holding them at arm's length but convincing ourselves that we are acting compassionately. Welcome requires embrace, and rarely do we willingly embrace strangers. Above all else, the stranger threatens our peacefulness, our sense of shalom. People with dementia threaten hypercognitive perceptions of shalom in deep ways. If peace (shalom) has to do with righteousness, holiness, and right relationship with God,[18] and if the orthodox way of knowing God is assumed primarily to be cognitive and intellectual, then those who come proclaiming that the standard ways of relating to God might not apply to them will inevitably create a dissonance that is at best disorienting and at worst offensive. It is easier to position people with dementia as strangers whose customs, worldviews, and experiences are alien to "us"; it might be easier for "us" to acknowledge their "value" in their difference than to face the challenge of what it might mean to love God when you no longer know who God is. Clearly, people with dementia bring strangeness in a myriad of ways and sit neatly within the role of stranger both culturally and spiritually.

Hospitality to Strangers?

In an odd way, recognizing the ways in which those involved with dementia become strangers is the first step toward developing a way of looking at

---

18. For a deeper exposition of the concept of shalom, see John Swinton, *From Bedlam to Shalom* (New York: Peter Lang, 2000), Chapter 4.

their strangeness which has healing possibilities. The idea of offering hospitality to strangers is a key theme that runs throughout the Old and New Testaments.[19] As one reflects on the ministry of Jesus, a constant dynamic was his hospitable movement between being a guest and being a host. Jesus spent time with rich people and powerful rulers, but he also spent much time offering hospitality and welcome to strangers, to those whom society rejected, marginalized, and refused to relate with. There is a strong tradition in Christianity that seeks to emulate this aspect of Jesus' ministry. In Romans 12:13 (NLT), Paul tells us, "When God's people are in need, be ready to help them. Always be eager to practice hospitality." The word "hospitality" means "stranger-loving."[20] To practice hospitality, then, is to learn how to love the stranger. If I am correct in identifying those involved with dementia as strangers, then this tradition could offer an important starting point for the shaping of a community that can see and respond to dementia in new ways. The question then becomes different: Does the tradition of offering hospitality to strangers provide an adequate model for finding room within Christian communities for people with dementia and those close to them?

The Stranger in the Bible

In his essay "The Stranger in the Bible," Elie Weisel draws attention to the significance of the stranger in the history of the people of Israel. He asks, "Who is a stranger?" He points out that the Hebrew Bible provides three terms for the stranger: *ger, nochri,* and *zar*. The *ger* lives among the Jewish people. He has adopted the Jewish faith, Jewish customs and values, and has made Jewish friends. The *nochri* is a *ger* who desires to remain separated from and aloof toward the Jewish people. The *ger* adjusts and assimilates; the *nochri* remains a friendly outsider. The *zar* is even further removed than the *nochri*. He is different and hostile.[21]

19. Arthur Sutherland, *I Was a Stranger: A Christian Theology of Hospitality* (Nashville: Abingdon Press, 2006).

20. The word in Greek is *philoxenos*, which means "stranger loving; being kind to strangers; being hospitable."

21. Elie Wiesel, *"Inside a Library"; and, "The Stranger in the Bible"* (New York: Hebrew Union College — Jewish Institute of Religion, 1981), p. 28.

The Ger as Stranger

Ian Cohen picks up on the importance of the idea of the *ger* and reflects on its implications for people with intellectual disabilities. He highlights the fact that a *ger*

> was a sojourner, or more technically a "resident alien," who in the He-
> brew Bible was "a person living in a mutually responsible association
> with a community not originally his own, or in a place not inherently
> his own." He was a "protected or dependent foreigner," a "protected
> stranger" . . . of another tribe or district who, coming to sojourn in a
> place where he was not strengthened by the presence of his own kin, put
> himself under the protection of a clan or of a powerful chief.[22]

The *ger* was looked upon with favor and enjoyed unusual privileges (Exod. 20:10; 23:12):

> One must be as charitable with the *ger* as with the Levite. One must not
> reject the *ger* or cause him harm or loss or distress; one must extend
> more assistance to him — or her — than to the average person; one
> must make an effort to understand the *ger* and make him feel welcome,
> at home; one must love him — or her. The term *veahavta* — and you
> shall love — is characteristically used three times in Scripture: and you
> shall love your God with all your heart; you shall love your fellow-man;
> and you shall love the *ger,* the stranger.[23]

To love the stranger is to love the *ger,* one who has come among the people of God and chosen to live with them, someone who is worthy of respect, hospitality, and welcome. The *ger* is to be treated in this way because the people of Israel know what it is like to be strangers, since they were once strangers themselves: "The stranger who dwells among you shall be to you as one born among you, and you shall love him as yourself; for you were strangers in the land of Egypt: I am the LORD your God" (Lev. 19:34, NKJV). In other words, as Cohen points out, "We must treat others the

---

22. Cohen, in *Encounter with Mystery,* ed. Frances Young (London: Darton, Longman & Todd, 1997), p. 155.
23. Cohen, in *Encounter with Mystery,* p. 29.

way we have been treated. We must show them compassion, charity, and love. Above all, we must not make them *feel* like strangers."[24]

We offer hospitality to the *ger* because the people of God (in this case, the Israelites) have been strangers and have experienced God's care and release. God raised up the Jewish people and remains true to God's promises. In the same way, the Jewish people are called to recognize their own history in the *ger* and treat her as God has treated them. It is important to notice that it isn't enough simply to *include* the *ger* within the community; she must be made to *feel* welcome, to feel that she is no longer a stranger. She remains a foreigner, but it is the task of the community to make her feel included.

Wiesel's and Cohen's analysis of *ger* is in some ways helpful for our understanding of dementia and strangeness. It opens up the biblical idea of the stranger and shows clearly that God is located in that place where the *ger* sojourns. The people of God at all times and in all places are people who accept and welcome the stranger. Christians are obligated to offer hospitality and welcome to the *ger* because they belong to the same story from which Israel emerged and worship the same God, a God who was with the people of Israel in their estrangedness and who views the stranger with care and compassion. For Christians, reflecting on the *ger* brings fresh poignancy to Jesus' words in Matthew 25:35: "I was a stranger and you welcomed me." If Jesus was a stranger, then our only response to the stranger can be welcome.

Cohen applies this understanding to the lives of people with intellectual disabilities. He perceives them as modern-day *gerim* whom the church must not only incorporate but also receive as messengers. Cohen argues that linking intellectually disabled people with the *gerim* helps one to understand the meaning of intellectual disability. God is with the *gerim, and they remind us of the social location of God. This is the true vocation of the gerim:* to remind all people where God is and what it means to share a soul with God, what it means to be a creature.[25]

The Problem with Being a Stranger

It wouldn't be too difficult to apply a similar argument to the lives of people with dementia who in a sense could, for the reasons outlined previously, be

24. Cohen, in *Encounter with Mystery,* p. 29.
25. Cohen, in *Encounter with Mystery,* p. 157.

construed as modern-day *gerim*. There is, however, a significant problem with trying to equate people with dementia and their carers with *gerim* and the idea of offering hospitality to them as "strangers." First, the *gerim really were* strangers. They didn't come from the communities into which they assimilated, and they were not, and never could become, true-born Israelites. They were forever strangers, forever different. People with dementia are not strangers in such a territorial and ethnic sense. They may become estranged, and indeed others may come to perceive them as strangers, but in reality they are very much a part of "us." They may have changed in some ways, but their status within our communities has not. If my mother were to develop dementia, I wouldn't be thinking of her as a strange incomer who had entered my camp and to whom I was obliged to offer welcome and protection. She is and will always be my mum. She might become strange, but she won't become a stranger in this sense. Likewise, the sense of strangerhood that carers experience doesn't mean that they *are* actually strangers — only that the experience of caring for persons with dementia has made them *feel* like strangers.

The idea of extending hospitality toward strangers as it emerges from the Hebraic tradition is clearly helpful, and the reflections on the special status offered to the *ger* clearly raises our consciousness about the way in which God perceives and responds to human difference: God welcomes the stranger, the disabled, the one whom society has pushed to the side. God repositions them from the margins of human caring to the center of divine love. This is a valuable counter to the forms of malignant social psychology that we have explored previously in this book. Likewise, the command not to allow the *gerim* to *feel* like strangers is important. If the role of stranger has more to do with perception than reality, then creating a context wherein people no longer feel like strangers is a first step to overcoming estrangement. Nevertheless, at best, the idea of the *gerim* can be applied only metaphorically or analogically to the lives of people with dementia and those who love them. As long as the metaphorical quality of the *ger* is kept in mind, there is much to be gained. However, if the metaphor becomes reified — that is, if we come to believe that people with dementia *really are* strangers — then its utility begins to be eroded, and strangeness is actually *created* rather than dissipated and countered. That being so, while the term *ger* and its associated understandings of how to treat the outsider are helpful in identifying some aspects of our approach to the strangeness of dementia, another level of analysis and reflection is required.

The Church as Strangers

In the *Letter to Diognetus,* a first-century apologist reflects on what is different about Christians:

> For Christians cannot be distinguished from the rest of the human race by country or language or customs. They do not live in cities of their own; they do not use a peculiar form of speech; they do not follow an eccentric manner of life. This doctrine of theirs has not been discovered by the ingenuity or deep thought of inquisitive men, nor do they put forward a merely human teaching, as some people do. Yet, although they live in Greek and barbarian cities alike, as each man's lot has been cast, and follow the customs of the country in clothing and food and other matters of daily living, at the same time they give proof of the remarkable and admittedly extraordinary constitution of their own commonwealth. They live in their own countries, but only as aliens.[26]

This is quite a striking passage. It not only points to the radically different way of life that the early Christians lived; it also shows clearly what their status was in the world:

> They have a share in everything as citizens, and endure everything as foreigners. Every foreign land is their fatherland, and yet for them every fatherland is a foreign land. They marry, like everyone else, and they beget children, but they do not cast out their offspring. They share their board with each other, but not their marriage bed. It is true that they are "in the flesh," but they do not live "according to the flesh." They obey the established laws, but in their own lives they go far beyond what the laws require. They love all men, and by all men are persecuted.[27]

The vocation of Christians is to live as foreigners in a world within which they have no true home. Their true home is in heaven. As the apostle Peter puts it,

---

26. "An Anonymous Brief for Christianity Presented to Diognetus: The Mystery of the New People," 5.2-6, Christian Classics Ethereal Library: http://www.ccel.org/ccel/richardson/fathers.x.i.ii.html.

27. "An Anonymous Brief for Christianity presented to Diognetus," 5.6-11.

Dearly beloved, I beseech you as strangers and pilgrims, abstain from fleshly lusts, which war against the soul; Having your conversation honest among the Gentiles: that, whereas they speak against you as evildoers, they may by your good works, which they shall behold, glorify God in the day of visitation. (1 Pet. 2:11-12, KJV)

The vocation of Christians is to live lives which change and transform the world without themselves being polluted by the values, perspectives, and assumptions of the world — to live among people but not to become like them. In other words, *to be a Christian is to live as a stranger.* The vocation of Christians today is to become strangers, or, perhaps more accurately, to become a community of strangers. Understood in this way, *the gerim are the church as it exists in the world.* Identifying the church as *gerim* reflects and stems from Jesus' own status as *ger.* Cohen puts it thus:

The early Church perhaps . . . thought of Jesus as *ger.* Matthew's story of the escape into Egypt (Matt. 2:13-23), linking with Hosea 11:1, makes Jesus clearly a *ger* in Egypt. Luke's story of the birth of Jesus contains within it the notion that Jesus was a stranger who found lodgings in a manger. When this can be linked (a link not often made) with Jeremiah 14:8 — "Why are you like an alien in the land, like a traveler who stays in lodgings?" — the picture becomes clearer.[28]

Jesus is the *ger,* the ultimate stranger. Significantly, the early church identified itself as *paroikos,* the Greek equivalent of *ger* (stranger/foreigner):[29]

The Church was the new Israel, and was therefore a nation of sojourners who lived as citizens of God's household. They were not in this world but lived in it. The people of God were *gerim* who were protected by God. Whether in their ancient or recent history, in Jesus, the people knew God to be *ger,* with whom they shared a soul.[30]

Thus strangerhood and being a Christian can be seen to be one and the same thing. To follow Jesus, the *ger,* is to be a disciple. *Gerim make up the*

28. Cohen, in *Encounter with Mystery,* p. 156.
29. Cohen, in *Encounter with Mystery,* p. 156.
30. Cohen, in *Encounter with Mystery,* p. 157.

community of God; we are strangers who are called to welcome strangers. Thus, it may be slightly inaccurate to suggest that the best frame for the church's attitude toward those affected by dementia is the church's key vocation of offering hospitality *to* strangers. It might be more appropriate to suggest that the church is called to offer hospitality *among* strangers. The difference is subtle but important.

Hospitality among Strangers

In Matthew 25:31-46, Jesus offers a picture of the final judgment. In this awesome apocalypse, there is a terrifying separation between the sheep and the goats. Those who have been faithful are blessed and sent off into glory. Those who haven't been faithful are sent off into the awful darkness. The criterion appears to be not only what people believed, but also the manner in which they put their beliefs into action. Whither and how they responded to the sick, the weak, the poor, the stranger, the prisoner became a criterion for salvation. Those who are invited into the kingdom are clearly surprised. They thought that their actions were simply what all people should do when they encountered sickness, strangers, poverty, or incarceration. All they had done was offer those who needed it food, water, visitation, presence, and hospitality:

> Then the righteous will answer him, "Lord, when did we see you hungry and feed you, or thirsty and give you something to drink? When did we see you a stranger and invite you in, or needing clothes and clothe you? When did we see you sick or in prison and go to visit you?" (Matt. 25:37-39)

Jesus' response is stunning: In ministering to people in such ways, they had actually been ministering to God!

In verse 35 we find a small piece of text that's helpful for our argument at this point: "*I was a stranger* and you invited me in . . ." The thing to notice here is the transformation that occurred: what Jesus was and what he became. Jesus *was* hungry, but he isn't anymore because the saints fed him. Jesus *was* thirsty, but those who cared for him gave him water. Jesus *was* sick, naked and in prison, but no more. Jesus *was* a stranger, but he is no more. Why? Because he was invited in and welcomed. When Jesus took up that invitation, he ceased to be a stranger even though he was in another sense the ultimate stranger. The hospitality that was now being offered was extended not to a stranger but to a friend, someone who had been invited in and welcomed. Paradoxically, he was no longer a stranger when he was held within the community of strangers.

This is an important observation with regard to how the church might go about redescribing the ways in which it should respond to people with dementia and those who seek to offer them love and care. The pattern of the Gospels reveals that Jesus, not unlike people with dementia, was clearly perceived as a stranger by the society around him even though he was in fact one of them.[31] People's simple act of inviting him in was a profound movement away from his socially ascribed role as "the stranger" and toward a repositioning of him as someone worthy of the offer of hospitality. Of course, according to the Matthew passage, Jesus resides within those whom society decides to name as strangers. To estrange the outsider is to make God a stranger. The key point is that *the object of extending hospitality to strangers is to stop them from being perceived as strangers, not just to offer them welcome.* Offering hospitality to those who have been made strangers is thus not simply a warm, charitable thing to do (although it can obviously be that). It is a radical invitation designed to strip persons of their current role as strangers and reposition them as valued members of a community that understands strangeness (because in many ways it is itself strange). The intention is *not* to continually minister to people with dementia as if they remain forever strangers. The intention is to welcome them in such a way as to overcome their strangeness and empower their status as friends. Ministering to people with dementia has the end goal of revealing that they are not in fact strangers at all, and yet, paradoxically, that in being accepted and ministered to by the community of strangers, they will become and remain strangers.

The idea of offering hospitality *to* strangers, in the sense of caring for people outside of the Christian community, remains important. However, when it comes to Christians who have dementia, the welcoming of strangers requires a parallel dynamic that focuses on hospitality *between* and *among* strangers. Hospitality between strangers begins with the assumption that people with dementia are irrevocably members of the community of

31. John 1:46 (NLT): "'Nazareth!' exclaimed Nathanael. 'Can anything good come from Nazareth?' 'Come and see for yourself,' Philip replied."

strangers. In this sense, such hospitality doesn't have to "invite them in" at all, as they are already fully present. But it does need to find them and recognize their existence. Malcolm Goldsmith makes this point well:

> I look back with shame on my five years as a rector of a busy church in the centre of an English city some twenty years ago. I don't think I can recall meeting a single person with dementia during that period. You see, if you don't look for them and if you are not ready to welcome and accept them, then they so easily go elsewhere — and in terms of the church that "elsewhere" invariably becomes "nowhere" — and we are all impoverished as a result.[32]

It is clear that the ongoing welcome of people with dementia and those who care for them isn't always available, or at least it doesn't always *feel* like it is available. I ask readers to reflect on their own experience of church and to think whether the act of welcoming people with dementia and their families has been central to the strategies of mission, evangelism, worship, and pastoral care that they have encountered. If not, I wonder why not? If the task of the people of Israel was to ensure that the *gerim* did not *feel* like strangers, then the task of the Jesus community will be to make sure that people with dementia and their carers do not feel like they are strangers.

A Theology of Welcome and Belonging

The key, then, is to create places of belonging where people with dementia and those who offer care and support to them can find a place that is truly theirs and within which they can express the full experience of dementia — its pain, its affliction, and its lament as well as its joys and its possibilities. Creating such places of belonging begins with thinking about dementia differently. If, as this book has tried to show, dementia is as much a relational and spiritual condition as it is a neurological condition, then overcoming destructive modes of malignant social psychology and negative theological positioning will require particular forms of personal relationships that make welcoming, belonging, and truly being in the moment with others a possibility. Jean Vanier talks about the importance of belonging:

32. Malcolm Goldsmith, "Through a Glass Darkly: A Dialogue between Dementia and Faith," *Journal of Religious Gerontology* 12, no. 3 (2002): 123-38; quotation on 136.

The basic human need is for at least one person who believes and trusts in us. But that is never enough; it doesn't stop there. Each of us needs to belong, not just to one person but to a family, friends, a group, and a culture.[33]

The ways in which people with dementia and their carers are framed and treated by society often function in precisely the opposite direction from Vanier's proposition. Rather than drawing people into community, they throw them into the role of strangers and destroy any sense of belonging for both the sufferers and those around them. Vanier asserts that "we do not discover who we are, we do not reach true humanness, in a solitary state; we discover it through mutual dependency, in weakness, in learning through belonging."[34] If this is true, then in order to be remembered well now and in the future, we must recognize how crucial it is to create places of belonging. But we must be clear about what is meant by the term "belonging." "Belonging" is not the same as "being included." To be included, one simply needs to be present "somewhere," wherever "somewhere" might be. Belonging is different. In order to belong, one needs to be missed if one isn't there. In order to belong to the community of strangers, people with dementia and their families need to be missed when they're absent. If they're not missed, they don't belong; and if they don't belong, there is no true community — for anyone.

The theological framework that has been laid out in this book makes it clear that creating such places of belonging is not an option for the church; it is an act of faithfulness and a living out of our true humanity. I challenge readers to reflect on their own experiences of people with dementia within their churches. Are they missed when they're not there? Are they there to begin with, so that they can be missed?

A Theology of Visitation

Learning how to miss people involved with dementia requires that we know that they're "there" in the first place. Goldsmith's comment above indicates that this might not always be the case. Everything that's been

33. Jean Vanier, *Becoming Human* (London: Darton, Longman & Todd, 1999), p. 33.
34. Vanier, *Becoming Human*, p. 41.

written in this book requires that the church not only include people with dementia and their carers, but also take time to be with them and get to know them. This is the way that we care well for them and show them love. In order to know them, we need to visit them. And it is as we learn what it means to visit one another that we start to overcome our estrangedness and begin to redescribe and learn to love one another, in the power of the Spirit, in ways that are constructive and healing.

The practice of visiting one another is both simple and complicated at the same time. The term "visit" has its origins in the Latin word "videre," meaning "to see, notice, or observe" (hence the word "video"). To visit someone is to *see* them. As we've moved through the various issues in this book, it's become clear that there is a tendency not to see people with dementia properly. This in effect is the essence of malignant social psychology. To visit someone properly requires that we learn to be with them physically and to see them in the right ways — to come close, take time, and listen carefully. In closing this book, I will make one final proposition: To learn to rethink dementia in fundamental ways requires that we learn the practice of *visitation*. It is as we visit one another that we learn what it means to offer and to receive hospitality among strangers. It is as we visit one another that we learn the true meaning of the words, "It's good that you exist; it's good that you are in this world."

The word "visitation" has three dimensions to it. Negatively, it can relate to forms of suffering or disaster that are visited upon individuals or communities — often by God. Such visitation can be punishment for sins or the infliction of illness, such as a visitation of the plague. So in Isaiah 10:1-3 (KJB) the prophet warns,

> Woe unto them that decree unrighteous decrees, and that write grievousness which they have prescribed; To turn aside the needy from judgment, and to take away the right from the poor of my people, that widows may be their prey, and that they may rob the fatherless! And what will ye do in the day of visitation, and in the desolation which shall come from far? to whom will ye flee for help? and where will ye leave your glory?

God can choose to visit the sins of others onto their offspring:

> "The LORD is slow to anger, abounding in love and forgiving sin and rebellion. Yet he does not leave the guilty unpunished; he punishes the

children for the sin of the fathers to the third and fourth generation."
(Num. 14:18)

Visitation in this mode relates to misfortune, sorrow, distress, chastening, calamity, and the imposition of suffering. This kind of visitation can be a source of suffering and an indication of God's displeasure.

It isn't difficult to see how dementia could be framed in this way. Last week I had a conversation with a friend who is a psychologist and a committed Christian. When I mentioned that I was developing a theology of dementia, her response was quite calm, but stark: "Is there such a thing as a theology of dementia? Is it not just demonic?" I nearly fell off my chair! My friend seemed to believe that dementia was a visitation from an evil spirit rather than a natural biological phenomenon. I might have been more surprised were it not for a recent encounter with one of my students whose grandmother has dementia. The grandmother had been a committed Christian all of her life, but now was beginning to lose sight of the spiritual things that used to be so dear to her. My student came to me quite distressed. "My grandmother can't remember Jesus anymore," she told me. "Is God punishing her for something? Is that it? Is she going to hell?" Critical as I have been in this book of overly medicalized perspectives on dementia, one thing that the medical model can do very well is help protect people with dementia from this kind of malignant spiritual positioning. Dementia is not a visitation from a malignant god. It is brain damage.

A second perspective on visitation relates to the creative appearance of God as God reaches into creation to minister to God's people. In Genesis 50:24-26 (WEB), Joseph speaks of God's promise:

> Joseph said to his brothers, "I am dying; but God will surely visit you, and bring you out of this land to the land which He swore to Abraham, to Isaac, and to Jacob." Then Joseph took an oath from the children of Israel, saying, "God will surely visit you, and you shall carry up my bones from here." So Joseph died, being one hundred and ten years old; and they embalmed him, and he was put in a coffin in Egypt.

God will visit God's people and enable them to fulfill that which is their destiny. And so, although he had been dead for three hundred years, Joseph still took part in the Exodus:

So God led the people around by way of the wilderness of the Red Sea. And the children of Israel went up in orderly ranks out of the land of Egypt. And Moses took the bones of Joseph with him, for he had placed the children of Israel under solemn oath, saying, "God will surely visit you, and you shall carry up my bones from here with you." (Exod. 13:18-19, NKJV)

When God visits, things happen. When God visited Mary, Jesus, we might say, "happened":

Then Mary said to the angel, "How can this be, since I do not know a man?" And the angel answered and said to her, "The Holy Spirit will come upon you, and the power of the Highest will overshadow you; therefore, also, that Holy One who is to be born will be called the Son of God. Now indeed, Elizabeth your relative has also conceived a son in her old age; and this is now the sixth month for her who was called barren. For with God nothing will be impossible." (Luke 1:34-37, NKJV)

God's visitations are profound and deep and designed to initiate change and transformation. When God comes to visit someone, God does so for a purpose, and that purpose is always revelatory and transformative. Ultimately God comes to visit human beings in Jesus — Immanuel, "God with us":[35]

Then fear came upon all, and they glorified God, saying, "A great prophet has risen up among us"; and, "God has visited His people." (Luke 7:16)

This visitation is both temporary and permanent. It is temporary insofar as Jesus' earthly ministry has been concluded.[36] It is permanent in that through the power of the Holy Spirit, Jesus continues to visit human beings: "And surely I am with you always, to the very end of the age" (Matt. 28:20). Jesus is the paradoxical visitor who has left but at the same time continues to visit with us. This dimension of visitation indicates that God

35. Matthew 1:23.
36. "But Jesus told them, 'I will be with you only a little longer. Then I will return to the one who sent me'" (John 7:33, NLT).

is with us and for us not only in terms of judgment, but also in terms of loving, guiding, creative presence. God's visitation of human beings is pure and graceful and bears no relation to the abilities or goodness of human beings. God visits his creation simply because God loves.

The third aspect of visitation relates to Jesus' statement in the passage from Matthew's Gospel that we have recently discussed. Here we find an answer to the question "Where is the God who visits today?" It is as we visit one another in and through the Spirit of Christ, as we learn to pay attention to the weak and the strong within the community of strangers, that God's visitation becomes flesh. The practice of visiting is motivated and undergirded by the recognition that the disciples of the God who visits have a vocation to do the same. As we have been visited, so in turn we visit. As we visit, as we find the time to be in the moment with our fellow strangers, so those we visit can encounter God in the sensitivity of our touch and our words, and a gentle presence that transcends all of time. God is with us as we visit. Visitation is an embodiment of God's actions toward creation. As we come close to others, as we visit the sick, the prisoner, the poor, the broken, so we carry within us and reveal the God who visits. As we visit those with dementia and those who care for them, so we bring God with us, so to speak, in our friendship, our thoughtfulness, and our enduring presence. As we visit one another and allow others to visit with us, so we can learn to see and to hold one another well.

Visiting the sick is thus seen to be a deeply theological Christian practice and a crucial way of offering hospitality among strangers. It is a simple but radical practice that takes us to the place where our souls can meet. None of the redescribing of dementia in this book would be possible without the simple practice of visiting. Theology makes sense only when it is practiced. If we visit the "wrong person," then our presence will not be healing.

Rethinking the Gestures of Love

Earlier we asked the question "Is love based on capacities?" In other words, do we love people only because of the pleasure we get from their having certain capabilities? The answer, of course, is no. Nevertheless, capacities matter. They may not define our humanness, but they do matter. This is evident to those among us who are close to people with dementia. It matters that they can now no longer remember or communicate with us. It matters that we feel that we're losing them in fundamental ways. It matters that we sometimes don't feel the same about them as we did when they were fit and healthy and unafflicted. Capacities may not define people, but they do have an impact on our relationships. Capacities are not the criteria for love, but they do inhibit its expression. The loneliness of dementia for all concerned needs to be recognized and articulated if it is to find any kind of healing and resolution.

Previously we reflected on Anastasia Scrutton's question: "If it is possible to choose to love, aren't there situations in which it becomes more healthy and helpful to everyone involved to stop loving someone (to let the person go, or to escape an abusive partner), or to stop loving in a certain way?" This is a difficult question. For all of the reasons laid out in this book it doesn't seem right to suggest that we stop loving a person even if that were in fact possible. It cannot be the case that our saying "It's *not* good that you exist; it's *not* good that you are in this world" can be the right response to our encounters with people who have dementia, even if there may be many times when we feel precisely that way. But it may be necessary to stop loving the person in certain ways. The manifestations of love are many and varied, and many of the ways in which we normally assume love to be expressed are challenged by those who see and experience the world of love differently through the experience of dementia. It may be that when it comes to the expression of love in the context of advanced dementia, we have to rethink the gestures of love. We will have to let go of some of the old ways in which we loved the person. We need to accept that things have changed and that the old modes of love are different. We need to learn to love through our gestures, through our presence, through touch and movement. Our act of faith — that place where we give people the benefit of the doubt — is to hold on to the person as he/she develops and changes through the disease process and to learn what it means to be with him/her and to love the emerging person. This will be painful, alienating, and difficult, but the cross of Jesus reveals to us that very often love is precisely this way. We may have to to learn to see love differently and to realize that the different forms of love that emerge are valid, just as our grieving for the old forms of love is also valid and totally justified.

The new forms of love may be very different, and although we can grow into them, they are inevitably filled with both joy and sorrow. However, it is absolutely crucial to remember that love remains love even if its shape shifts and changes. Caring for the bodily needs of a person is a deep expression of love, but it isn't the same as sharing in his/her emotional life, planning together for the future, or sharing dreams. What we need to remember is that love isn't always romantic. Love is more than a feeling; it is a way of being in the world. Sometimes it is hard, willful, intentional, and deeply disappointing. This is so in a general sense, but it is often profoundly the case when we're faced with the losses that accompany dementia. But if we can recognize the way that our love remains real even if it has to adapt to the rhythm of the disease process, we need not feel guilty when our feelings shift, change, and oscillate. Freed in this way, we just might be able to discover new and hopeful ways to love as the old and tested ways move on. As Barclay has pointed out in her meditation on Psalm 88, such a process begins with weeping.

It is my hope and my prayer that this book has offered a positive, hopeful, and realistic place to begin to rethink the practices of love within the context of dementia. There is much room for hope and joy to run alongside grief and lament. That, I suppose, is the nature of love.

"May Your Will Be Done on Earth, as It Is in Heaven"

It is important that readers of this book do not read this final chapter as negative in any sense. Throughout this book I have made an effort to present a fair, honest, hopeful, positive, and challenging perspective on dementia. I have tried to present it in a different light (I hope without romanticizing it) — to describe it in new ways. Dementia may be a tragic affliction, but there is much to be hoped for as long as we can create the types of relationships and communities that will allow us to see properly, hope realistically, and remember with a love that drives us into the presence of people with dementia. In this chapter I have simply attempted to show that no matter how much one might try to redescribe dementia, the elements of pain, tragedy, and affliction cannot be avoided or written out of the story. Healing begins with an honest acknowledgment of this truth. Only when we recognize the pain of dementia can the things that I have offered in this book begin to make sense and initiate change. The sadness of dementia need not and indeed must not be allowed to have the final word. Even in the midst of the pain and affliction that can accompany dementia, there are hidden possibilities if we trust God and allow the challenge of our sadness to stimulate new ways of thinking and being with one another.

This book has highlighted a number of important practices that have the potential to bring healing out of the brokenness of dementia. These practices aren't complicated. We just have to learn to recognize them:

- Critical thinking and redescription
- Care as a reflection of Godly action
- Recognition of holiness in the other
- Presence and being with the other
- Remembering well
- Lament
- Hospitality among strangers
- Visitation

At the heart of these practices lies the practice of visitation. If we don't visit one another, if we don't take time to be present for one another, we will never see dementia for what it really is. So, my concluding thought would be quite simple: We must visit one another — spend time together and offer friendship, respite, relief, listening, and loving presence to both sufferers and carers. We must give people with dementia the benefit of the doubt, and not allow the stories that we assume to be so convincing to prevent us from seeing the face of Jesus in these struggling ones. As we do these things, as we practice in such ways, God is worshiped and attended to. As we do these things, so a little piece of heaven is revealed on earth. Our actions may be deeply dusty, but our *nephesh* reminds us of the presence of glory.

It is interesting that Matthew, as he records the Lord's Prayer, offers us the words "May your kingdom come soon. May your will be done on earth, as it is in heaven" (Matt. 6:10, NLT). Many of us tend to read this as a prayer for the future. It is not. We can experience something of heaven here on earth. When God's will is done, heaven is revealed. When we visit the sick, when we learn to see one another properly, position one another well, hold one another gently, and act in accordance with our renewed vision, we come to see God more clearly and act more faithfully. Heaven truly is in our hearts, even when our hearts are afflicted and broken. We are remembered. So, to quote the words of the Deuteronomist, "Be strong and courageous! Do not be afraid and do not panic before them. For the LORD your God will personally go ahead of you. *He will neither fail you nor abandon you*" (Deut. 31:6, NLT; italics added). When we encounter dementia in others or in ourselves, we can find solace and hope in Jesus' words: *"Be sure of this: I am with you always, even to the end of the age."* It is in the gestures of your body as it meets mine, it is as our souls collide even in the midst of deep forgetting, that these promises are felt, touched, and lived into truth. To quote Russell Moore's touching words again: "Somewhere out there right now, a man is wiping the drool from an 85-year-old woman who flinches because she thinks he's a stranger."[37] He is not a stranger, she need not become a stranger, and yet, in the power of the Holy Spirit, to-gether they are strangers. In that strangeness they find salvation now and in a future that is firmly held within the memories of God. Small gestures reveal great truths. *Trust.*

---

37. Russell D. Moore, "First Person: Alzheimer's, Pat Robertson, and the True Gospel." Access: http://www.bpnews.net/BPFirstPerson.asp?ID=36119.

Index

Adam, 167-69, 179, 185

Adams, Trevor, 107n, 138n

Advanced directives, 120-21, 132

Affliction of dementia, 264-67

Albert, Martin L., 37n

Alzheimer's Association, 118

Alzheimer's disease, 40; history and context of the diagnosis, 36-37; Keck on loss of memory as "deconstruction incarnate," 190-93; linguistically representing other forms of dementia, 9n, 36-37; "Loneliness and Risk of Alzheimer's Disease" (Wilson et al.), 85-86; losing and finding one's self, 98-107, 112-13, 141; as "theological disease," 9

Alzheimer's Research Trust, 85

Alzheimer's Research UK, 187

American Psychiatric Association's Diagnostic and Statistical Manual (DSM-IV), 34-36, 38-42, 50-51, 55, 64

Anderson, Ray S., 167, 173, 174-77, 178

Anselm of Canterbury, 12-13

Augustine, St.: *Confessions,* 11-12, 202-3; on finding/seeking God, 11-12; and humans as *terra animata* (animated earth), 166; on time and contingency, 230-32; understanding of mind/self and memory, 202-3

Baggini, Julian, 113

Baldwin, Clive, 24n, 72n, 73n, 74n, 76n

Barclay, Aileen, 261-64, 265, 285

Baron-Cohen, S., 61n

Barth, Karl, 16, 25

Bayley, John, 113

Beck, C., 6n

Behuniak, Susan, 114n

Belonging, 278-79

Bender, Michael: on diagnostic criteria for dementia, 33-34, 36-37, 39-41, 52, 53-54; and the standard paradigm of dementia care, 39-41, 67

Bengt, Winblad, 137n

Berry, Wendell, 167, 169, 176, 184

Beuscher, L., 6n

Beyond Belief (BBC Radio 4 program), 1-2

Boden, Christine, 23

Bodily subjectivity, 244-47. *See also* Embodiment

Bogdan, Robert, 56-58, 60

Bonhoeffer, Dietrich, 2, 4-5, 163n, 201, 206; and the suffering God, 201; "Who Am I?", 2, 4-5, 218

Bono, G., 7n

The Book of Eli (film), 206-7, 209

Bower, P., 138n

Brain development and function:

54; and higher cortical functions, 63-65; impaired thinking, 55-63; linguistic confusion, 58-59; loss of mind, 54-65, 82-83; as relational and socially constructed, 71-98, 107-9; and the social construction of thinking and humanness, 56-58, 93n; types (subcategories), 39-41. *See also* Redescribing dementia

Dementia with Lewy bodies, 40

Descartes, René, 93n

Deterritorialization, process of, 24-25, 47

Dewing, Jan, 144

Diagnostic and Statistical Manual (DSM-IV) and diagnostic criteria for dementia, 34-36, 38-42, 50-51, 55, 64; diagnosis of Alzheimer's, 50-51; higher cortical functions, 50-51, 63-65; impaired thinking, 55

Diagnostic criteria for dementia, 49-54; creation of "typical" patients, 51-54; cultural context and politics of, 33-38, 35n; as diagnosis by exclusion, 52-54; DSM-IV, 34-36, 38-42, 50-51, 55, 64; emphasis on defects, 41-47, 49-54; as epistemological process, 52; etiology-changes over time, 37n; and fragmentation of persons into components, 50-54; as hermeneutical process, 52; higher cortical functions, 50-51, 63-65; ICD-10 criteria, 33-34, 38-42, 55, 63-65; impaired thinking, 55-63; and mind reading, 56, 60-62; Sabat on, 50-51; and subjectivity, 36-38; and types (subcategories), 39-41. *See also* Standard medical/neurological paradigm

Divorce, 112, 115-20

Dominion, practice of, 170-72

Eccles, Sir John, 78-79

Eckholm, Erik, 117n, 118n

Edge, Kenneth, 115-17

Edvardsson, David, 137-38

Egan, M. F., 254-55

Einstein, Albert, 27

Ellor, James W., 199n

Embodiment, 165-78; bodily subjectivity, 244-47; and care (giving and receiving care), 171-72, 177-78; and contingency, 165-66; corporate spirituality, 238-39; and creation, 165-69; the embodied soul, 175n; and God's life-giving *nephesh*, 167-69, 173-75, 185, 214-15, 223-25; identity and bodily memory, 243-48; Merleau-Ponty's idea of "body-subjects," 244-47; our bodies as holy ground, 169-72; personhood and humanness, 165-78, 243-48; spiritual identity and bodily change over time, 174-78

Euthanasia, 3-4, 113, 121, 125, 126-27, 131-34; and question of compassion, 3-4n; Singer and the ethical debate about, 126-27, 131-34

Evans, G. R., 12n

"Excess disability," 87. *See also* Malignant social psychology and negative positioning

Fox, Patrick, 36-37n

Franzen, Jonathan, 69-71, 147; "The Long Slow Slide into the Abyss," 69-71

Fronto-temporal dementia, 40

Genova, Lisa, 220

George, Daniel R., 36n, 68

Ger/gerim: the church as, 275-76; people with intellectual disabilities as modern-day *gerim*, 270, 271-73; and significance of the stranger in Hebraic tradition, 270-73

Gift, dementia as, 162-63

God: Augustine on, 11-12, 230-32; Barth on knowledge of, 25; Bonhoeffer on, 5, 201; Calvin on knowledge of, 10-11;

Williams, Bernard, 133
Wilson, Robert S., 85-86
Wittgenstein, Ludwig, 56n, 62-63, 92, 245
Wood, Rebecca, 85-86
World Health Organization's International Classification of Diseases (ICD-10), 33-34, 38-42, 55, 63-65
Wyatt, John, 127-29

Yoder, John Howard, 8n
Yuen, Wayne, 113-15

Zizioulas, John, 158n
Zombie metaphors and "missing person" language, 114n, 212n
Zschech, Darlene, 9-10n